Rob's Guide to Using VMware

Second Edition

Rob Bastiaansen

September, 2005

Copyright © 2005 by Rob Bastiaansen
Published by Books4Brains, September 2005

P.O. Box 345
3830 AJ Leusden
The Netherlands

ISBN 90-808934-3-9

Table of Contents

Introduction

It is unbelievable what can happen in the IT industry over the course of only one year. In July of 2004, the first edition of Rob's guide to using VMware was published. It is now September 2005 and in just over one year a lot has happened. The first VMware conference (VMworld) was held in San Diego in October of 2004, VMware shipped a new product called ACE, VMware Workstation version 5 became available and earlier this year the VMware Technology Network for Developers went live. Last but not least, in August of 2005 VMware announced that they will drive the development of Open Standards on Virtualization in a joint effort with many leading companies in the IT industry. Part of the deal includes sharing the ESX Server source code with those partners in a new program called VMware Community Source. Also in August of 2005, Sun Microsystems announced that they will support VMware ESX Server for use on their Sun Fire x64 systems.

As you can see, these are interesting times for the virtualization community. And there is more to come. A new version of VMware ESX server (v3) is around the corner and new processors from Intel and AMD will contain support for virtualization, which will bring this technology to an even higher level of performance, scalability, and stability.

With this second edition of Rob's guide to using VMware, I hope that I have succeeded in helping you get the most out of your VMware products and to give you a good overview of the VMware software that is available today.

What this book covers

This is the second edition of my VMware guide. The feedback that I received on the first edition was great and gave me a lot of insight into what I could add or change for this new edition. Of course, I have updated the VMware Workstation sections to support version 5, which was released in April of 2005. However, I have also made a lot of progress on the Linux platform and have added a lot of new material about VMware on the Linux platform, in this new edition.

In this new edition, the physical to virtual conversion, clustering, and the operating system specific chapters about installation and configuration have been updated.

New parts of this book are VMware ACE and the VMware server products: GSX Server and ESX Server. Several new books on VMware ESX server became available in the summer of 2005. For an in depth technical discussion about this product, I suggest that you read one of these new books. I have tried to write a comprehensive introduction to VMware ESX Server, which will help you get started and will also help you decide what VMware product you should choose.

About the author

Rob Bastiaansen is well known in the international VMware community. He has dedicated his website to VMware products since he started working with VMware version 2 in 2000. He was the first person to describe how to set up a cluster within VMware for the NetWare and Windows operating systems. Since then he has answered many questions on VMware products and clustering and he published the first edition of his VMware guide in July of 2004. He has also published articles on VMware technology for technical magazines in The Netherlands, where he resides.

In 2005, Rob published his second book called The NetWare Toolbox. Also, in early 2005 he started his own publishing company called Books4Brains. In addition to publishing his own books, Books4Brains offers a framework for other authors to publish their books under conditions that no large publishing houses offer.

Rob owns his own company and works as a consultant and instructor. Most of his work is focused on Novell software and VMware technology. He is a Master Certified Novell Instructor, Certified Directory Engineer, and a Novell Certified Linux Engineer. He is also certified for the Linux Professional Institute and as a Microsoft Certified Systems Engineer. Rob works with all major operating systems including NetWare, Windows, and Linux.

About the reader

Clearly, you are reading this book because you are interested in VMware technology. Whether you want to get started with VMware Workstation, or want to set up an advanced configuration with NetWare or Windows clustering, this book is for you. In writing this book, I have assumed that you are knowledgeable about installing the operating systems that you want to use in VMware. Therefore, you will not find detailed instructions on how to set up Windows, Linux, or NetWare. I am also assuming that you are able to read documentation manuals, so I have chosen not to cover too much basic information, such as how to add USB devices or other equipment to your virtual machines.

However, if you are new to VMware products, you will find a section which describes what VMware technology is and how to set up your first virtual machines. This information was not included just because it is not covered in the manuals; instead, it is included because many people need just a few basic guidelines to get started and they may want to get up to speed quickly. An example of this is: How to get started with clustering in VMware when you have not worked with VMware before.

If you are an experienced ESX server administrator, the introduction chapter in this book does not teach you anything new. However, the configuration tips for the entire range of VMware products covered in this book will contain at least some material that you will find useful for your environment.

Finally, you may be looking for tips on using VMware, such as how to create Virtual Floppy Disks. Also, you may need troubleshooting tips on VMware, or you may want to set up routing with virtual machines. You will find all of this information in this book.

Acknowledgements

Like many authors, I have to thank my family for the support they have given me during the period of writing this book. It is fun writing about VMware technology, but enjoying a day in the woods or playing games is really helpful in keeping you focused on what is really important in life.

A special thank you goes to Ron van Herk and Robert Zondervan at Novell for sharing their information with me about the updated clustering configuration for VMware Workstation. And I would like to thank Ronald Beekelaar for sharing his knowledge on Virtual PC with me for the conversion process.

I hope that you will enjoy the virtualization comics in this book. They were made especially for this second edition of Rob's guide to using VMware by Howard Tayler, the creator of Schlock Mercenary, the on-line comic space-opera found daily at www.schlockmercenary.com.

Part 1

Introduction to VMware Workstation and VMware ACE

1   VMware Overview

This chapter will introduce you to VMware's line of products. These products range from solutions for the desktop to the enterprise server environment. I will start out with an overview of what VMware technology is and will follow it with the description of individual VMware products.

1.1   How VMware Works

There are several VMware products available. This book focuses primarily on the so called hosted products. These are the products that require Windows or Linux to run as a host for the virtual machine environment. I have also included an introduction to VMware ESX Server, which does not require a host operating system but it comes with its own OS to run the virtual machine environment.

It does not really matter which version you choose to work with; VMware operates in a very similar fashion in all its versions. What you need to know about creating virtual machines is basically the same for all VMware products. I will focus on the desktop products first, and will follow with a brief overview of the server versions later in this chapter.

By using VMware technology, you can create one or more PCs on your computer, which can run simultaneously. Your host computer still runs its own operating system (Windows or Linux), and the virtual machines can run with other operating systems (Windows, Linux, NetWare). They all use memory from your PC and their processor instructions are processed by the CPU in your host computer.

Hosts and guests
This brings us to some terminology that you must understand when working with VMware. We call the computer on which you run the VMware software, the host. This host PC can have either Windows or Linux operating system. You will have to choose what operating system you will be using as your host, because you have to buy a specific version for either Windows or Linux.

The virtual machines that you run on your host are called guests. They can run with many operating systems and therefore it does not matter what operating system your underlying host is running. Because of this, you can run Linux on a Windows PC, NetWare on a Linux PC, or just another version of Windows on your Windows host. The next section describes some usage scenarios for VMware.

Host and guest hardware usage
The guests that you run are completely new PCs. When you start working with VMware, you must keep in mind that what can be done on a real PC can be done in VMware. The only limitation is the hardware; you can not add physical devices, such as a video capture card in a virtual machine. However, you can do everything else, such as networking, disk imaging, and so on. Nothing you do infects the host

PC; Of course the PC performance will be compromised, because you are sharing resources between the host and your guests.

This brings us to the hardware aspect of using VMware. VMware technology does not work like an emulator. That is what you see with software that creates a virtual PC on a Macintosh for example or a Macintosh on a PC. When using VMware products, we are committed to the Intel architecture; the software creates virtual machines that run their instructions on the same Intel based processor (or AMD if you prefer it more) that you have on the host PC. The CPU in your virtual machine will show up as the same one in your host computer.

For the rest, your virtual machine has its own set of hardware that is not related to the device types that you have in your host PC. Your virtual hardware is somewhat limited to what you have installed on your computer. For example, you will not be able to store more physical data in your virtual machine than what you have available on your host PC.

Hardware configuration
A virtual machine always has the same hardware, which is unrelated to your host PC. It always uses the same AMD network adapter, the same VGA adapter, and a virtual IDE or SCSI hard disk in every virtual machine. This makes it simple to move virtual machines to another hardware box. You can even move virtual machines from a Windows to a Linux host and vice versa. There will be no changes to the virtual hardware in your virtual machine. The complete machine is stored in a simple set of files:

- .vmx file

  This is a text file that contains the configuration of your virtual machine. It stores information about the hard disks that are used by your machine and the type of networking you have chosen, etc.

- one or more vmdk files

  The virtual hard disk you create for your machine is in fact a file on your file system which stores everything you do in your virtual machine. You can partition and format your virtual disk, defragment it and so on, and nothing affects the underlying hard disk of your host PC. It all happens inside the .vmdk files.

- nvram file

  Every PC has a BIOS and so does a VMware virtual machine. A PC stores its information in Non-Volatile Random Access Memory area. This file performs a similar function and stores the BIOS information with the boot order of your virtual hard disk, floppy, and CD-ROM.

Because the entire machine is stored in these files, it is very simple to move it to another location. You can copy the files to a second directory and voila! You have two identical PCs. You will of course have to take care of unique names and IP addresses within the guest operating systems.

Also, because the entire machine is stored in a set of files, it is simple to create a back-up or archive set. After installing a new guest operating system, you close the virtual machines and create a ZIP archive that you store on your server. If you ever need to do anything, for example on a Windows 2003 Enterprise Edition server, you just need to unpack the archive to your computer and you can get started with your project.

1.2   Usage Scenarios for VMware Software

Every time I meet people who are new to VMware, they are impressed with what the software can do, but they also discover new ways of using VMware which I did not even think of before. This section describes a few common scenarios for the use of VMware technology, for either the workstation or server versions.

Software and OS testing

System administrators, trainers, and consultants are continuously challenged with new releases of software and operating systems. They have to install the new software and to test it for their production environment, customer projects, or for educational purposes. Installing new operating systems normally requires an extra PC or requires making an existing PC multi-boot. With VMware, you can run multiple operating systems on one PC and they can even run simultaneously. But software testing also requires multiple PCs. In an environment where multiple systems are used, new software must be tested for all platforms in use.

Using VMware software to accomplish this task saves time and money. Time: because with a click of a button (the Revert to Snapshot button) you can reset your environment to the same baseline starting point for every test. Money: because you do not have to pay for extra PCs to do all of the testing.

Software development and support

The same reasons mentioned before also apply for software developers and support personnel. They very often have to test the solution they are building or the software they are supporting on the same environment as their customers are using. With VMware software, they can start the operating system of their choice without having to place multiple PCs on their desk.

Secure and standards based desktop management

With VMware Workstation you can create virtual machines that are configured with your corporate operating system environment. Those machines can then be given to end-users to run the standardized environment from their own PCs at work, at home, or on their laptop. In early 2005, VMware introduced a new product called Assured Computing Environment (ACE). With this product, virtual machines can be created the same way as with VMware Workstation, but as an administrator you get full control over the way these machines are used. The user's working environment can be secured by only allowing authorized users to access the virtual machines or by limiting access to specific servers on your network. With ACE, VMware has introduced a completely new way of working with operating system environments for end users.

Education

For training delivery where PCs are involved, there are many advantages to using VMware software. In the first place, it makes the job of the instructor easier, because setting up the baseline for training requires no more than copying the correct virtual machines to the student PCs. When a student crashes his environment, it does not take too much time to revert back to the starting point with either using the Snapshot feature, or by copying a new PC.

Most of this could be done with imaging software, but the possibility of creating a snapshot and returning to a point where it was working, without having to do all of the exercises from day one is something that only VMware can do for you. Something else that makes VMware the preferred technology over imaging is that it runs on all hardware platforms. For a trainer working at multiple locations there is always the challenge of finding the correct drivers for the video adapters and network boards. With VMware software, installing VMware and copying the virtual machines to the computers is all that it takes to set up the classroom.

Also, it can be advantageous for the students to work with VMware because you can run the full environment for the training including multiple servers and workstations on a single PC. You are not impacted by other students who can not keep up with the pace. However, therein lays the challenge for the instructor since you lose the benefits of students teaming up and learning from each other. This is easy to overcome by using a virtual machine per computer that still gives you the benefits mentioned earlier, but allows you to create teams of students as well.

Consolidating servers

The VMware GSX Server and ESX Server products can be used to consolidate servers into one general hardware platform. There are many reasons to do this; some companies do it to save on the cost of hardware, other companies want to make it easier to maintain their environment. Also, some customers want higher availability and buy the full virtualization platform with ESX Server, VirtualCenter, and VMotion.

1.3   Choosing the Right VMware Product

The entry level product that VMware offers is the VMware Workstation version. It is intended to be a product for a single user on a single computer, running multiple virtual machines for any of the purposes described in this chapter. People very often ask me: 'Can I use VMware Workstation to consolidate my servers into one hardware box?' My answer is yes, but! The technology that you get with VMware Workstation or any of the server versions is very similar. You can run multiple operating systems, and you can assign multiple network adapters and separate disk channels so you can even run multiple servers with an acceptable performance. Here comes the But!! As I have mentioned earlier, the product is intended for single user usage. Only one user can manage the virtual machines at any given time, and you will have to be present at the physical machine to work with the machines (or you will have to remote control the host PC). This is again limited to one administrator accessing the host computer.

 Note: not only are there technical and usability issues with using VMware Workstation in this way. You also do not comply with the End User License Agreement for VMware Workstation that is very specific that the product is intended for one specific individual user only.

VMware ACE gives you the same capabilities as VMware Workstation, but it also gives you full control over how virtual machines are being used by end-users.

VMware Server products
In the VMware GSX Server and ESX Server sections of this book I will explain the differences between these versions in more detail and will explain why you should consider buying them. At this point, I would like to give you a brief overview.

Among other benefits of these products, both server versions come with a Management Interface which you can use to manage the virtual machines via a web based management interface and from a Remote Console. With these management solutions you do not have to rely on the remote access to the operating system; you can access the VMware GSX or ESX virtual machines directly on the hardware level. Therefore, you can enter the BIOS of the virtual machines, power the machines on and off, and even change the VMware configuration. With these solutions you can manage your machines with multiple administrators simultaneously.

When you are serious about running multiple servers for your production environment on a single hardware platform, it is not only the management of virtual machines that makes it interesting to look into server versions. It is also the ability to monitor the performance of your virtual machines and act accordingly.

There are many tools and products available for the server versions that can help you create a professional virtual environment. An example is physical to virtual conversion, such as when you move your servers from the existing environment into your virtual infrastructure. Other examples are VirtualCenter and VMotion applications which can help you manage your virtual machines and move them from one hardware platform to another, if they are stored on a Storage Area Network.

Last but not least, the server products come with support for your virtual environment. This is possibly the most important feature of the server products if you plan on using VMware technology in your production environment. You will likely have support for your operating systems and your hardware, so it is very important to have a supported virtual infrastructure as well.

2   Fast Track to VMware Workstation

This chapter contains everything you need to know when you get started with VMware Workstation. Experienced users may find the new information on upgrading from a previous version interesting. Chapter 3 explains what is new in VMware Workstation version 5 in detail.

In this chapter, I will cover the basics and will make sure that you have the important information that you need to get your virtual machine up and running. All other basic information is covered in the VMware manual; therefore, I will not discuss the basic information, such as how to add a USB device or a printer to your virtual machine in detail. The people at VMware have done an excellent job of explaining the day to day operations in their documentation and in the products' help files.

2.1   Set Up the Hardware and Host OS

VMware Workstation runs on almost any PC that you have available, starting with Pentium II and Celeron versions. A full list of hardware specifications and requirements can be found at VMware's website at the following url: `www.vmware.com/support/ws5/doc`. The two most important items that you need when getting started with VMware Workstation are memory and disk space; you need lots of memory and lots of disk space. You can read more about optimization steps that you can take as well as advanced configurations for working with virtual machines in part 2, which covers general configuration and tips. The minimum amount of RAM that you need to start working with VMware and to have acceptable performance is 512 MB. If you run a virtual machine that uses 256 MB, it leaves the other 256 MB for your host operating system. For every virtual machine that you install, you need at least 1.5 GB of disk space.

As a host, you need either Windows or Linux. You will have to decide on one of these before you buy the software, because every operating system requires its own version of VMware Workstation and both require their own license.

Windows

Simply put, the only Windows versions that are not supported in VMware are Windows 9x and Windows NT. All the other versions can be used ranging from Windows XP Home Edition to Windows Sever 2003. If you have a 64 bit system, you can also install a Windows XP or Windows Server 2003 64 bit edition to use the VMware Workstation. The software itself is still 32 bit so you will not gain any benefits. Also, your guest will run in 32 bit legacy mode inside the virtual machine.

 Tip: At the time of writing this book the beta version of VMware Workstation version 5.5 supports running 64 bit operating systems as a host and as a guest.

Linux

The list with supported Linux distributions on VMware's website is rather long. If you need detailed information about the distribution on which you want to install VMware Workstation, you can check the full listing at the following URL: www.vmware.com/support/pubs. Most current versions of Mandrake, Red Hat and SuSE are supported. Not only the professional workstation and server version, but also the 'consumer' editions like Red Hat Linux 9 and SuSE Professional 9.x are supported.

 Tip: When installing your Linux host, make sure to select the packages for the C compiler and Kernel development. These are not enabled by default. I suggest that you install them because it is very likely that there are kernel modules for VMware or other products that you want to install, which do not match the kernel you are running and will need to be compiled. Installing these packages after your host has already been installed is time consuming and you could run into some inconsistencies. An example of this is when your kernel is updated by an update process and the packages that you install from the CD-ROM are from an older version.

2.2   Get the Software

First, you will need to get the software. You can start out with an evaluation version that you can download from: www.vmware.com/download. You can also apply for a 30 day evaluation copy. The software that you download is the same for both the evaluation period and when you buy a license. So you do not have to re-install the VMware Workstation.

At the time of writing this book, September 2005, the most current version is VMware Workstation 5.0, build 13124. This is also the version that is used for all configurations and examples in this book. Many of the tips and configuration options also apply to the VMware server versions.

Get a discount

VMware Workstation is available for Windows or Linux. You choose the host operating system when you buy your copy. So, if you buy the Windows version and decide to switch to Linux, you will have to buy an additional copy, and vice versa.

The price for each (Windows or Linux) is USD 189.00 for electronic distribution and USD 199.00 for packaged distribution. An upgrade to version 5 from version 4.x costs USD 99.00 (these prices are as of September 2005). You are eligible for a 5% discount if you enter the following discount code when you buy your product on-line at the VMware Store: VMRC-ROBBAS389. This code is valid for VMware Workstation and VMware GSX Server purchases.

 Note: Do you have the latest version? VMware includes an auto update feature that checks the availability of new software. Open **Edit → Preferences** to configure this feature on the **Workspace** tab. You can configure this check to be performed daily, weekly (default), or monthly. It does not automatically install the new software, but it does warn you when a newer version is available for downloading. The automatic check can also be disabled by selecting **Never** in the update configuration.

2.3   Upgrading From a Previous Version

For computers with a Windows host operating system, where an existing version of VMware is already installed, the upgrade process has become much easier with version 5. For previous upgrades, the older version had to be deleted and the entire process, including the new installation required at least two reboots. This has been greatly simplified, because the upgrade now removes the current version and installs version 5 without the need to reboot.

For computers with a Linux host, it depends on the installation method that you used for the previous installation. If you used the tar installation method, then there are no extra steps that you need to take. You can start the installation process from the distribution files. The only thing that you must do first is to delete any old tar installation files that may still be in your present working directory. If the directory vmware-distrib exists, delete it first, before extracting the installation archive.

When you use the RPM installer, you must first uninstall the current version before you can install a new one. To find out whether your installation was made with the RPM package, use the following command to query the RPM database:

```
rpm -qa | grep VMware
```

If no entry from the database is shown, then you can assume that the installation was done with the installer from the tar archive. If you need to uninstall the application when it was installed with the RPM package, use the following command:

```
rpm -e VMwareWorkstation
```

The RPM database listing that you performed with the query command shows all the installed software. The keyword VMwareWorkstation is used to uninstall the Workstation. It could also be another keyword from the database, depending on the version you are running.

Preparing for the upgrade
Before upgrading the software, virtual machines must be prepared.

1. Make sure that all virtual machines are in the Power Off state. If your machines are suspended, resume them first, shut down the guest operating system, and then power them off. After installing the new GSX Server software, you will need to upgrade the virtual hardware. See the GSX Server

Administration Guide if this applies to you. Also check the explanation about VMware generations on page 98.

2. Save all the undoable disk mode information into the virtual disks. When you have disks that are in the legacy undoable mode, make sure to save all the changes into the virtual disks or discard the changes when powering off.

3. Remove any current snapshots that the virtual machines have.

After taking these preparatory steps, the software can be installed on your computer. The individual virtual machines still need to be upgraded.

Upgrading from a version released prior to version 4
If you are working with a very old version, then additional steps are necessary. For version 2, you need to upgrade the virtual machines to version 3 or 4. Afterwards, they can be upgraded to version 5. VMware version 3 machines need to be upgraded to version 5 before they can be used with version 5.

Upgrading from version 4
Virtual machines that have been created with version 4 of Workstation can run directly with version 5. There will be some limitations because the new features of version 5, such as using multiple snapshots, are not available. Also, the performance benefits that version 5 offers are not available, if you do not upgrade your virtual machines. If you choose not to upgrade the machine, do not forget to install the newer version of the tools inside the guest operating system. That is the minimum action that you must take after upgrading your host to version 5.

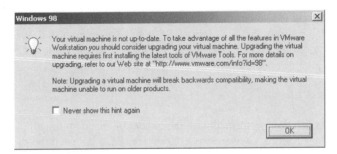

Figure 2.1: This message will warn you if your machine is not already upgraded to a version 5 virtual machine.

As you can see, it is best to upgrade your entire virtual machine to version 5. This is an irreversible operation so make sure to create a backup of your virtual machine first. Upgrading the virtual machine must be done while it is in a power off state. When the machine is powered off, select the **Upgrade Virtual Hardware** from the **VM** menu.

After the upgrade has been performed, install the new version of the tools inside the virtual machine. Depending on the version of VMware Workstation that you were running and the operating system inside the machine, additional steps may be necessary for your specific guest. For example, in a Windows 9x machine the display driver needs to be upgraded after upgrading the virtual hardware.

2.4   Install VMware Workstation for Windows

The installation of VMware Workstation for Windows is very straightforward. When accepting the license agreement, you will get the usual questions, such as where you would like to place your software. One of the specific questions that will be asked may need some clarification. This question is displayed in Figure 2.2.

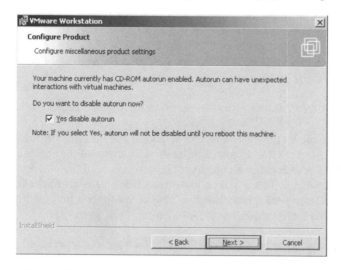

Figure 2.2:   Prevent unwanted behavior and disable
Autorun during installation.

If you leave the CD-ROM autorun enabled, and you run operating systems in your virtual machines which also auto mount CD-ROMs, you will end up with multiple PCs accessing the same CD-ROM. This is not a desirable situation. It will cause strange behavior and will slow down both the host and the guest. Therefore, leave the default setting to disable autorun enabled.

The final step for finishing your installation is to add your VMware Workstation for Windows license. In VMware Workstation, select **Help → Enter Serial Number** to add the license.

Once the installation has been completed, you can create your first virtual machine. Before you do so, make sure that you understand what types of disks and networking you can choose. Continue with section 2.6 to read more about disk types and networking options.

2.5   Install VMware Workstation for Linux

At this point, I am assuming that you have downloaded the installation files, copied them to your computer, or mounted the CD-ROM that contains the installation files. VMware Workstation for Linux is available in two formats: tar archive and an RPM package. I will explain how to install the VMware Workstation for both types of installation files.

Follow these steps to install the software:

1.   Log on to your Linux host and open a terminal window.

2.   You need to install the software as a root user so use the `su` - command to become `root`.

3.   For the RPM version, there are two installation methods. One method is to execute the following command to install the software:

```
rpm -Uhv VMware-gsx-3.2.0-14497.i386.rpm
```

Another method to install the RPM package is to click on the file in a file manager in the GUI. Figure 2.3 shows an example of a SuSE 9.3 host, where the RPM is selected in Konqueror. The description of the package is displayed to show what software will be installed. Click on **Install package with YaST** to install the package. Package managers on other Linux distributions may look different from this, but the installation is just as simple.

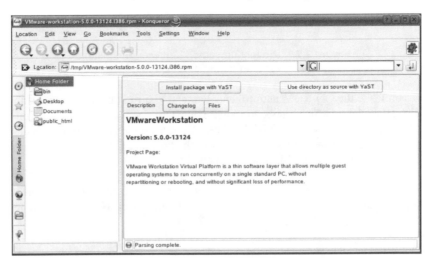

Figure 2.3: The RPM package can also be installed from the GUI.

4. For the tar archive version, execute the following commands to install the software. First, make the /tmp directory your present working directory or choose another directory where you want to extract the files. This eliminates the need to copy the archive to your hard disk first.

```
cd /tmp
```

Extract the archive with the following command:

```
tar -zxf <path>/VMware-workstation-5.0.0-13124.tar.gz
```

Change the present working directory to the location of the installation files:

```
cd vmware-gsx-distrib
```

Start the installation script:

```
./vmware-install.pl
```

5. After the package is installed or when the installation script from the tar archive has completed running, start the VMware Workstation configuration script with the following command:

```
vmware-config.pl
```

6. The first action that you have to take is to read and accept the end user license agreement. Read through it and when you are finished, press q to exit the reader. Then type yes, if you agree with the EULA.

7. The configuration script will ask you several questions that you need to answer. Here are the default directories that you will be prompted for as well as the default paths that are suggested by the VMware configuration script. They originate from an installation on a SuSE 9.3 professional host. The paths can be different on other Linux distributions.

mime type icons	/usr.share/icons
desktop meu entry files	/usr/share/applications
application icon	/usr/share/pixmaps

8. At this point in the configuration process, it will try to find a suitable vmmon module for the kernel you are running. If it finds one, the following message will be displayed and the configuration will continue:

```
The module loads perfectly in the running kernel.
```

When the pre-compiled modules for your kernel are not available, the following message will be displayed:

```
None of the pre-built vmmon modules for VMware
Workstation is suitable for your running kernel. Do
you want this program to build the vmmon module for
your system (you need to have C compiler installed
on your system)?
```

At this time you need to have a C compiler and the kernel source files installed. If you have not installed these during the initial Linux installation, you can do that now.

Tip: Be aware that if you install the kernel source from your installation CD-ROM, that version may be different from the one that you are already running. This is because the current one may have been updated by an automated update process. In that case, go through the same update process to update the added kernel development package including the kernel sources.

When a C compiler and kernel source files are available, you will be prompted with the following question:

```
What is the location of the C header files that
match your running kernel?
```

The default location is: `/usr/src/Linux/include`.

When it was necessary to build the vmmon module it might show messages saying: `Module.symvers is missing'` modules will have no modversions and `Unable to build the vmmon module`.

If that is the case, run the following commands from the Linux source directory, but make that directory the present working directory first:

```
cd /usr/src/Linux

make cloneconfig
make modules_prepare
```

After running these commands, execute the `vmware-config.pl` configuration script again. Whether the modules will now compile, really depends on your distribution. However, in most cases they will compile. When it does not work after this step, I suggest that you search the VMware knowledge base and the VMware Community Forums for information on your specific installation.

9. When the modules are loaded, the configuration script will prompt you with questions regarding networking. Answer these questions according to your needs.

- Do you want networking for your virtual machines?
  (default: yes)

- Do you want to be able to use NAT networking in your virtual machines?
  (default: yes)

  If you select to install NAT:
  Do you want this program to probe for an unused private subnet?
  (default: yes)
  You will also be prompted with a question to configure additional NAT networks. The default answer is: no.

- Do you want to be able to use host-only networking in your virtual machines?
  (default: yes)

  If you select to install host-only networking:
  Do you want this program to probe for an unused private subnet?
  (default: yes)
  You will also be prompted with a question to configure additional host-only networks. The default answer is: no.

10. After the configuration script has finished successfully, you can start the VMware Workstation. There is no need to do that as a root user, so execute the `exit` command to return to your previous user environment. Start the application with the following command from the command line:

`/usr/sbin/vmware &`

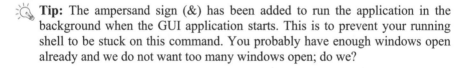 **Tip:** The ampersand sign (&) has been added to run the application in the background when the GUI application starts. This is to prevent your running shell to be stuck on this command. You probably have enough windows open already and we do not want too many windows open; do we?

11. The final step to finish your installation is to add your VMware Workstation for Linux license. In the VMware GUI application, select **Help → Enter Serial Number** to add the license.

After the installation is complete, you can create your first virtual machine. Before you do so, make sure that you understand what types of disks and networking you can choose. Continue with paragraph 2.6 to read more about disk types and networking options.

2.6   Disk Types for your Virtual Machines

Before you can create your first virtual machine, you will have to understand your options for using hard disks and networking first.

VMware Workstation virtual machines will run with virtual disks which will not in any way affect your host computer's hard disk. You can create partitions in your virtual machine, format your disks, and defragment them. None of these actions will directly interfere with your physical hard disk. Everything happens in one or more virtual disk files that form your virtual hard disk.

The only relationship with your host hard disk is that your host operating system is transferring data to and from your physical disk. Your guest operating system is accessing the same physical disk by using the virtual disk files. You can imagine that disk intensive operations will slow down your PC dramatically if you are running multiple PCs simultaneously on a single disk channel.

You have three hard disk options when creating new virtual machines.

- A virtual disk that will **grow dynamically** to the maximum virtual hard disk size.

  This is the default option, as well as the option that is used when doing a typical creation of a virtual machine. **I recommend using this disk type if you are just getting started with VMware Workstation.** A .vmdk disk file that is only a few kilobytes in size will be created. The .vmdk file grows dynamically; this is only the case if you start putting data on the hard disk from the guest operating system, during installation and afterwards (when working with the machine).

  The advantage is that your virtual machine will only take as much space as is really needed by your guest operating system and its applications and data. You can create a 100 GB disk that will start small and grow to 1 or 2 GB after installation without ever using the entire 100 GB on your host PC.

  The disadvantage of this disk type is that with the file becoming larger over time, it will become very much defragmented on your host PC's hard disk and will make it slower. Growing the disk also has a negative impact on performance.

  These dynamically growing disks are not automatically shrunk. You will have to go through a manual process described elsewhere in this book to decrease the size of your virtual disk file.

- A virtual disk that has a **fixed size** equal to the maximum virtual hard disk size.

  When creating a virtual disk from the New Virtual Machine Wizard, you can enable a check box for your virtual machine to **Allocate disk space now**. This option allows the VMware Workstation to create a virtual disk file which has the same size that you specify for the virtual hard disk on the host PC. Creating a 100 GB virtual hard disk would take up 100 GB of hard disk space on your host PC's hard disk.

  The advantage of this disk type is that even though it may take longer to create the disk, running the virtual machine is still faster because the disk will not be so defragmented on your host PC's hard disk. This is only true if you make sure that there is enough space to sequentially create the entire file. Use the Windows Defragment utility to analyze this before and after you create the file.

  You will need to use this type of disk if you want to use a clustering solution with a shared disk, as explained in a later section of this book.

- Use a physical disk in your virtual machine.

  This is considered to be a configuration for advanced users. It allows you to use a disk partition from your existing physical disk, from within a virtual machine. The advantage is that it is the fastest type of disk access you can obtain for your virtual machine, but the disadvantage is that you need to partition your hard disk just as you would with a multi boot PC. Also, you will not be able to save the virtual machine easily with its configuration and disk files into an archive for back-up. In addition, it can not be used for future installations based on the same virtual machine copy.

  It could be a useful installation if you have a dual boot PC, because you can start your extra operating system from the boot loader or from within a virtual machine.

 Tip: I recommend the type of virtual disk that grows dynamically (the default selection when creating new virtual machines). It does not take up too much hard disk space, the performance is acceptable, and it is very easy to create an archive of a virtual machine by just copying the files to a safe location.

2.7 Networking Options for your Virtual Machines

Nowadays, all computers as well as your virtual machines come with a network adapter. It is important to know what types of networking you can use, because choosing the wrong type can prevent you from accessing your services in the virtual machines. It can also have undesired effects on your existing network.

In general, you have two types of networking options available: bridged and host-only.

Bridged networking

This is the default type of networking that is selected when you create your virtual machine. It allows your guest operating system to communicate with the physical Ethernet network that your host is also using. The virtual machine has its own MAC address (a unique address for every networked machine) and will need to have its own IP address that it will either receive automatically from your DHCP server or that you will manually configure.

Accessing the network (and via that, the Internet) is very simple and straightforward. You must of course be aware that everything that you run inside your virtual machine will be accessible from the network. Therefore, installing a server of some sort (Domain Controller, DHCP server) will have serious implications for other users on your network. Unless if the plan was to run these services inside of the virtual machine in the first place. Just be aware of this, because you would not be the first one to run an extra DHCP server at a customer site, after accidentally running the wrong virtual machine.

Host-only networking

If your virtual machines do not have to communicate with the network, or if you want to prevent this because you want to test network services that may not leak out onto the network, you can select this type of networking. All network traffic will be handled by an internal VMware process and nothing will leave your host PC. Virtual machines will be able to communicate with each other, and by using the virtual host-only adapter, your host operating system can also communicate with the guests. VMware comes with a DHCP service for your host-only network. The VMware manual describes how to use and configure this in detail.

What networking option to use

If you will be running a simple workstation with Windows or Linux, then your best choice is bridged networking. You can access the network and, if available, the Internet, and update the machines with the latest patches.

Switching between bridged networking and host-only networking can be done on-line, when your virtual machines are up and running.

You can either select **VM →** **Settings** from the menu and then configure the networking option, or you can double click the network adapter icon on the right lower corner of your virtual machine. This will also bring up the networking control panel.

If you need advanced configuration options and tips on networking, go to section 11: "Networking configurations"

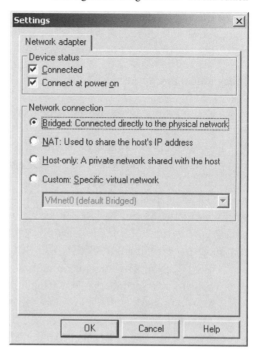

Figure 2.4: The networking configuration can be modified when a machine is on-line.

Tip: I have met a lot of people who have problems with accessing virtual machines and the LAN when they start configuring their physical and virtual adapters. It is very important to make sure that all adapters (physical, including wireless, host-only VMnet1 and VMnet8) are in different IP subnets. A real PC with two network adapters on different Ethernet segments, but with the same IP subnet used on both LANs will not know where to send its packets.

Compare it to a junction with two signs pointing to Paris. You would also be confused as to what direction to choose (unless they both point to Rome, of course, since we know that all roads lead to Rome!).

A PC with a physical adapter and or more virtual adapters that have been configured for the same subnet will have the same problem and will prevent you from accessing hosts on either the physical or virtual networks.

2.8 Virtual Machine Hardware Specifications

A great advantage of virtual machines is that they always provide you with the same hardware. Independent of the hardware in the host system, the hardware inside the virtual machine stays the same. The only component that will be different is the processor, since the virtual machine will work with the underlying processor from the host machine. It also does not matter whether you have installed your virtual machine on a Windows or a Linux host; you can transfer it between these two supported host operating systems.

Every virtual machine has these hardware specifications:

- Same processor as on the host computer
- Intel 440BX-based motherboard with NS338 SIO chip and 82093AA IOAPIC
- PhoenixBIOS™ 4.0 Release 6 with VESA BIOS
- A maximum of 3.6 GB of RAM for each individual virtual machine (with a limit of 4 GB maximum for all virtual machines).
- VGA adapter that supports SVGA
- A maximum of seven SCSI devices
- SCSI controller: Mylex® (BusLogic) BT-958 compatible host bus adapter or an LSI Logic Ultra320 LSI53C10xx SCSI controller)
- Virtual SCSI disks with a maximum size of 950 GB
- A primary and secondary IDE channel for up to four devices
- Virtual IDE disks with a maximum size of 950 GB
- A maximum of three AMD PCnet-PCI II compatible Ethernet adapters
- Creative Labs Sound Blaster® AudioPCI emulation
- Virtual floppy drives (maximum of two), parallel and serial ports, and two USB ports
- Two-port USB 1.1 UHCI controller
- Keyboard and PS/2 mouse

2.9   Creating your First Virtual Machine

It is now time to create your first virtual machine. I will walk you through the steps in the Wizard and will explain all your options. I will also explain what the implications are when selecting settings other than the default.

You create your virtual machine after starting VMware Workstation by selecting **New Virtual Machine** from the **File** menu or from the main window. This will start the New Virtual Machine Wizard.

1. The first option that you have to select is whether to use the typical or the Custom configuration. I am assuming that you are the investigative type or an advanced user, so we will use the Custom configuration and go through it step by step.

2. The next window will be new to users that have worked with version 4.x. You are prompted with the choice (Figure 2.5) to either create a new virtual machine or a legacy machine that is compatible with version 4.

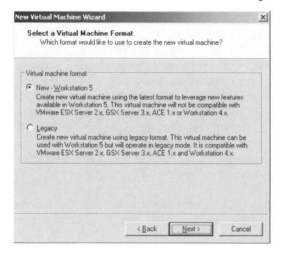

The default selection for version 5 is to create a new machine. The legacy machine can be used in version 4.x but also in VMware GSX Server, ACE 1.x and ESX Server 2.x. For more information about VMware virtual machine generations, checkout section 0.

Figure 2.5: You can still create VMs that are compatible with version 4 and GSX Server.

3. Next, select the operating system that you want to install in this virtual machine. Your selection will create the most optimized configuration for your guest operating system.

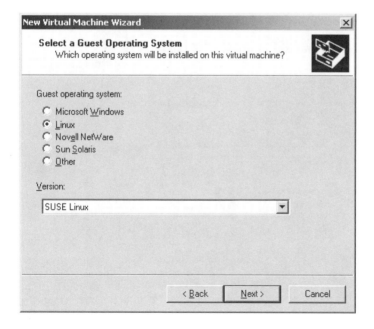

Figure 2.6: Always select the correct OS to get the right settings.

Selecting the incorrect operating system does not cause too many serious problems. The OS will actually run, but it could have a negative impact on the performance. You can also change the operating system later on from the virtual machine configuration settings. Based on your selection, VMware sets the defaults for your machine to what is best for your guest OS. For example, if you select Windows XP, the Wizard will propose to use an IDE disk by default, because SCSI drivers for VMware are not supported by default. If you choose SuSE Linux, VMware will propose SCSI because drivers for the VMware SCSI storage adapter are supported by this operating system. VMware will also set the amount of memory to use, such as to 256 MB, because that is enough memory to run Windows XP or SuSE Linux.

The selected operating system is also used to select the tools that you need to install in the guest, and to display additional tips if required for that operating system.

4. After selecting the guest operating system, you are prompted for the location of your virtual machine files. Create a directory per virtual machine to store all the files.

5. Your next choice is to decide how much memory to use for your virtual machine. The default of 256 MB of RAM shown below is the default for Windows XP and SuSE Linux.

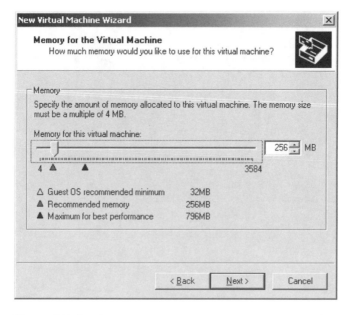

Figure 2.7: Set the memory to your needs or accept the defaults.

The maximum amount of memory for any virtual machine is 3584 MB. If you do not have this amount of RAM in your host PC, then it is useless to select this amount of memory. Do not set the memory too low, especially during installation. The installation process of a virtual machine may notify you about insufficient memory and the performance will be very poor. A general rule for VMware virtual machines is to use as much RAM as you can, but of course not more than what you have in your physical machine. The total amount of RAM to be used in all virtual machines that run concurrently is 4 GB. More detailed explanations about memory optimization can be found in chapter 8: "Performance tuning and optimization".

6.   Next, select the choice of networking that you want for your virtual machines.

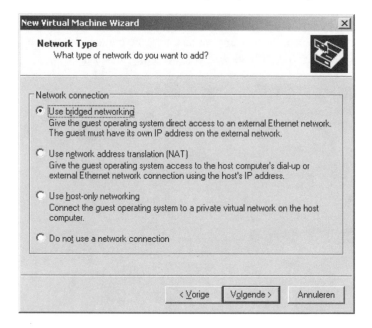

Figure 2.8: Select the network type for your virtual machine.

When installing Windows or Linux, it is a good idea to run them in a bridged mode during the installation. That way, they have access to the Internet (when available) on your network. You can then update them via the web during or right after the installation. It is easy to download new drivers or other software that you need for your guest operating system directly into the virtual machine.

7.   Every virtual machine will support normal ATAPI IDE devices, but you will have to decide whether you want to use the Buslogic or LSI Logic SCSI adapters for your virtual SCSI environment. VMware will set a default choice based on the operating system that you have selected. There is a separate

---

chapter on using SCSI devices for Windows, Linux, and NetWare later on in this book.

8. Next, you will have to select the type of disk that you will be using. You can choose to create a new virtual disk (which is what I suggest you do to get started), use an existing disk if you already have one, or use a physical disk. This last option is not recommended for most common installations.

9. In the next window, you have to select the Virtual Disk Type: IDE or SCSI. If you are not sure if SCSI is correctly supported by your operating system, then set it to IDE because that is supported by any known operating system.

10. If you have chosen to use a virtual disk in step 8, you must now select the size of the disk. Also, select if you want the disk to grow dynamically to that size, or if the disk space should be allocated when creating the virtual disk.

Figure 2.9: Specify the disk size and other features for your virtual disk.

The minimum size of a disk is 100 MB and the maximum is 950 GB for both IDE and SCSI.

If you have a file system that only supports files to a maximum of 2 GB (such as FAT), you will have to split the disk files onto separate 2 GB files. However, they will, form a set of files that have the same name prefix and are sequentially numbered. When looking at Microsoft's file systems documentation, they list the FAT32 file system to be able to hold files with a maximum capacity of 4 GB. With VMware workstation you are required to split your virtual disk up into 2 GB files on both traditional FAT and FAT32.

Tip: I always split my disk files up because it makes them more flexible to zip in pieces; this is advantageous if I ever have to write them on to CDs or DVDs. Also, if you need to copy a large virtual disk from one computer it is easier to do that when copying smaller chunks. It gives you the flexibility to restart a failed copy or move cycle.

11. Do not click on **Next** too fast on the screen where you specify your virtual disk name. I would like to draw your attention to the **Advanced** button. This is explained in the next step.

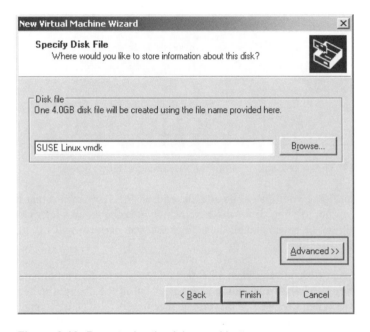

Figure 2.10: Do not miss the Advanced button.

Typically, the name that you enter here does not have a path. This means that the virtual disk file will be stored in the same directory where the virtual machine is located. VMware Workstation uses relative paths and always loads virtual disk files from its own directory. You could still specify another location on your hard disk to store the file. This would include the full path in this field.

12. If you click the **Advanced** button, you will be able to specify two additional settings. The first one is the location where the disk will be located on the IDE or SCSI channel. The second setting option is to change the disk mode.

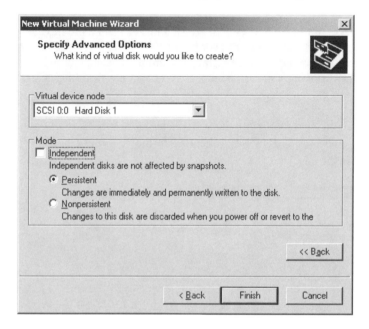

Figure 2.11: These settings are from the Advanced settings screen.

You can configure your disk to be an independent disk. This means that if you create a snapshot of your virtual machine, which is explained in a later chapter, the disk will not be saved and all the actions that you perform will still go into the disk file.

The **persistent disk mode** writes all actions directly into the virtual hard disk file. The **Nonpersistent disk mode** keeps track of all the changes in separate REDO-files. When you power the virtual machine off, all your changes are discarded. You can switch between these modes later from the virtual machine Settings configuration.

The non-persistent disk mode is useful when you are working with software testing. You can start with the same unchanged environment after every restart (power-off/power-on).

Tip: If you want to use this feature, set this disk mode after installing the operating system. By the way, working with Snapshots is the preferred method of using the same starting point over and over again.

You have now created your first virtual machine. Before getting started with the installation of your operating system, I will explain some useful information about the VMware Workstation interface. While most of it is self explanatory, I want to make sure that you know the basics in order to get started. Figure 2.12 shows an overview of the main control options and access to configuration options.

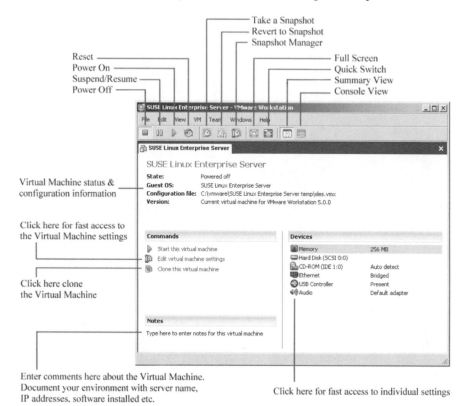

Figure 2.12: Overview of the main virtual machine control and configuration options.

Suspend and Resume

The Power On, Power Off, and Reset buttons are the same as with a real PC. Suspend and Resume, however, may need some clarification. You can compare this feature with the Hibernate feature of laptops. If you click Suspend, the virtual machine state will freeze. In addition, hard disk activity will be stopped and the contents of the virtual machine's memory will be saved to a file on your hard disk. This .VMSS file compares to the HIBERFIL.SYS file, which Windows creates in the root of your hard drive when you use the hibernate feature.

Suspending a virtual machine for the first time (when it has been down or has been reset), used to take a long time with previous versions of VMware; sometimes up to a few minutes. This was because the .VMSS file was created on your hard drive with the same amount of RAM that was assigned to your machine. Creating that file took a lot of time. The performance of the Suspend and Resume processes has improved dramatically with version 5. This is accomplished by creating a .vmem file as soon as the virtual machine is powered on and by not waiting for you to suspend the machine.

3 What's New in VMware Workstation 5

In this chapter, I will introduce the new features for VMware Workstation version 5. In the chapter 2 from this book you can read how to install this version. There are some topics that are new in this version which I have not covered in this chapter, such as isochronous USB support. Another feature that is covered in this book is the new command line interface, which is covered in section 6.2.

The topics covered in this chapter are:

- Using multiple snapshots

- Cloning virtual machines

- Teaming virtual machines

- Movie Record and Playback

- Virtual Machine Importer

What's new in VMware Workstation version 5.5
This chapter covers the new features of VMware Workstation version 5. However, when you are reading this, there is good chance that VMware has already released version 5.5. These are the features that will be included in the new release:

- Support for multiple (two) CPUs for virtual machines

- Support for 64 bit host and guest operating systems

- Integrated conversion for virtual machines from other vendors

3.1 Using Virtual Machine Snapshots

There is a reason that this functionality is on top of the list of new features and it is discussed first in this chapter. It has been the most requested new feature since snapshots were first introduced. It is now possible to create snapshots at multiple points in time which will give you the capability to go back to different points in the life cycle of your virtual machine. You can even branch off at the point when the snapshot was made to create a second timeline based on that snapshot. This will give you the capability to try several scenarios based on one virtual machine while having the flexibility to go back to any saved snapshot in the snapshot-tree.

I will first discuss what snapshots are and after that I will go into the details of working with the new and previously existing features of the snapshot technology.

3.2   Introduction to Snapshots

While working with real PCs, you might have come across this scenario: you are at 90% completion point of your new server installation and an error message appears which prevents you from continuing with the installation. Or, a blue screen appears, or the installation just hangs up. Or, maybe you are working on a new software installation and you want to try it with several options but still use the same starting point, such as a clean Linux or Windows workstation.

Due to the fact that VMware acts just as a real PC, you can find yourself in the same situation during the installation of your guest operating system. VMware Workstation contains a snapshot feature that can help you go back to a point in time that you can preset when you install your new guest operating system, or that you may have chosen as a base for all your testing.

3.3   What Snapshot is

When you take a snapshot of a virtual machine, the state of the machine is saved at that particular point in time. Both the disk and the memory are 'frozen' at the point where you create the snapshot. The configuration of the virtual machine and the state of your BIOS are also saved.

All the operations that you perform on the virtual machine from the point of taking the snapshot will be saved in separate files on the file system.

You can check the directory where the virtual machine is stored for these files:

* <name>-Snapshotn.vmsn

  This file contains the configuration information about the snapshot. It is also this file which keeps track of your virtual machine configuration. The snapshot files will be numbered Snapshot1.vmsn, Snapshot2.vmsn, and so on. The online documentation points out that more than 100 snapshots are being supported. How much more than 100, it does not specify. But of course, it will be limited by hard disk space.

* <name>-Snapshotn.vmsn

  Contains the memory dump of your virtual machine

* <name>-nnnnnn.vmdk

  Multiple files contain the changes to your virtual hard disk. These files are numbered 000001.vmdk, 000002.vmdk, etc.

3.4   Using Snapshots

You can take a snapshot when the virtual machine is either in a Powered On or Powered Off state or even when it is suspended. Click the snapshot button or select **VM → Snapshot → Save Snapshot**.

Figure 3.1: The toolbar provides easy access to the snapshot feature.

From this point forward, everything you do in your virtual machine will not affect the original files. All changes to the hard disk will go into separate files, and what was in RAM at the point of taking the snapshot is saved in a separate file.

To go back to the same point where you took the snapshot, just click the Revert button or select **Snapshot → Revert to Snapshot**. With the new multiple snapshot feature, you can select to which snapshot you want to revert to if you have more than one.

⚠ **Note:** Be careful about using the snapshot feature in a distributed virtual machine environment. If an application in one machine is communicating with another application in a second virtual machine, then reverting to a snapshot in one of the machines will create an inconsistent data set. This is also true for Active Directory and eDirectory synchronization and replication.

Reverting to the snapshot point will delete everything that happened since taking the snapshot and will start out with the disk from that snapshot point. It will restore the RAM which was in the virtual machine's memory when the snapshot was created.

⚠ **Note:** You will still be using the snapshot, so everything you do will still be saved in separate files. Clicking **Revert** one more time will delete everything again.

⚠ **Note:** Using the snapshot feature results in an overhead to the normal operations of VMware Workstation. If you do not need snapshots for a particular machine then do not create any snapshots or if they already exist, delete them.

3.5 Working with Multiple Snapshots

Starting with VMware Workstation 5, you can work with multiple snapshots. This feature helps you to return to any point in time, when you were using a specific configuration.

 Note: Virtual machines which where created with an older version of VMware Workstation (prior to version 5 or with other VMware products) can be used in this version, but the snapshot feature will not be available. Upgrade the virtual machine hardware to use this new feature.

The example I will discuss here takes place in a training situation, where the students can go to any exercise in the training by reverting to the snapshot point for a particular exercise. By using snapshots this way, students can go back to a previous exercise when they have messed up their environment. Also, when there is a need to skip an exercise, the students can start at any given point without the need for going through the other exercises first. This is a great solution for modular training delivery.

Tip: Of course students who perform all the exercises without problems do not have to go to any of the snapshots. They can start out with the starting virtual machine and just work their way through the exercises for the duration of the training. Only when something does go wrong, they will not have to start all over again.

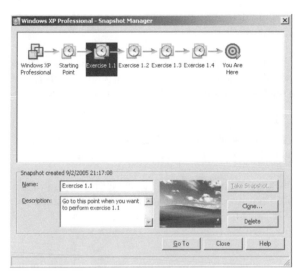

The first possibility to work with snapshots is linear: you start out with your first snapshot and keep creating sequential snapshots.

Figure 3.2 shows an example of this approach. You can go back to any point in time. In this example, it is to start a specific exercise. The description box is useful in helping users identify the status of the virtual machine.

Figure 3.2: The simplest way to use multiple snapshots is the linear approach.

There can be some scenarios, when you not only want to follow a single line of snapshots, but you may also want to branch off at any given point in the line of snapshots. This can be done and will result in a snapshot tree.

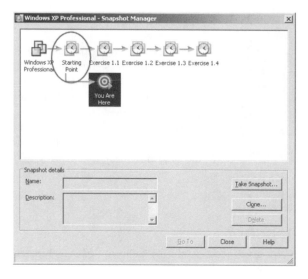

In the example where exercises are created for students, you can click the initial snapshot and revert to that snapshot in **Snapshot Manager** by clicking the **Go To** button.

This will result in a new line of snapshots that can also be branched off at any given point. Just click the snapshot, revert to it and select **Take Snapshot**.

Figure 3.3:   Click the initial snapshot and revert to it to start a new branch.

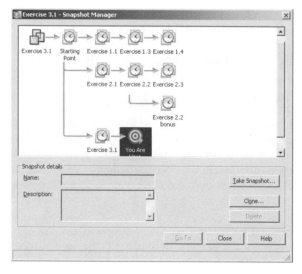

Figure 3.4 shows an example of a snapshot branch that was created for the exercises in section 2 of a training course. In this example, there is an extra exercise that the students can perform for which an extra snapshot is created at the **Exercise 2.2** snapshot point.

They can go to that snapshot, when they want to perform that specific exercise.

Figure 3.4:   A snapshot tree can be branched off at any point.

While working with many snapshots, it is possible to loose track of where you are. To find out what the active snapshot is, you need to go into the **Snapshot Manager**.

You can rename the virtual machine in the settings to the same name as the snapshot. Since the snapshot feature also keeps track of the configuration changes, the VMware Workstation window will show the name of the machine, which will also be the name of the snapshot.

Figure 3.5: Rename the virtual machine in each snapshot to keep track of where you are.

3.6 Deleting a Snapshot

You can delete a snapshot at any given time. From the Snapshot Manager, select the snapshot that you want to remove and click the **Delete** button. This will start a process of optimizing the snapshot tree and linking the children of the deleted snapshot to their parents.

 Tip: If you do not want to save the changes that you made since creating the snapshot, first revert to the previous snapshot and then delete the snapshot.

It is also possible to delete an entire snapshots branch at once. To do this, right click the snapshot and select **Delete Snapshot and Children**.

3.7 Configuring the Snapshot Feature

In some situations you might want to disable one of your disks from the snapshot. You can do that by configuring the disk as an independent disk. To do that, go into the settings of the virtual machine, select the disk that you want to set to independent, and click the **Avanced** button in the disk configuration panel. Set the checkbox to make the disk an independent disk. You can only do this when there are no snapshots already.

You also have to choose between a persistent disk and a nonpersistent disk. The first mode saves all the changes into the original disk file and the second mode saves all the changes in a separate REDO-file, which will be removed when you turn off your virtual machine.

Disabling Snapshots

The snapshot feature can be disabled on a per virtual machine basis. This only works when the virtual machine does not have a snapshot. To disable taking snapshots, open the virtual machine settings, select the **Options** tab, and select the **snapshot** entry. In the right panel, you will see a checkbox to **Disable Snapshots**.

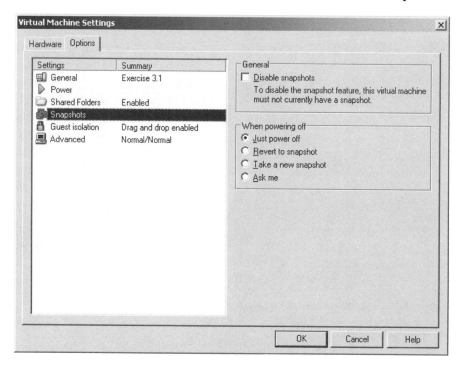

Figure 3.6: Snapshot behavior can be configured on a per virtual machine basis.

The default configuration for snapshots is that they will not be affected by powering off or resetting the virtual machine. This behavior can be changed from the virtual machine Settings to any of these options:

• Just power off	Does nothing and leaves the snapshot intact.
• Revert to the snapshot	Always removes the snapshot when powering off and always starts with the same state.
• Take a new snapshot	Takes a new snapshot when the machine powers on, and adds all changes you made to the original file.
• Ask me	Asks you which of the above actions to take.

Changing snapshot priority

With VMware Workstation, virtual machine snapshots are created and restored as a background process. This is a great feature because you can almost instantaneously continue working with the guest OS while the snapshot process is finishing up. If you try to start a new snapshot process when another one is not finished, you will receive a message about it.

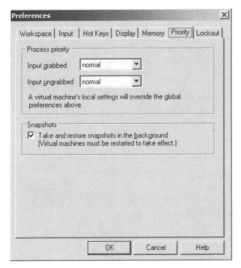

It depends on the usage scenario of the virtual machine whether you want to keep this feature turned on. In a classroom environment for example, students who revert to a snapshot can start working immediately. However, when they do this, the machine might be slow in the beginning. Depending on the audience, it might be better to let them wait until the process is finished as a foreground process.

To change the way that the snapshots are created, select **VM** → **Preferences** and enable or disable the checkbox in the **Priority** tab.

Figure 3.7: Snapshots are created as a background process by default.

3.8   Cloning Virtual Machines

This new feature allows you to create a copy of a virtual machine. It is different than using snapshots. With multiple snapshots on a virtual machine only one of the snapshots can be active, whereas you can boot one or more clones that you have created of a virtual machine at the same time.

There are a wide in variety of usage examples for virtual machine clones. For an instructor who has to set up a classroom with virtual machines, this wizard helps him to easily create unique machines for each student. With the linked clone setup, explained later, the parent could reside on the network, while the student's clone machine is on his own computer.

Other uses are for software testing where at any point in time, or even at a given snapshot in a snapshot tree, you need to have someone else work on the same environment to perform tests for you. Clone the virtual machine and provide them with that copy to work on.

Creating a clone of a virtual machine duplicates the machine and creates a new identity. The Clone Virtual Machine Wizard takes care of creating a new unique identifier (UUID) and MAC address for the virtual machine. So, you can safely run multiple clones of a parent machine without any networking problems.

Guest operating system specific identity information will not be changed by the cloning feature. You still have to change that from within the guest OS yourself. The simplest action to start out with is to use the DHCP to assign IP addresses. What are left to be changed, for any guest OS, are the workstation or server name and possibly the SDI on Windows. You can use Microsoft's SYSPREP tool to take care of preparing the parent virtual machine before you create a clone. For Linux hosts changing the name is something that can easily be scripted.

 Tip: there are many tools available that can help you to set a new identity for your computer without running SYSPREP. Sysinternal has a freeware tool called NEWSID, which can set the security identifier and hostname on a Windows machine (www.sysinternals.com). Another freely available utility is called Zcnc Lite from ENGL (www.engl.co.uk). This utility can set the computer name based on your own input but it can also read Windows Management Instrumentarium (WMI) information. For example, In VMware, it can read the BIOS serial number that returns the machine's UUID.

Linked versus full clones

There are two sorts of clones that you can create. The full clone can operate completely independent of its parent. This type of clone does not need to have access to the parents' virtual machine files. This is different for the linked clone, where it will always stay dependent on the parents' virtual machine files. A full clone uses the same amount of disk space as its parent. A linked clone only takes a small amount of disk space to start out with because the entire parent virtual disk will be used to work with. Eventually the disk space that the clone takes will grow once the data is modified and is added inside the clone.

 Note: Using a linked clone is faster when you create it but the performance is negatively impacted, just as with the snapshot feature. A full clone runs entirely on its own virtual disk and provides better performance.

Preparing the parent for cloning

You can create a clone of a virtual machine when the machine is powered off. A clone can be created at any point in the snapshot tree of a virtual machine. But when snapshots of the parent are deleted, it will break the link with the linked clone and will make it unusable. To prevent this scenario from happening, you can set the parent to be a template for cloning. With this feature enabled you can not delete a snapshot or the virtual machine to prevent from accidentally breaking the link with the clone.

To set up a machine as a template, open the virtual machine settings and on the **Options** tab in the **Advanced** menu select the checkbox for **Enable Template mode (to be used for cloning)**. This does not disable the delete control in the snapshot manager but when you try to delete a snapshot, the warning message in Figure 3.9 is displayed.

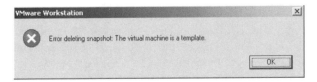

Figure 3.9: When enabled as a template, snapshots can not be accidentally deleted.

3.9   Creating a Clone

The virtual machine must be in the power off state before you can create a clone. It does not matter if you are at a snapshot in the snapshot tree or not. The clone can be based on a snapshot too.

 Note: Virtual machines which were created with a VMware Workstation version prior to version 5, or with other VMware products, can not be cloned until their virtual hardware is upgraded to version 5.

You start the Clone Virtual Machine Wizard either from the VM menu or from Snapshot Manager.

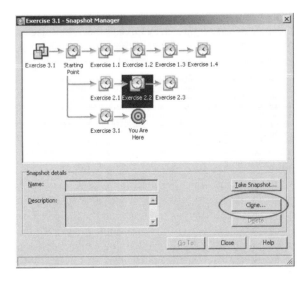

To clone a virtual machine when it is in a snapshot state, open the **Snapshot Manager** and select the snapshot point that you want to clone. Click the **Clone** button. This starts the Virtual Machine Clone Wizard, where you can select this snapshot point to be cloned. You can also select any other snapshot point from the wizard's drop down list.

Figure 3.10: Snapshots can also be used for cloning.

Cloning a clone

It is possible to create a clone of a linked cloned virtual machine. Be aware that this new linked clone needs access to all linked clones in the chain including the parent. Also keep in mind that using the linked clone feature negatively impacts the performance and linking linked clones brings even more overhead to your virtual machine environment.

3.10 Teaming Virtual Machines

With VMware Workstation you can run multiple machines that have a relation, such as for a demonstration, or for a testing project. For example, you always want to demonstrate the combination of a server and a workstation. Or you perform testing on a pair of servers that compose a cluster. In this case, you used to always have to open the individual machines and start them. Now, you can just bundle those machines into a team and start off all of them with on click.

The teaming feature also adds the feature to assign the machines to a specific (virtual) LAN segment and define how that network is being used. You can configure the speed of the network and possible packet loss to simulate a real world scenario.

Managing teams

Create a new team from the File menu. The **New Team Wizard** will guide you through the creation of the team. You can create a team with an entirely new virtual machine and you can also add existing virtual machines to a team.

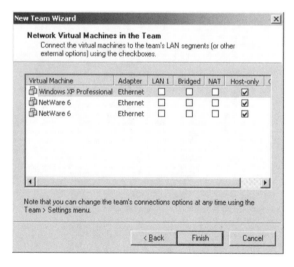

During the creation process you can specify the networking configuration for all machines in the team. Figure 3.11 shows an example of a team that is configured for host-only networking. To throttle the bandwidth or set other networking features, the virtual machines must be assigned to a LAN segment. That would be LAN 1 in this example.

Figure 3.11: Teamed virtual machines can be configured for networking from the wizard.

After creating the team, you can now power on the entire team at once or you can power on individual machines from the team. You can not start virtual machines outside of a team but you can start them individually form the team window.

Once a team is created, you can manage it from the **Team** menu. It allows you to add virtual machines to the team or remove them from the team. You can also delete the entire team including the virtual machines or you can delete the team and leave the virtual machines on your hard disk.

Team configuration
A team can be powered on with one click of a button. That is convenient, but it may also cause some performance problems if more than one virtual machine is booting at the same time. Also, you can have a setup where you first need the server to be fully booted before you can start a workstation. The starting interval can be configured from the **Team Settings** configuration screen.

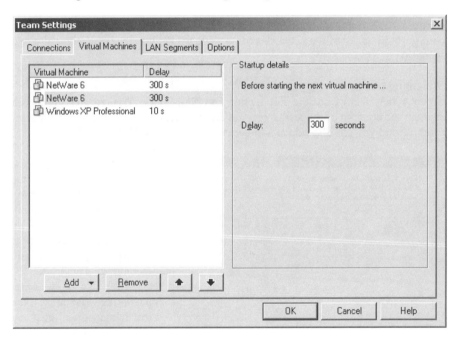

Figure 3.12: Virtual machines in a team do not have to start at the same time.

In the example shown in Figure 3.12, the first NetWare server is started when the team is powered on. VMware Workstation waits for 5 minutes (300 seconds) to allow the server to boot. When the second server is booted, another waiting period of 5 minutes starts before the Windows workstation is powered on. The starting order can also be configured with the up and down arrows at the bottom of the list.

Teams, Clones and Snapshots

Virtual machines which are part of a team can be cloned; however, the new clone will not become a member of the team. It is possible to create a team from cloned virtual machines. So, if you are planning to create an efficient set of machines that share a virtual disk, you can first create the machines and then create the team and add the virtual machines to it.

You can create a snapshot of a virtual machine inside a team. But it will only be a snapshot of that machine, not of the entire team. Of course, you can create snapshots of the machines individually or have a snapshot of the entire team, but if consistency is important then you might want to take a snapshot of the machines in the team when they are in the suspended or power off state.

Team networking configurations

Virtual machines in a team can be configured to use normal host-only, NAT, or bridged networking. But it is also possible to assign them to a special LAN segment which is used only by the team. You can configure this on a per virtual machine basis in the machine's settings or from the Connections tab in the **Team Settings** window.

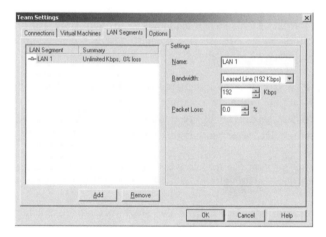

Adding machines to a LAN segment not only isolates them from any other networks but you can also configure the network bandwidth for the LAN segment. This is a great feature too; for example, testing a client server application that would run over a leased line. You can also configure packet loss to simulate network problems.

Figure 3.13: Network bandwidth can be throttled for a team.

3.11 Movie Record and Playback

Earlier versions of VMware Workstation already contained a feature to create a screenshot of a virtual machine. That feature is still available today but has been extended to capture an entire video of what is happening inside the virtual machine.

To capture a movie, select the **Capture Movie** option from the **VM** menu. Provide a filename for the file, which will be stored in an AVI file format. You can enable the checkbox **Omit frames in which nothing occurs** to only capture video fragments if something is really happening inside the machine. If you are working on building a demonstration and you leave the virtual machine running with the video capture enabled to configure something on your host computer, then that time will not be added to the movie file.

Figure 3.14: During the movie capture, an icon will be displayed in the status bar.

You can right click the icon displayed in Figure 3.14 to stop the movie capture or stop the capture from the **VM** menu.

To play a captured movie, you need the VMware Movie Decoder. It is my experience that most DVD player applications already play the AVI file anyhow. But other players, including Windows Media Player require this decoder. You can download it from the VMware website. The most recent version at the time of writing this book is `VMware-moviedecoder-5.0.0-13124.exe`.

3.12 Virtual Machine Importer

There is a product from Microsoft, named Virtual PC, which competes with VMware Workstation. The format of their virtual machines is different from that of VMware so they are not interchangeable. If you want to move a Virtual PC machine to VMware Workstation, then you can run the Virtual Machine Importer.

This application (Windows only) comes as a separate download from VMware. The most recent version at the time of writing this book is `VMware-VMimporter-1.0.0-12997.exe`. The utility and full PDF manual can be downloaded from the following URL: `www.vmware.com/download`.

 Tip: In VMware Workstation version 5.5 this conversion wizard is integrated in the VMware Workstation software by default.

After installing the program, you can start it from the **Start** menu from outside VMware Workstation. The application does not depend on Workstation to perform the conversion process.

You can select between a custom or typical installation. When you use the custom method, you can create virtual machines that are compatible with older versions of VMware Workstation or other VMware products. You can also configure a linked virtual machine in the custom method. For the example in this paragraph, I have used the custom method.

1. The first step to perform the conversion is to select the .VMC file from the Microsoft Virtual PC machine.

2. Next, provide the virtual machine name and location for the destination virtual machine.

3. If you have selected the custom method, you will be prompted to create a new VMware Workstation version 5 compatible machine or a legacy machine.

4. Next, you can choose to create a full copy of the virtual machine or to link to the original file

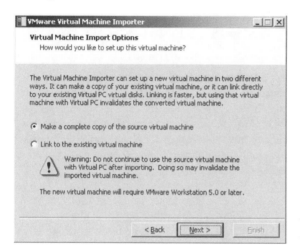

Copying the full machine will result in a .VMDK file containing the full virtual machine. When linking to the original Microsoft .VHD file, it will work as a snapshot with .VMDK files which only contain the changes. Creating a copy takes longer than linking to the machine, but the linked machine will be dependent on the original file.

Figure 3.15: You can copy the entire source virtual machine or link to the original virtual PC hard disk file.

With a linked virtual machine the original file will remain intact but you must not use it inside Microsoft Virtual PC anymore. If you do, the VMware virtual machine will become corrupt because it only contains changes to the original file.

5. Once the conversion is complete you can start the virtual machine directly and close the Virtual Machine Importer.

6. When the guest operating system starts, Windows in many cases, it will detect new hardware and will require a reboot. Before you reboot, it might be a good idea to install the VMware tools, which also requires a reboot.

The application keeps a log file of its actions in your temporary directory, typically c:\documents and settings\username\local settings\temp. The file has a v2vapp prefix and uses the date and time as the remainder of the file, with a .log extension. For example: v2vapp.2005-08-25.08-30.log.

4   Install Operating Systems and VMware Tools

This chapter starts with the installation of Windows, Linux, and NetWare in your virtual machine. In addition, installing the VMware tools is explained, and you will find instructions on using your virtual machines effectively by optimizing the machines and shrinking your hard disks.

4.1   Installing Operating Systems General Tips

So, how do you normally install an operating system on a new PC? You put in the floppy disk or the CD-ROM and power it on? That is exactly what you do to with a virtual machine. However, you have a few extra choices in this case.

Whatever operating system you will be installing, the fastest and easiest way to do it is to use an ISO image instead of a CD-ROM. If you have to install virtual machines on a regular basis, it is a good idea to create ISO images of your operating system CD-ROMS. For some of the operating systems, you can download ISO-files from the Internet; sometimes even with an integrated service pack. But, you can also create ISO files yourself. This is explained in section 7.7: "Working with CD-ROM and DVD image files".

Depending on your CD-ROM drive, it will be faster to use an ISO file from your hard drive than your physical CD-ROM drive. Using floppies is always faster from floppy images than from real diskettes. How to work with virtual floppies is also explained in chapter 7.

If you have problems booting from a CD-ROM, read the tip in section 7.8: "My virtual machine does not boot from a CD-ROM". This may be caused by a problem with the boot order in your virtual machine BIOS.

4.2   Installing your First Windows Guest

You install Windows from the bootable Windows CD-ROM or ISO-file. Place the CD-ROM or assign the ISO and power the virtual machine on. The installation of Windows starts and you can go through the setup as you normally would do with a real PC. Use the normal procedure to create and format partitions.

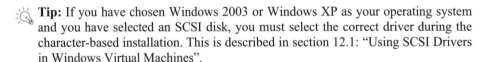 **Tip:** If you have chosen Windows 2003 or Windows XP as your operating system and you have selected an SCSI disk, you must select the correct driver during the character-based installation. This is described in section 12.1: "Using SCSI Drivers in Windows Virtual Machines".

Let the Windows setup finish its job, including rebooting the machine. When Windows is up and running again, the first thing you need to do is to install the VMware tools; this will be explained later. After installing the tools, make sure that all the hardware is detected and is working properly. If applicable, also install any service packs you are planning to use, at this point and run Windows Update to get your machine updated with the latest software and patches.

 Tip: At the point, before adding new hardware or patches to the machine, take a snapshot of where the machine is installed. This way if one of the new components breaks, in your Windows environment, you can easily switch back to the point where it all worked fine.

Windows XP and Server 2003 Activation

Microsoft introduced a mechanism with Windows XP that is now also implemented in Windows Server 2003, where you have to activate Windows. This process generates a checksum based on the hardware in your PC, and uses that to activate Windows via the Internet or via a telephone dialog with a Microsoft representative. If you change pieces of the hardware, Windows will recognize that it is running on a different hardware and requires you to re-activate Windows. You will have to keep that in mind, if you are installing hardware into a Windows XP workstation. You will be reminded by VMware about this with the following dialog box.

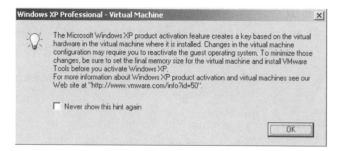

Figure 4.1: Install Windows completely before activating your copy.

Adding a single piece of hardware is not a problem, but if you activate Windows before finishing the installation, it could require you to re-activate even before you are finished. So, make sure that you have all your disks configured, that the amount of memory is set to what it needs to be, and that extra network or sound adapters are added before you activate your copy of Windows.

4.3 Installing your First Linux Guest

Linux is available in many different distributions, but the installation procedure is similar for almost any of the distributions and uses a CD-ROM or DVD. There are Linux operating systems that you can install over the Internet and as I mentioned earlier, a virtual machine is just like a normal PC, so if you could do it from a hardware box you can also do it from a virtual box.

When booting from the Linux installation medium (CD-ROM, DVD, or ISO), you must select the components that you wish to install and partition and format your hard drive. Let the installation program finish its job, including any reboots, until it is finished. It is advisable to run your virtual machine in bridged mode, so that available patches and updates can be downloaded during installation, if your distribution supports this.

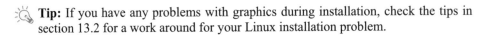 **Tip:** If you have any problems with graphics during installation, check the tips in section 13.2 for a work around for your Linux installation problem.

When the installation is complete, install the VMware tools into your Linux guest operating system. After that has been completed, you are finished and now you have a completely functional Linux system.

Tip: At the point where you enter the Linux configuration for users etc., right after copying the files (if your distribution has that order) take a snapshot. That way you can also go back to the point where all was fine without having to go through the entire installation.

4.4   Installing your First NetWare Guest

Just as with Windows and Linux, your NetWare installation starts with a CD-ROM or an ISO file. During the installation, you create a DOS partition and a NetWare system partition (pool and volume SYS). Let the installation go through the entire process, including a reboot, and when the process is finished, install the VMware tools for NetWare.

Tip: While installing NetWare, take a snapshot at the point where the GUI installation asks you for the server name. If anything should go wrong during the installation process which creates your environment, it is easier to go back to this point instead of starting the installation all over again.

4.5   Installing the VMware Tools

Without the additional tools available for VMware, your virtual machines will still run any of the supported operating systems; however, you could miss important functionality and the performance could suffer. The tools take care of several issues, and add features to the virtual machine, depending on the guest operating system that you are running.

Some features and benefits that the tools provide you are:

- The ability to automatically grab or release the virtual machine's input when the mouse is pointed at the virtual machine.
- Enhanced graphics performance with the SVGA video driver.
- Improved mouse input performance.
- Time synchronization between the host and the guest.

- Shared folders for sharing files between host and guest (Windows and Linux).
- Drag and drop of files to and from the virtual machine.
- Copy and paste operations between the host and guest clipboard.
- Preparing your virtual disks for shrinking operations.

The tools come as ISO files with the VMware software and are stored in the VMware program directory. If you open the ISO file, you will see that the VMware tools software is inside the virtual CD-ROM image in the native application format of the guest operating system they are for: setup.exe for Windows, setup.ncf for NetWare, and a compressed tarball and RPM package for Linux, which contains the installation script.

The installation of the tools is started for every operating system by selecting **VM → Install VMware Tools**. This will add the VMware Tools ISO-file to your virtual machine as a CD-ROM device. Dependent on the settings in your guest operating system, the setup application will automatically start or will have to be started manually. How to continue the installation for your operating system is described in the next section.

VMware tools for Windows guests
After starting the VMware Tools installation from the menu, the CD-ROM will become available in your Windows guest and will automatically start, if you have not disabled autorun. Otherwise, you can start the setup.exe from the root of the virtual CD-ROM.

For Windows NT/XP/2000/2003, you will have to be logged in as an Administrative user inside the guest, to be able to install the tools.

Continue the installation of the VMware tools via the Wizard. The tools will be installed and the drivers for your display, mouse, SCSI controller, and the VMXnet driver will be added to your environment. Depending on your version of Windows, you may have to reboot to finish the installation.

Tip: The tools will show up on the system tray of your Windows machine. If you run VMware in an environment where you do not want users to know that they are inside a virtual machine, you may want to disable the system tray icon. You can do that by right-clicking the system tray icon and selecting **Disable Icon**. To access the tools settings, or to enable the system tray icon, you can open the VMware tools configuration from the Control Panel in the Windows guest operating system.

The Control Panel application can be disabled by a Windows policy that prevents access to the control panel. Or you can rename or delete the VMControlPanel.cpl file in the VMware tools program directory in the Windows guest, or the VMControlPanel.cpl value in the following registry key: HKEY_CURRENT_USER\Control Panel\MMCPL.

VMware tools for Linux guests

The tools for Linux come in two formats. These tools are the RPM package and the compressed tarball. When using the tar installation, the install can not be started immediately. You will first have to extract the files to a temporary location in your Linux guest. It may be necessary to mount your CD-ROM. You will have to run the installation as root.

The steps to install the VMware tools for Linux are included in the following sections. There may be small differences with your Linux distribution. For many Linux distributions, the CD-ROM is a device called /dev/cdrom. This is used in the next command line example. Use another device name if applicable for your Linux guest.

1. Change your user environment to the root user with the su - command.

2. You may need to mount the CD-ROM, if it was not automatically mounted.

   ```
   mount /dev/cdrom /media/cdrom
   ```

   If /media/cdrom does not exist, create it first. Your distribution can also use /mnt/cdrom or a directory called /media/cdrecorder as the mount point.

3. When using the RPM installer, start the installation with the following command:

   ```
   rpm -Uhv /media/cdrom/VMwareTools-5.0.0-13124.i386.rpm
   ```

   Use the correct path and file name for your actual installation.

4. When using the tar installation option, extract the installation files to a temporary directory and run the installation script. If you make the temporary directory your present working directory, you do not have to copy the files to your hard disk first. Use the following commands to perform this task:

   ```
   cd /tmp

   tar zxf /media/cdrom/VMwareTools-5.0.0-13124.tar.gz

   cd vmware-tools-distrib

   ./vmware-install.pl
   ```

The installation script will prompt you for the directories where the software and documentation will be installed. Here is a list of the default directories that are suggested during installation:

binary files	`/usr/bin`
init directories	`/etc/init.d`
init scripts	`/etc/init.d`
daemon files	`/usr/sbin`
library files	`/usr/lib/vmware-tools`
documentation files	`/usr/share/doc/vmware-tools`

5. When you have finished installing the RPM or extracting the archive, you can unmount the virtual CD-ROM that contains the tools with the following command:

```
umount /media/cdrom
```

You can also use the correct path to the mount point for your specific installation.

6. The next step is to run the configuration utility for the VMware tools. To perform this step, execute the script with the following command:

```
vmware-config-tools.pl
```

You may encounter errors with the script about compiling the vmhgfs (virtual machine Host-Guest File System) or VMXnet (network adapter) driver. If that is the case, make sure that you have a C compiler and the kernel sources are installed. The VMware Workstation for Linux installation is explained in detail on page 29.

The script will prompt you for a screen resolution for your X-environment. From the proposed resolutions, select one that fits your needs.

Tip: If the tools configuration script suggests that you need to install from outside the GUI, you can end the graphical environment by executing the `init 3` command from a command line prompt, or by pressing **Ctrl-Alt-Backspace**.

When the script is finished, the configuration will be written to disk and the guest operating system daemon will be started.

7. You can now run the VMware tools application from within the GUI environment by executing the following command:

```
vmware-toolbox &
```

Use the ampersand character to start as a background process.

VMware tools for NetWare guests
The CD-ROM with the VMware tools will be mounted automatically after starting the installation from the menu. You can execute the `volumes` command to verify that the volume (VMWTOOLS) is indeed mounted.

When the CD-ROM is not mounted automatically, verify whether the `cd9660.nss` driver is loaded (`modules cd9660.nss`); otherwise load this module (`load cd9660.nss`). This will auto mount the CD-ROM.

To start the installation of the tools, run the NCF file from the VMware tools CD-ROM.

```
vmwtools:\setup.ncf
```

You can check the progress of the installation on the Logger Screen in NetWare 6.x. The command to load the tools will be added to your server startup file (`autoexec.ncf`) and the `vmwtool.nlm` will be loaded. There is no need to restart the server.

Tip: The tools are also available in the Graphical User Interface on NetWare. As an example, you will find options for shrinking disks and configuring time synchronization. You can load the tools for the graphic environment from the Novell start menu in the GUI, but if you want them to be loaded automatically, you can add the NCF file that loads them (`vmwtoolj.ncf`) to `sys:\java\nwgfx\bin\startx.ncf` which loads the GUI.

4.6   Setting the Power On and Power Off Modes

First time users have to get used to seeing the virtual machine as a real PC which can do everything you normally can do with a PC, including powering on and off. VMware virtual machines can even be configured to look more like real PCs. Nowadays, pressing the power off button of a PC does not just power off but also shuts down the operating system. VMware can also do that.

To configure this option, open the Virtual Machine Settings and on the **Options** tab, select the **Power** entry. The following settings, displayed in Figure 4.2, are available:

- Power off button: Power off or Shut Down Guest

- Restart button: Reset or Restart Guest

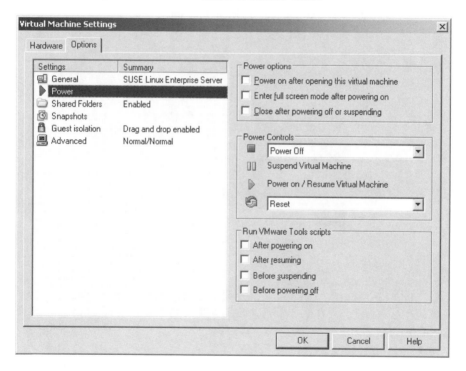

Figure 4.2: The machine can be powered off but a graceful guest OS shutdown can also be configured with the Virtual Machine Setting Power Options.

Note: The behavior of these settings depends on the guest OS that you are using. The Power Off setting always turns the virtual machine off, but the Shut Down Guest setting sends a signal to the guest operating system to perform a shutdown. If your guest OS does not support this feature, then you must manually stop the guest the same way as on a physical machine. This is also true for running the VMware tools scripts with the Power Off options; not every OS with VMware tools installed supports this feature.

The other Power Options from the settings screen in Figure 4.2 are self explanatory:

- Power on after opening this virtual machine.

- Enter full screen mode after powering on.

- Close after powering off or suspending.

Use these options to configure a machine that runs without the user controlling it. By automatically starting and entering full screen mode, a user would never have to know that he or she is working inside a virtual machine.

5   Introduction to VMware ACE

This chapter introduces you to VMware's latest addition. Based on VMware Workstation, this product provides an Assured Computing Environment: ACE. I will start out with an introduction to ACE, and will then introduce some usage scenarios. I will also explain how to get started and how to use the product.

There are two ways to explain VMware ACE in a single sentence:

1)   It is a product that is used to distribute virtual machines to end-users in a controlled way.

2)   It is a product that combines the functionality of VMware Workstation, imaging software, and desktop management applications.

The first explanation is the condensed version of what the VMware website uses to describe ACE. To find out what functionality VMware ACE really gives you, let us take a look at the second explanation which is one that I came up with.

First, VMware ACE provides you with VMware Workstation technology: you can run a virtual machine on a host system providing you the flexibility and capability to run on all hardware platforms. The only limitations compared to VMware Workstation is that it runs on Windows only and that you do not have all features available, such as snapshots or shared folders.

With VMware ACE, you can provide your users with a virtual machine that contains a working copy of your company's standard computing environment. There is no need to modify it for their hardware. This is where the comparison with the imaging software feature comes in. Companies use imaging software to easily install a copy of their standard computing environment on all workstations.

The problem with imaging software is that you will have to take care of the hardware differences between different types of workstations. With VMware ACE, you can leave the default Windows installation which is already installed in place and run a virtual machine to provide the needed functionality to the user. You actually only need one virtual machine for the entire organization, compared to multiple different images that you need to maintain.

Workstation management does not only mean that you need to deploy the software to computers. You also need to manage and secure the computers that are in use. Windows policies can take care of part of that. Third party software such as Novell ZENworks, Altiris, or LANDesk Management Suite can take care of the more advanced workstation management.

Depending on the level of security that is required, the use of additional software may still be needed. But with the functionality of VMware ACE several important tasks have already been taken care of. It is possible to configure what network connections can be used from the virtual machine. The machine can be set to its default state with every power on, etc.

And there is more; with VMware ACE it is possible to configure who can use the virtual machine, based on Active Directory user accounts when needed. Passwords can be used to secure the use of virtual machines and the use can be further restricted by setting an expiration date.

What do users see?
When everything is configured and deployed, what will the end users' experience be? He or she will only see an application window containing yet another Windows environment. It looks much like running a terminal services window. The main difference is that the actual processing is performed on the local machine. But that is not of much interest to the user.

5.1 VMware ACE Usage Scenarios

Every system administrator who looks at VMware ACE will see a new way of using this product, just as is the case with those being introduced to VMware Workstation for the first time. But I will describe a few usage scenarios here to give you an idea of the power of the product:

- By distributing a virtual machine to workstations in a controlled way, you have full control over the functionality that is available to users on their workstations.

- In an educational environment, virtual machines can be distributed to student workstations providing them with a complete working computing environment, while controlling what can be used from the workstation.

- Temporary workers can be provided with a full working copy of the company's computing environment, while controlling what can be used and what will the expiration date be.

The usage scenarios above give you an idea of what you can do with the product and hopefully will help you start thinking about how VMware ACE can be used in your environment.

5.2   Getting Started with VMware ACE

The software package that you work with as an administrator is called VMware ACE Manager. You will have to start out by installing this software to your workstation in order to create your ACE projects and to prepare the deployment to end users' workstations.

 Note: It is important to know that VMware ACE Administrator can not be installed in combination with other VMware products. Also, it is not possible to run existing virtual machines directly. The machines can be left intact, but you will always have to configure a VMware ACE project to point to the existing configuration. Therefore, if you want to keep using the VMware Workstation functionality as you are used to, you need to use a separate computer to manage your ACE environment (and no, you can not install the product inside a virtual machine). VMware ACE Manager does not interfere with VMware VirtualCenter and the remote console utilities for GSX Server and ESX Server.

 Tip: If you need additional reading material on VMware ACE, you can check the online documentation. However, there are also a few very good resources available at the following URL:
`www.vmware.com/support/resources/ace_resources.html`.

Because you will not be using ACE Manager to run a large number of virtual machines at the same time, the hardware requirements are a little less. You can run multiple machines at the same time, but typically you just use one project with one machine at any given time. A PC with 1 GB of RAM should work well unless you are creating ACE workstations with larger amounts of RAM. For the client computers, it really depends on the machines you will be deploying and how much resources you need. However, for a typical Windows virtual machine with 256 MB of RAM which you want to run on a user's computer, the user's PC should have 512 MB of RAM.

 Note: It is possible to use existing virtual machines from VMware Workstation version 4.5 in VMware ACE version 1.01, but VMs created with version 5 of VMware Workstation can not be used as VMware ACE machines.

 Tip: If you already have a version 5 virtual machine which you want to use in VMware ACE, do the following: create a new virtual machine in version 5 and select to use legacy mode. Then use any of the physical to virtual conversion technologies described in this book to copy one machine to the other one. If you use a bootable Linux CD-ROM, you do not even have to buy any tools.

Most of the technical features of VMware ACE are identical to VMware Workstation. Some exceptions will be mentioned later in this chapter. But the hardware inside the virtual machines is the same and the list of guest operating systems is also very complete, and it is comparable to VMware Workstation version 4.5.

Installing ACE Manager

The software for VMware ACE can be downloaded from VMware's website at the following URL: www.vmware.com/download. You can obtain an evaluation copy that is valid for 30 days. VMware ACE is licensed on a per user basis. You can buy a Starter Pack containing ACE manager and four user licenses for USD 995. A separate ACE Manager license is USD 795 and individual user licenses cost USD 99 (prices are as of September 2005). The most recent version at the time of writing this book is version 1.01 (VMware-ACE-1.0.1-14996.exe).

Compared to the initial release in January 2005, version 1.0.1 includes the following new features:

- BIOS password

- Drag and Drop Support

- Enhanced full screen display

- New guest operating system support

The installation itself is rather straightforward. It does not require a reboot, so you can get started right away.

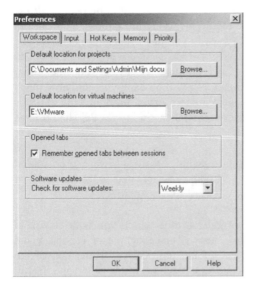

One of the things you want to look into after the installation is complete, is the basic settings for VMware ACE Manager. You access these from the **Edit** menu under **Preferences**.

You can configure the default path where you would like to place the ACE project configuration files and the location of your virtual machines. VMware ACE Manager can also check for updates automatically.

You can also configure the same memory settings as for VMware Workstation.

Figure 5.1: VMware ACE Manager settings.

5.3   Creating VMware ACE Projects

Virtual machines do not run inside ACE directly; they must be organized in projects. To start a new project, click the icon in the ACE Manager home window or select **File → New Project**.

1.   Provide a name for your project and a location where you would like to store the project files.

2.   Next, you are asked if you want to start the **Add Virtual Machine Wizard**. For this example, I have selected to do so.

3.   The wizard that is used to add new virtual machines is very much like the one in VMware Workstation. An important different first step is that you can choose to create an entire new machine or to use an existing machine. Creating a new virtual machine is identical to this process in VMware Workstation, except that you can not use raw physical partitions for your virtual machine since these can not be copied to end user computers.

     If you choose to use an existing virtual machine, browse to the .vmx file of that machine to add it to your project.

4.   When the Add Virtual Machine Wizard is complete, you will be prompted to configure policies for the virtual machines in the newly created project. Configuring policies is discussed later in this chapter.

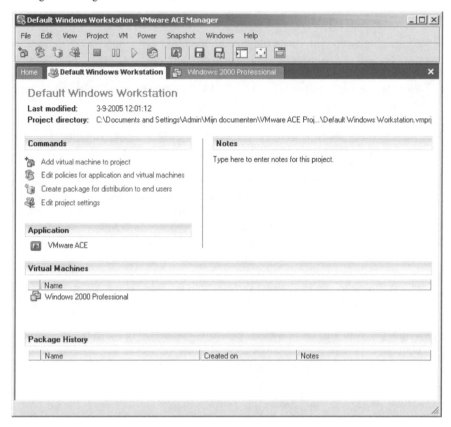

Figure 5.2: A default VMware ACE project typically contains one virtual machine.

5.4   Customizing a VMware ACE Project

In the main project window, click **Edit project settings** or select **Settings** from the **Project** menu. You can configure typical settings such as the project name and a description for the project. Other, more advanced topics are:

Selecting a policy domain
VMware ACE machines can be configured to read their authentication and policy information from an Active Directory domain. Configure the domain in the **Policies Domain** tab of the **Project Settings** window.

Defining offline policies
Typically, VMware ACE machines read their configuration from a web server or from Active Directory. If users do not always have access to the network, you can configure the policies to be cached on their local computer for a period of time to allow them to work with the ACE machine when they are not connected. For offline policies the following information is cached:

- Authentication policy: The key only

- Expiration policy: The expiration date only

- Devices policy: he list of allowed users only

- Network quarantine policy: All settings

Enable a recovery key for your project

If you will be using password protection for your virtual machines, you need to create a recovery key for this project. The recovery key enables you to process password changes. I will discuss how to do this later. At this point, select Create New Recovery Key in the Recovery Key tab of the Project Settings window. Or, select Browse for existing key if you wan to use another project's key for this project.

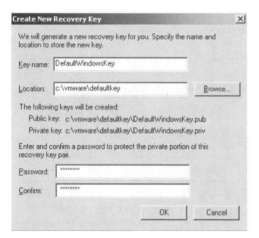

To create a new key, specify a name for the key that will help you identify it later and specify the path where you would like to store the file that contains the key.

Enter a password that will be assigned to the key file and that will protect the private portion of this public/private key pair. You need this password later when you need to process a password request from a user.

Figure 5.3: Create a recovery key for your project if you will be using password control.

5.5   Configuring Policies for a VMware ACE Project

An important reason to use VMware ACE for deploying virtual machines to end users instead of using regular VMware Workstation machines is that you can configure policies for your ACE environment. With normal virtual machines, the use of a machine can not be restricted. With VMware ACE, policies can be defined to:

- Allow only specified users to work with the virtual machine
- Specify what network resources can be used from within the virtual machine
- Configure the use of removable devices for a virtual machine
- Control the life cycle of the virtual machine

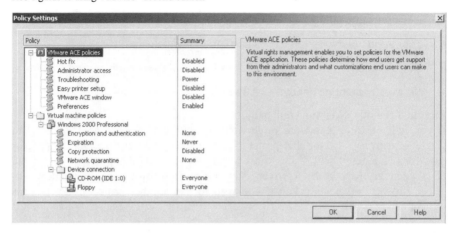

Figure 5.4: An overview of the available policies in VMware ACE.

There are two policy categories: VMware ACE policies that define how the ACE application works and virtual machine policies which define the behavior of the virtual machine that runs in ACE. Table 5.1 contains a brief description of the available policies.

Table 5.1: A brief description of all available ACE Policies.

VMware ACE Policy	Default	Description
Hot fix	Disabled	Use this policy to allow a user to request help with a lost password or an expired or copy protected machine. They can send an e-mail directly with an installed e-mail application through MAPI or create a file and send it themselves. Requires recovery to be enabled for the virtual machine.
Administrator access	Disabled	With this special Administrator password you can run the virtual machine on the end users' computer in a special application to change its configuration. Start this mode with the vmware -k command and provide the path and filename for the .vmx file.
Troubleshooting	Power	Power and reset controls are enabled

		by default. Reverting to the original state is disabled by default. When enabled the original image is created when the virtual machine is deployed to the user.
Easy printer setup	Disabled	When enabled, it allows users to select host printers to assign them to the virtual machine.
VMware ACE Window	Disabled	When enabled, it runs the VMware ACE machine in full screen mode.
Preferences	Enabled	Allows users to change these settings for the virtual machine: Confirm before exit yes/no, either suspend or power off the virtual machine and specify where to display the device connection icons.
Virtual Machine Policies		
Encryption and authentication		Use this policy to define security for the end user's virtual machine. This policy is described in detail later.
Expiration		Use this policy to specify if the policy will expire and if it does expire, specify the length of time such as how many days or the expiration date.
Copy protection		Users can copy the virtual machine files to a different location or another computer. With this policy enabled they can not run the virtual machine when copied to another location.
Network quarantine		Control access to the network from the virtual machine. This policy will be described in detail later.
Device connection CD-ROM	Everyone	Defines who can connect CD-ROM devices to the virtual machine: everyone, selected users, or defined by a script.
Device connection floppy	Everyone	Defines who can connect floppy devices to the virtual machine: everyone, selected users, or defined by a script.

From the list of available policies in Table 5.1 there are two that need further explanation. The encryption and authentication policy and the network quarantine policy allow you to secure the VMware ACE virtual machine environment. They are discussed in the following sections.

5.6 Virtual Machine Encryption and Authentication

This policy allows you to define the local security level for the virtual machine as well as who can access this machine. Figure 5.5 shows an overview of this policy's settings.

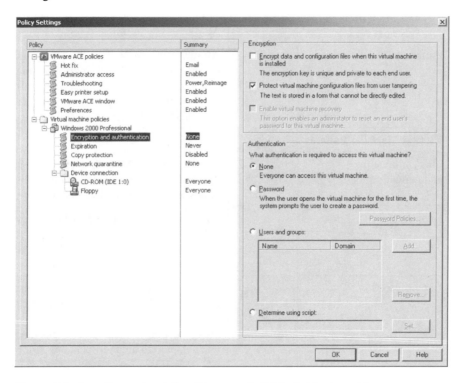

Figure 5.5: Security can be defined for every individual virtual machine.

The encryption feature encrypts the entire virtual machine's hard disk contents. If you enable this option, you must configure authentication for the virtual machine. Content encryption is performed when the virtual machine is deployed to the end user. This increases the deployment time. Depending on the size of the virtual machine's hard disk and the speed of the end user's computer, it can take anywhere from just a couple minutes up to ten or more minutes.

The other checkbox for this part of the policy, **Protect virtual machine configuration files from user tampering**, stores the virtual machine's configuration file (.VMX) in a non-editable format. You should always leave this setting enabled. If you do not leave it enabled, then the user can copy the virtual disk file including the vmx file and run it with another version of VMware, such as Workstation.

When the encryption feature is enabled, it is required to assign password management. You must also specify if recovery is possible for the virtual machine. With this setting enabled, the user can request a hot-fix and ask for a new password or to re-enable an expired or copy-protected virtual machine.

Password protection
A virtual machine can be secured with a password. It is required to start the virtual machine. With the simplest setting, the user will be prompted for a password when he or she starts the machine for the first time.

Figure 5.6: Password restrictions for the ACE virtual machine.

You can configure the restrictions that you want to apply for the virtual machine. The configuration allows you to enforce a minimum length and the use of a mixture of characters: uppercase, lowercase, numbers and symbols and punctuation, such as the exclamation mark and colon when choosing a password. If you need more complex rules or the password expiration feature, you must connect the virtual machine to Active Directory.

To enable password management for virtual machines through Active Directory, you must specify the domain that you want to connect to. You can do this from the **Project Settings** window. Or, you will automatically be prompted to do so when you choose to specify users and groups for the virtual machine and you have not configured the domain already.

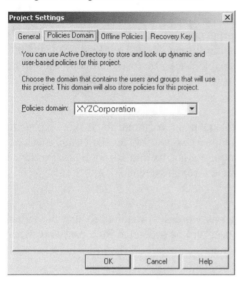

Figure 5.7: Define the domain where you want to store the policies for the virtual machine.

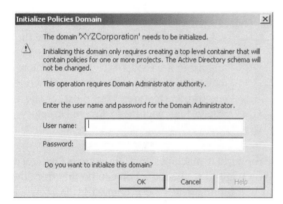

The Active Directory domain which you want to use to store the virtual machine passwords must be initialized. This creates a container where the policies will be stored. You most log into the domain with administrator privileges to create this configuration.

Figure 5.8: Create a container to store policies.

5.7 Virtual Machine Network Quarantine Policy

WMware ACE can control the network access from the virtual machine with the local network based on IP-addresses and other TCP/IP settings. This is called network quarantine. Table 5.2 lists the available quarantine types in VMware ACE.

Table 5.2: VMware ACE Network Quarantine Types.

Quarantine Type	Description
Static quarantine	Defines a fixed list of networks and machines that can be accessed from the virtual machine. Requires redeployment to change them.
Dynamic quarantine	Connects the virtual machine to Active Directory or a web server to read network access policies.
Version-based quarantine	Defines network access based on the virtual machine's version. For example, with an outdated machine that is not patched, you can allow access to the patch management server only.
Custom quarantine using a script	Advanced option to script access to the network.

The simplest quarantine setup is to define a static configuration that defines IP addresses or networks that can be accessed. This allows you to configure access to specific servers or networks only, or to deny access to those resources. An example of using these policies is when you use ACE to provide students with a safe and secure learning environment and you only want them to access the classroom server that runs an educational application. Or, you can provide a temporary employee with a virtual machine which can only access the database server that he or she needs to work with.

Static quarantine
Figure 5.9 shows a simple example of a configuration setting that only allows access to the machine on IP address 192.168.1.254. You can also specify a network address and subnet mask, such as 192.168.1.0 and 255.255.255.0, to allow or deny access to machines on that network only.

 Tip: You must configure to either allow access or deny access. You can not mix these two options in one policy configuration.

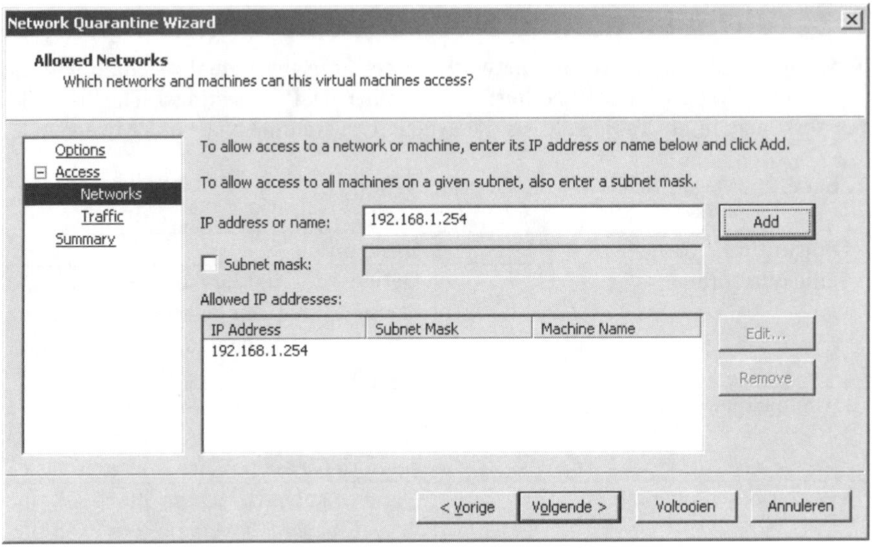

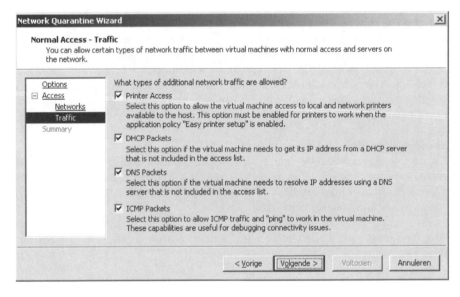

Figure 5.9: An example of a static network quarantine configuration.

After setting up the host's access configuration, you can specify additional protocols such as to allow or deny interaction with the virtual machine. These protocols are: Printer Access, DHCP Packets, DNS Packets, and ICMP Packets.

Figure 5.10: Four types of TCP/IP packets can be disabled for the virtual machine.

Dynamic quarantine
This type of configuration allows for the same settings to be specified, except that there is also the feature to simply allow all access or deny all access. For the rest, you specify the same networking features as described for the static quarantine. You can either point to Active Directory or to a web server.

For this to work, you must configure your own web server and deploy the .vmpl file which the wizard creates on the server. In the dynamic quarantine policy, you then specify the URL of this file on the web server, for example:

`http://policyserver/ACE/Windows2000Prof/netqpolicy.vmpl`

This URL can be anywhere on your server, where the users have access to the file.

Version based quarantine
With this type of quarantine, you can configure the same network settings as with the previous two quarantine types. You can also deploy this policy through Active Directory or through a web server. The additional configuration capability here is that you can configure a separate rule with restricted access which will be used if the virtual machine is of an older version.

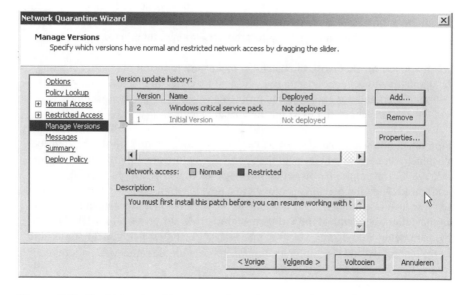

Figure 5.11: Restrict networking access based on a version number.

For this policy to work, you need to configure two different access levels. The normal level is the one that will be used if the virtual machine is up to date. The restricted level is the one that will be used if the version number does not match the one configured in the policy. For example, you can allow access to the patch management server only for the virtual machine to be updated.

Custom quarantine using script

In this quarantine scheme the same rules apply as for the previous ones, but a script file is used to define what level of access will be used. Scripts can be created in any language that is supported on the end users' workstation. Writing or modifying these scripts is beyond the scope of this introductory chapter. Sample scripts are provided with VMware ACE and full documentation is available in the ACE online documentation at the following URL: `www.vmware/com/supports/pubs`.

5.8 Deploying the ACE Virtual Machine

When the entire project is configured and the policies are set, it is time to prepare the virtual machine for deployment. Install the guest operating system the usual way and install all the applications that need to be included in the end users' environment. Also, add the VMware tools to the guest.

The virtual machine can be started with the regular control. I suggest that you use this option when you are installing the guest operating system, applications, and VMware tools inside the machine. It allows you to work with all normal VMware features for adding devices, shared folders, etc. Also, shrink the virtual disks to make sure that your deployment package is as small as possible.

When you are finished with the machine and you are almost ready to deploy it, run it with the option **Run in VMware ACE**. This will show you how it will look at the end user's machine and you can test the networking and other policies.

When you are finished with the machine, make sure to turn it off before creating the deployment package. Suspending a virtual machine on one machine and resuming it on another may result in problems when you start the machine. Also, remove any snapshots that exist for the virtual machine.

 Tip: When you want to add any VMware Workstation features to the ACE virtual machine, you need to add them to the .VMX file before creating the deployment package. For example, if you get the message about a UUID already being configured when the machine is moved to a new location. You have probably used a VMware Workstation virtual machine as the source when this happens. You can set the default behavior of the virtual machine to always create a new UUID with this parameter: `uuid.action = "create"`. I suggest that you do not use the `keep` feature because it could result in machines with the same MAC address on your network.

Creating a package

The actual deployment to the end user's computer is performed from a packaged installation of the virtual machine. It will result in a set of installation files and a subdirectory containing the virtual machine files. The files and paths are listed in Table 5.3.

Table 5.3: Overview of files inside a VMware ACE Package.

File or Path	Description
autorun.inf	When a user inserts a removable medium into a device such as a CD-ROM player, the installation defined in this file will start.
app.vmpl, config.ini and preferences.ini	These files contain information needed for encrypting the virtual machine at deployment time.
instmsiw.exe	This is the installation package for the Microsoft Windows Installer. If it is not already there, it can be installed to perform the installation with the .msi file.
package.msi	This is the Microsoft Windows Installer package to install the VMware ACE package.
setup.exe	This file can be used to start the installation of the package manually.
VMware ACE.msi	This is the Microsoft Windows Installer package for the VMware ACE runtime environment.
Project (directory)	Contains any custom scripts needed for the virtual machine.
Virtual machine directory	A directory with all the virtual machine's files.

The **New Package Wizard** will guide you through the process of creating the deployment package. Start the wizard from the **Project** menu, or click the link **Create package for distribution to end users** in the project's main window. Perform the following steps to create the package:

1. Provide a name for the package and enter the location for the new package. You can also provide some descriptive text for the end user to see when he or she executes the package.

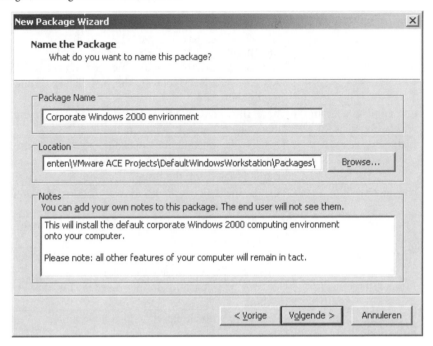

Figure 5.12: Provide a name, path and description for the new package.

2. In the next window, you must specify what you want to include in the package. This will typically be everything. Or, you can have one project with multiple virtual machines where you can select the machine that you want to deploy in this window.

3. At this time the wizard will check for any problems with the project and virtual machine that would prevent a successful deployment. For example, when you have not installed the VMware tools inside the virtual machine, it will warn you about that.

4. Next, you need to select if you want to create a network package or a package that is split in files which will fit on a CD-ROM or DVD. You can also choose a custom media and define a custom size. For example, whether you can write to larger CD-ROMs than the default 650 MB ones. You must also specify a prefix for the media (DISC by default). You will see a warning when the wizard is finished (see Figure 5.13). Make sure to label the CD-ROMs or DVDs you burn with this correct label for the VMware ACE installer to identify the media.

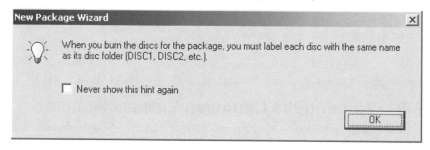

Figure 5.13: Use the directory names from the package as media labels.

Tip: If you have split the image for removable devices and would like to install it later from a network location, copy or move all virtual machine files into the `DISC1` directory.

5. The wizard will now display a summary about the package that it is about to create. This summary will also show the size of the package.

The package is now ready for deployment. You can deploy this package to the end user by placing it on the network or by placing it on a removable medium. The end user simply runs the setup executable and he or she is ready to go.

Note: A user can only have one VMware ACE project on his or her PC. A VMware ACE package must first be uninstalled before another package can be installed. Also, you can not test the package on the computer where you already have VMware ACE installed. You must use a computer without any current installations of a VMware product.

Tip: The package will be in the Add/remove programs list. But it will not be named VMware ACE. It will be installed with the name of the initial project name used in VMware ACE Manager.

The installation can also be started without any user intervention with the use of Microsoft Windows Installer executable.

```
msiexec -i package.msi DESKTOP_SHORTCUT=1
    INSTALLDIR="E:\Packages"
        APP_PROPERTIES="INSTALLDIR=""C:\VMware ACE""" /qr
```

In this example, the application is installed from `E:\Packages` into the `C:\VMware ACE` directory. The desktop shortcut will be enabled (default) but can also be disabled when you specify 0 (zero) as a parameter. You can specify the /q parameter for a silent installation. I have added the r parameter as well to allow for a limited user interface to make sure that the user sees that something is being installed. This will still allow the user to cancel the process. Use the /passive parameter to display only a progress bar.

 Tip: To uninstall the package, run the Microsoft Windows Installer with the following command: msiexec -uninstall package.msi /qr.

5.9 Running the Deployed Virtual Machine

After the package is deployed to the end user's computer, it can be started from the start menu or the shortcut on the desktop. When the virtual machine is configured for password management, the user is prompted for a new password the first time that the application runs.

When the machine is running, a user will see a status bar that is somewhat similar to a terminal services window. The user can access the host by just clicking on the window. Because the tools will be installed, the mouse pointer will seamlessly go out of the virtual machine and into the host operating system.

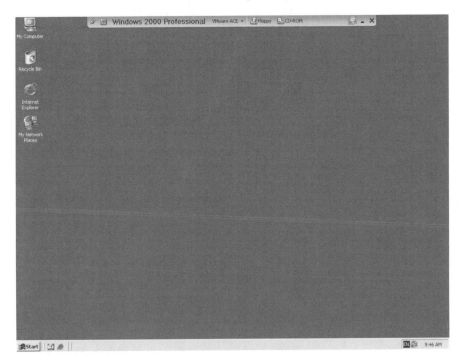

Figure 5.14: A virtual machine running in VMware ACE looks similar to a terminal services window.

 Tip: If you want users not to be able to use Ctrl-Alt-Del inside the virtual machine, specify the following command in the .vmx file before packing it for deployment: mks.ctlAltDel.ignore = true.

Depending on the level of access that you have specified, the user can select features such as adding a printer to the virtual machine or attaching a CD-ROM device from the menu at the top of his or her screen.

5.10 Responding to a User's Hot Fix Request

When you have configured the virtual machine with a policy that allows the user to request a Hot Fix, you must process these requests from VMware ACE Manager. A Hot Fix can be a request for a password reset, to re-enable an expired virtual machine, or to re-enable a machine that was copied to another location.

In the following example, a user tries to start a password protected virtual machine but has forgotten the password.

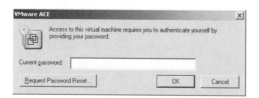

The user clicks the Request Password Reset button to start the **Request Hot Fix Request Wizard**. This will walk the user through the process of creating a file or sending an e-mail.

Figure 5.15: When a user forgets the password a Hot Fix request can be sent to the administrator.

The wizard will ask the user for his or her name and e-mail address. This information will be used to return the host fix request when it is processed by the administrator. If the feature is enabled to send the request via e-mail in the policy, then the user's e-mail application will be used through a MAPI call to send the e-mail to the administrator's address which is specified in the policy. For example, when the policy is configured to save the hot fix request in a file, the user can save the file on his or her network home directory.

To process the request, select **Open Hot Fix Request** from the **File** menu in VMware ACE Manager. Click the appropriate button to either select or deny the Hot Fix request and after processing it, send it back to the user (see Figure 5.16).

 Tip: You can also open the e-mail attachment directly from your e-mail application. It will start VMware ACE Manager and load the .VMHR file to directly process the request.

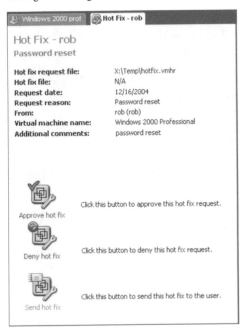

The window will show additional information about the user, the virtual machine involved, and the type of request. Depending on the type of request, an approved Hot Fix dialog box will be provided.

In case of a password reset, you must open the recovery key file that you created earlier for your project and provide the recovery password. Enter a new password for the user (twice, to confirm the password) and provide the password to the user. It will not be included in the Hot Fix response automatically.

You can store the file or send it via e-mail directly from VMware ACE Manager.

Figure 5.16:   Process a user's Hot Fix request.

When the user receives the Hot Fix request, he or she can open the .VMHF file directly from the e-mail attachment or from the file system. It will then be processed by the VMware ACE application.

Part 2

VMware Configuration and Tips

BOB GETS MORE STOCK OPTIONS.

6 General VMware Configuration and Tips

This chapter covers configuration settings and tips that are useful for all VMware technology users, who use VMware Workstation, GSX Server, or ESX Server. It will help you regardless of the host or guest operating systems you are using: Windows or Linux. The first section will point you in the direction of documentation and support, while the rest of the chapter will cover a collection of useful tips, tricks, and directions.

6.1 Documentation and Support

If you are new to VMware, I strongly advise you to download the official VMware Workstation, GSX Server, or ESX Server manual and go through the one that pertains to you before you start deploying your VMware solution. The VMware people have done a very good job of describing how to get started with creating virtual machines. They describe how to install guest operating systems, the accompanying tools, and much more.

VMware Technology Network
All official VMware resources on the web are now bundled in the VMware Technology Network (VMTN). This is a service that is available anonymously on the Internet for free. It is also possible to buy a subscription to VMTN. This is a service that was created for developers and provides a powerful suite of VMware products, support, and upgrades for a convenient, low-cost annual subscription.

The VMTN subscription includes licenses for Workstation, GSX Server, ESX Server with Virtual SMP, and P2V Assistant (Enterprise Edition). GSX Server, ESX Server, and Virtual SMP licenses are for two-processor servers. The VMTN subscription is designed and licensed for development use with only some licensing restrictions on ESX Server. Please review the terms for VMTN subscription licenses and support at www.vmware.com/vmtn_eula.

VMTN subscription privileges include web-based support and product upgrades. Each subscriber has access to VMTN community and technical resources plus two web-based support requests with VMware's support experts. The annual cost for a VMTN subscription is USD 299. An optional media kit with CD-ROMs and documentation costs USD 99 (prices are as of September 2005).

Online documentation
Access to the documentation is provided via VMware support website at www.vmware.com/support/pubs. You can access the online documentation for each product in HTML format or download the entire manual in PDF format.

If you need support beyond the documentation, you can use one of the following four official sources:

1. The **VMware support website** contains a very good Knowledge Base with support information from the VMware support team. You can access the knowledge base directly at the following URL: www.vmware.com/kb.

2. The **VMware Community Discussion Forums** is a good place to go when the knowledge base does not provide the answer you are looking for. There are forums on all product categories where many VMware enthusiasts are actively participating in helping others get the most out of their VMware products. The community forum is available at www.vmware.com/community.

3. Just like the forums, the **VMware Newsgroups** are a place on the web where you can go to get support from other VMware users. Point your NNTP newsreader to news.vmware.com to access the newsgroups.

4. At the VMworld conference in October 2004, the first VMware User Groups (VMUG) was started. These user groups are supported by VMware but are run by local VMware enthusiasts. The user groups have their own meetings and events and their own Internet forum. Information on all user groups can be found at the following URL:

    www.vmware.com/vcommunity/usergroups.html.

Other resources on the web
sHere is a list of some useful website that you can check out when you want to read more about the current status of virtualization technology in general and VMware specifically. These websites also contain tips and tools for your VMware environment.

Virtualization.info by Alessandro Perilli	www.virtualization.info
Virtual Strategy magazine	www.virtual-strategy.com
Site dedicated to virtualization	www.run-virtual.com
Dominic Rivera's site on certification	www.vmwareprofessional.com
Ulli Hankeln's VMware tips site	sanbarrow.com
Massimiliano Daneri's VM pages	www.vmts.net
Ken Kato's tools project	chitchat.at. infoseek.co.jp/vmware
The author's website	www.robbastiaansen.nl

6.2 Running Virtual Machines from the Command Line

You can start virtual machines from the command line in several ways. One of them is by using the VMware executable itself. There are also two separate executables that you can use: vmrun and vmware-fullscreen.exe (for Windows). All three options are explained in this chapter.

Parameters for the VMware executable

It can be very useful to start virtual machines when your host starts. You can do this by adding commands to a startup script or you could start virtual machines from scripts, or trigger them from other applications in your host system.

The syntax for starting VMware Workstation from the command line is:

```
vmware [OPTIONS] [\<path_to_config>\<config>.vmx]
```

Table 6.1: Listing of command line switches for VMware executable.

Command Line Switch	Description
-x	Automatically powers the virtual machine on when VMware starts.
-X	Automatically powers the virtual machine on when VMware starts and switches to full screen mode.
-q	Closes the virtual machine's tab when the machine powers off, and also exits VMware Workstation if no other virtual machines are running at the same instance as vmware.exe.
-s NAME=VALUE	Sets the specified variable to the specified value. Any variable names and values that are valid in the configuration file may be specified on the command line with the -s switch.
-p parentDisk childDisk	Points disks to the correct parent disk
-m (Linux host only)	Starts the program in quick switch mode on a Linux host.
-k KVM_FILE	Specifies a list of virtual machines.
-v	Displays the product name, version and build number of VMware Workstation.
\<path_to_config>\<config>.vmx	Do not forget to use quotes around file names that have spaces in them; otherwise parts of the path will be seen as separate parameters.

Using the vmrun executable
VMware Workstation version 5 comes with a new executable which you can use to work with virtual machines from the command line.

The syntax for this command is:

```
vmrun COMMAND [PARAMETER]
```

Table 6.2: Commands and parameters for vmrun executable.

Command	Parameter	Description
list		Lists all running VMs.
start	Path to vmx file[*]	Starts a VM
stop	Path to vmx or vmtm file	Stops a VM or Team
reset	Path to vmx or vmtm file	Resets a VM or Team
suspend	Path to vmx or vmtm file	Suspends a VM or Team
upgradevm	Path to vmx file	Upgrades a VM to a new hardware version

[*] Starting a team with the vmrun command is currently not supported.

Using the vmware-fullscreen executable (Windows only)
With this utility, virtual machines can be started and moved to full screen mode right away. This can be useful in scenarios where virtual machines must be started without user intervention or when you do not want the users to know that they are running with a virtual machine.

The syntax for this command is:

```
vmware-fullscreen <command> ["path to config file"]
```

Table 6.3: Commands for the vmware-fullscreen executable.

Command	Variables	Description
poweron[*]	-s variable=value	Sets the specified variable to the specified value. Any variable names and values that are valid in the configuration file may be specified on the command line with the -s switch.
	-name=<alias>	Specifies an alias to be used in the **poweroff** and **switchto** commands.
	-directkey=<keyspec>	Specifies a key which can be used to switch to this machine directly.[*]
	-fullscreen	Powers on and switches to full screen immediately.
poweroff	alias or path to vmx file	Powers off the specified virtual machine.

switchto	alias or path to vmx file	Switches control to the specified virtual machine.
listvms		List virtual machines
query		Checks the status of the virtual machine.
exit		Stops all virtual machines that where started with the vmware-fullscreen command.

* Add the following parameters (explained in the online documentation) to your configuration file: FullScreenSwitch.cycleKey, FullScreenSwitch.hostDirectKey and FullScreenSwitch.cycleHost.

Log file information for the vmware-fullscreen utility is written to a log file in the temporary directory of the user who is running the application. By default, this will be: `c:\documents and settings\<username>\local settings\temp`.

The path can be changed by adding the following entry to the general VMware Workstation configuration file (`C:\Documents and Settings\All Users\Application Data\VMware\VMware Workstation\config.ini.`):

`fullScreenSwitch.log.filename="<path>"`

6.3   VMware Files Reference

A virtual machine is made up of a set of files. The configuration, the BIOS, and the contents of the virtual hard disk all go into files on you host PC's file system. Table 6.4 contains an overview of the files that are used for your virtual machines and for general VMware purposes. The list is not complete since not all the files are documented. The overview is created by analyzing VMware Workstation and the files that it creates.

Table 6.4: Virtual Machine File Reference.

File or Filetype	Description
.vmx	A text file that contains the virtual machine's configuration. The parameters are configured via VMware application. If needed, the parameters can be modified via a text editor. Close the VMware application before editing it manually. VMware Workstation verifies the validity of this file for missing quotes, duplicate entries, etc.
.vmxf	This is an additional configuration file that stores team specific information for a virtual machine when it is a member of a team.

.vmtm	Configuration file, for a team of virtual machines.
.vmdk	Extension of all virtual disk files.
diskname-###.vmdk	REDO file where all changes to the original disk file are stored after creating a snapshot.
<vmxconfigname>.nvram or just .nvram	File containing the Non Volatile Random Access Memory for BIOS.
.vmsd	This file contains meta-data about snapshots.
vmsn	This is the actual snapshot file which stores the running state of the virtual machine.
.vmss	Virtual machine Suspend State file. It contains the memory dump when suspending a virtual machine.
.vmem	Memory swap file for your virtual machine.
.lck	Lock file created for configuration and disk files.
.log	Log file for all activities in the virtual machine. Logging can be turned off by adding `logging = FALSE` to the .vmx configuration file. The name and location of the log file can be modified with this parameter: `log.filename = "c:\patch\name.log"`. **Note:** Without logging, it will be very difficult for VMware to analyze any problems you might encounter.
vmware-core	Dump file created in the situation of some kind of fatal error.
C:\Documents and Settings\All Users\Application Data\VMware\VMware Workstation	
config.ini	General configuration file.
C:\Documents and Settings\All Users\Application Data\VMware	
vmnetdhcp.conf	VMware host-only DHCP server configuration file.
vmnetdhcp.leases	File containing the assigned IP addresses by DHCP.
vmnetnat.conf	VMware NAT service configuration file.

6.4   VMware Product Generations

If you have worked with VMware products for a few years, you probably know that virtual machines are not always compatible between virtual machine products or between different versions of the same product. In this section, I will discuss how to work with different product generations and how to find out which generation a virtual machine belongs to.

 Note: The information in this section is an abstract from the official VMware Virtual Machine Mobility Planning Guide, available at the following URL: www.vmware.com/pdf/mobility_guide.pdf.

Table 6.5 lists the four current VMware product generations. Converting virtual machines between VMware products that are of the same generation is simple in most cases. In some special cases such as moving from VMware Workstation to VMware ESX Server, some additional steps are required.

Table 6.5: The VMware products and their generations.

Generation level	Products that belong to this generation
Generation 2	GSX Server 1, ESX Server 1.0 and 1.1
Generation 3	Workstation 3, GSX Server 2, ESX Server 1.5
Generation 4	Workstation 4, GSX Server 3, ESX Server 2
Generation 5	Workstation 5

 Tip: When products are not from the same generation, you can certainly follow the official guideline and upgrade the virtual machine. However, it is sometimes easier to just use the physical to virtual conversion methods described in part 3 of this book to perform a virtual to virtual migration.

If you want to do some research on a virtual machine when you are not sure of its generation, here are some tips that are useful:

First, the virtual machine configuration file (.VMX) contains an entry called config.version that will specify a version number for the VMware product that it was created with. This is a list of what I have extracted out of virtual machine configurations that I have collected over the years:

```
config.version = "2"    VMware Workstation 2
config.version = "6"    VMware Workstation version 3 / GSX Server 2.x
config.version = "7"    VMware Workstation version 4/ GSX Server 3.x
config.version = "8"    VMware Workstation version 5 and 5.5.
```

There is also an identifier that is being used for the hardware generation. This is a list of what I have found in my virtual machines over the years:

```
virtualHW.version = "2"     VMware Workstation 3 / GSX Server 2.x
virtualHW.version = "3"     VMware Workstation 4 / GSX Server 3.x
virtualHW.version = "4"     VMware Workstation 5 and 5.5
```

A VMware Workstation version 2 virtual machine can easily be recognized by the .dsk extension for its virtual disks. The .vmdk extension was introduced with VMware Workstation version 3.

If you have a copy of a virtual hard disk only (.VMDK) and you do not know what hardware generation it belongs to, then you can search the file for the appropriate string. The hardware identification is stored in the first .VMDK file of the virtual had disk set.

Use Windows's find command or Linux's grep command to find the virtual disk generation identifier inside the file:

Windows
```
find "virtualHWVersion" <path to .vmdk file>
```

Linux
```
grep 'virtualHWVersion' <path to .vmdk file>
```

This will result in a string, such as this one which displays version 4, belonging to VMware Workstation 5:

```
ddb.virtualHWVersion = "4"
```

 Note: For older versions of VMware Workstation, I did not find this string in the configuration file. It is there for VMware Workstation 4 and 5. Therefore, since version 2 uses .DSK files the remaining .VMDK files where this string is not found will probably be from Workstation version 3 or GSX Server 2.

6.5   VMware Windows Services Overview

VMware Workstation adds three services to your Windows. If you install the VMware DiskMount utility, a fourth service will be added. The image below shows the services overview from the **Services** application in **Administrative Tools**.

Name /	Description	Status	Startup...	Log On As
VMware Authorization Service	Authorization and authentication service for starting and accessing virtual machines	Started	Automatic	Local System
VMware DHCP Service	DHCP service for virtual networks		Automatic	Local System
VMware NAT Service	Network address translation for virtual networks	Started	Automatic	Local System
VMware Virtual Mount Service Extended	Part of the VMware Virtual Image Editing Framework		Manual	Local System

Figure 6.1: VMware Services in Windows.

The DHCP and NAT services take care of these respective VMware features on your host PC. They are explained in chapter 11: "Networking configurations". The Virtual Mount service belongs to the VMware DiskMount utility, discussed in section 7.4: "Using the DiskMount Utility".

VMware Authorization Service
This service needs clarification. The authorization service takes care of running VMware when the user who starts the application is not an administrative user. This service detects that a user is not an administrative user and starts VMware as the Local System Account. Figure 6.2 shows a screen capture of the Sysinternals Process Explorer

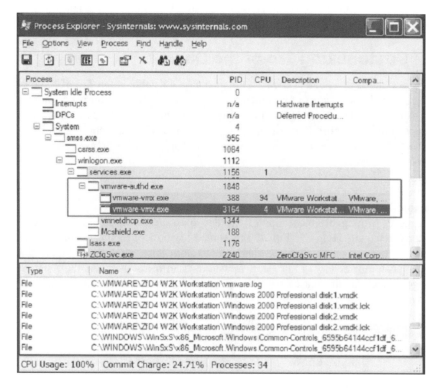

Figure 6.2: Sysinternals Process Explorer.

The vmware-vmx.exe is started as a child of vmware-authd.exe under services. The operation of the service can be tracked by enabling logging in the general VMware configuration file. This file is called config.ini and is located at C:\Documents and Settings\All Users\Application Data\VMware\VMware Workstation. To enable logging, add the following lines to this text file:

```
vmauthd.logEnabled = "true"
log.vmauthdFileName = "C:\authd.log"
```

The following is part of a log file where a virtual machine is started by user Simple:

```
app| Username associated with named pipe: simple
app| Allocating a new session
app| CreateLogonSession: spawn with username: simple
app|   (Account is NOT administrator)
app|   (Account is interactive)
app| Not mapping drives for acct
```

 Note: Do not leave the logging turned on by default. Use it only when analyzing or troubleshooting this service and turn the logging off when you are finished.

6.6   Customizing Tip of the Day

As an experienced user, one of the first things that you disable is the **Tip of the day** screen. If you do not want to be bothered with this information, you need to press Ctrl-Alt-Ins to send Ctrl-Alt-Del to the guest. Depending on how VMware is used, these tips could be useful. For example, they are useful when students are working with the software in an educational environment. The messages VMware displays can be customized to meet the need of your users or to be translated in their native language.

Re-enable Tip of the Day

If you regret turning off these tips of the day messages, you can re-enable this feature by selecting **Help → Tip of the Day**. This will open the tip of the day window, where you can enable the checkbox to **Show tips at startup**. Figure 6.3 shows a customized Tip of the Day message. It informs users in their native language (Dutch in this case) on how to send a reset keystroke to the virtual machine.

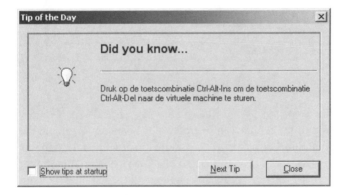

Figure 6.3: The tip of the day feature can be customized.

Customizing Tip of the Day

The tips that VMware Workstation shows are stored in the file `tip_list.vmsg`. For Windows, it is stored in directory `C:\Program Files\VMware\VMware Workstation\messages\en`. For Linux, the file is stored in directory `/usr/lib/vmware/messages/en`.

These messages can be customized by modifying the text in the default tips or by adding new messages. The file has the following format:

```
# en-tips-ws-windows
tip.0="To send Ctrl-Alt-Del to the guest press Ctrl-
Alt-Ins."
tip.1="Press F11 to enter quick switch mode."
tip.2="Press Ctrl-Alt-Enter to enter full screen mode."
...
```

The tips are processed in sequential order starting with `tip.0`. You can add tips by continuing the numbering at the end of the file. Tips can also be removed from the file, or can be commented out (# at the beginning of the file) to prevent them from being displayed. Make sure that all other lines are ordered sequentially, because when the numbering sequence is broken, the tips after the missing number will not display.

 Note: The new tips will be displayed after restarting VMware. The application reads the tips at startup.

 Note: This file may be overwritten when installing a newer version of VMware Workstation. So, make sure to keep a back-up copy of your modified file and verify and restore your modified environment after an upgrade.

6.7 Restricting and Customizing VMware Workstation (Windows Only)

There are two features in VMware Workstation that are useful when end-users work with VMware Workstation. These features are useful in an educational environment or when end-users use VMware in a migration scenario; they may be using an older version of Windows to migrate to another operating system on their desktop (either Windows or Linux).

 Tip: For the functionality described in this paragraph, it is important that users have limited rights to the Windows environment. Users that are not configured to be administrators can start virtual machines because of the VMware Authorization Daemon. How that works is described in section 6.5, "VMware services overview"

Administrative lockout feature
With the use of this feature users can be prevented from doing the following:

• Create new virtual machines and teams
• Edit virtual machines and team configurations
• Manage virtual networks

These three options can be individually selected from the **Lockout** tab via **Edit** → **Preferences**. (See Figure 6.4.)

In this screen, you also provide a password that will be needed by the users to perform any of the locked out features.

This configuration by itself is also secured with the same password.

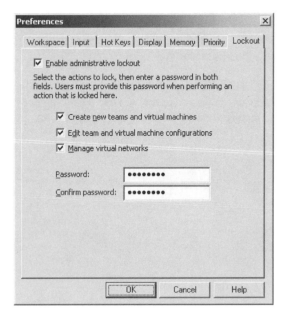

Figure 6.4: Administrative lockout prevents users from modifying the VMware environment.

If the password is forgotten, you can follow the directions described in the note below.

⚠ **Note:** The VMware documentation points out that in case of a lost password the entire application needs to be uninstalled and re-installed. However, there is a configuration file that stores the password. In a previous version of VMware Workstation the password was stored in clear text, but with version 5 it is stored in an encrypted format. But, if a user has write access to the VMware configuration file, he or she can still disable the lockout feature by modifying the lockout.enabled option in the file.

For Windows the configuration file is called config.ini and it is located at:

`C:\Documents and Settings\All Users\Application Data\VMware\VMware Workstation.`

The following text is an example of the administrative lockout configuration parameters from the config.ini file:

```
lockout.enabled = "TRUE"
lockout.createVM = "TRUE"
lockout.editVM = "TRUE"
lockout.manageNetworks = "TRUE"
lockout.passwordHashed = "TRUE"
lockout.password = "ik47fsVUv60uf/oXpD8sSw=="
```

You can configure the settings in this file, but doing so is not recommended. The Preferences panel is the only supported means of configuring these settings in VMware Workstation.

Restricting the user interface
This is a feature that can be enabled on a per virtual machine basis to restrict the VMware user interface. It will disable the menu options and toolbar buttons. The effects of using this setting are described below. It is only available for Windows hosts:

- The toolbar is hidden from the end user.
- All options in the **Power** and **Snapshot** menus are disabled.
- Access to the virtual machine configuration is disabled. Both via the **Settings** menu option and via the icons in the status bar.
- Users can open other virtual machines via the .vmx file. If the user interface is not restricted for that virtual machine then the interface will be only available for that machine. It is still restricted for the virtual machine which was opened with the restricted setting.

- The virtual machine will automatically power on after opening it. A virtual machine is stopped, by shutting down the guest operating system. The user can click the close icon in the upper right corner or choose **File → Exit**. This will ask the user to power the machine off. Suspend and resume is not available in this mode. You can use the Snapshot feature to always start at the same point. This will be discussed in more detail later.

The restricted user interface is activated via a parameter in the virtual machine configuration file. Close the VMware application for the virtual machine that you want to configure and open the .vmx configuration file with a text editor. Add the following line to the file:

```
gui.restricted = "true"
```

Starting VMware with this parameter restricts the user interface as described above.

 Note: Using this setting is not a total security feature to disable users to modify the VMware environment. You will have to configure the configuration file for read-only access, so that the users can not modify the contents of the file. However, they can still copy the file or its contents to a new location or file, where they have full access and remove the gui.restricted parameter.

The restricted user interface can be unrestricted by removing the gui.restricted parameter from the .VMX file or by setting it to gui.restricted = "false".

Using Snapshot to always start the same configuration
The Snapshot feature can be combined with the restricted user interface to create a configuration where a user always starts the virtual machine with the same guest operating system state.

To create this type of configuration, perform the following steps:

1. Create the Snapshot of the virtual machine while it is in the Power off state. The VMware manual notes that any state can be used, but when taking a Snapshot of a running machine and setting the machine to revert to the Snapshot after Power off, the machine continues to go to that state after powering off.

2. Turn your virtual machine off and configure the virtual machine to always revert to the Snapshot after Power off.

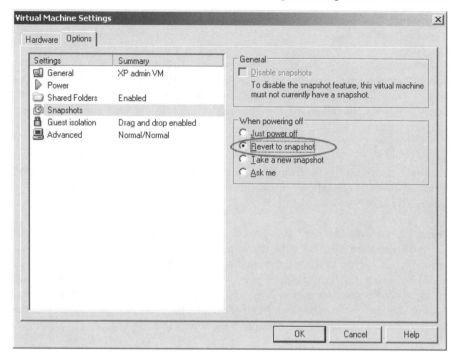

Figure 6.5: Always return to the same starting point with snapshots.

3. Close the VMware application and enter the `gui.restricted` = "`true`" parameter in the `.vmx` file.

From now on, the virtual machine will always start with the same state of operating system that it was in when the snapshot was created.

6.8 VMware Guest Time Synchronization

Time synchronization between the host computer and the guest is a mechanism which either: always works for you, or always gives you a headache. Let's get it over with, and look at the details of configuring time synchronization.

A new virtual machine boots and takes over the time from the host operating system. It creates a NVRAM BIOS file which is also used to store the values of the CMOS clock of the virtual machine. Just as with a real PC, the virtual machine uses its internal clock, and your guest operating system in turn uses that time.

So far so good; but there can be many reasons why the clock in your guest starts to drift off from the time of your host's clock. This is mostly hardware related. One issue, for example, is encountered when using laptops with Intel SpeedStep technology. These computers vary the speed that the processor runs with, to the power state of the PC.

Your best strategy to get the time synchronized between the host and the guest is to enable the time synchronization feature in the VMware tools. You can enable this feature from the graphical configuration window for the tools in your operating system, or to set the following parameter in the .vmx file for your virtual machine.

```
tools.syncTime = "true"
```

However, there is a strange behavior about this synchronization which is mentioned in the VMware Workstation manual somewhere, but which is not well known. It is described in the following note:

 Note: You can synchronize the time in the guest operating system with the time on the host operating system, only when you set the clock in the guest operating system to an earlier time than the time set on the host. This can very simply be tested by setting the local clock of your virtual machine a few minutes ahead, and enable the time synchronization. You will see that the time will stay in the future. Setting the time to a time that lies before the time on the host, will start the synchronization and within a few minutes the time will be in sync.

 Note: It is very important to use only one method of time synchronization for your virtual environment. Do not enable the VMware tools time synchronization if your virtual machine is synchronizing time with an outside time source, or with other virtual machines (via NTP for example).

7 Virtual Disks, Floppies and CD-ROMs

Working with VMware is addictive. Once your start working with virtual machines, you will want everything to be virtualized. You do not want to swap CDs anymore or format floppy disks. This chapter describes how to work with your virtual disks, how to create virtual floppies, and how to work with CD-ROM images.

7.1 Working with Virtual Floppy Disks

With VMware Workstation and VMware GSX Server you can use virtual hard disks. That is the first virtual component of VMware that every user creates when he or she starts working with VMware. You can also create virtual floppy files. This makes it easier to access files in a guest operating system if, for example, file sharing between the host and guest is not possible.

One method of creating virtual floppy disks is via standard features supported by VMware.

You just add a virtual floppy file to a virtual machine and format and access the floppy from within the guest operating system. The following image shows you how a virtual floppy is created.

The configuration in Figure 7.1 creates a virtual floppy disk with the extension of .flp. If you now boot a Windows or Linux guest, you can format the floppy disk. Virtual floppy disks are pre-allocated by default so the file created with the above setup will be 1.4 MB in size.

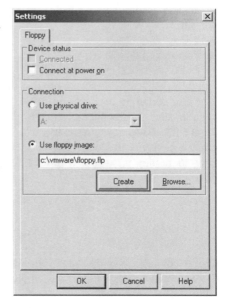

 Tip: a formatted virtual floppy (VirtualFloppy.zip) is available for download at www.robbastiaansen.nl.

Figure 7.1: Creating a virtual floppy disk.

WinImage

One other method to work with virtual floppy files is the WinImage application, available at www.winimage.com. It supports the virtual floppy file format. This enables you to create new floppy disks from scratch or to manage existing virtual floppy disks. The only thing to be aware of with using virtual floppy disks from WinImage is to save them as **non-compressed** disk files. The normal image type for WinImage is a compressed file type with the .IMZ extension; see Figure 7.2). So, use the non-compressed .IMA format and save the files as .FLP files, or rename the .IMA files to .FLP files.

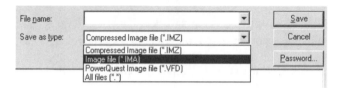

Figure 7.2: Use the uncompressed format from WinImage.

Virtual Floppy Driver by Ken Kato

There is also a tool available that can mount your virtual floppies in Windows with a drive letter. The utility is created by Ken Kato from Japan and it is available from his website at:

chitchat.at.
    infoseek.co.jp/vmware

The tool comes in a command line version and a graphical version. Figure 7.3 shows how simple it is to browse to a virtual floppy file and how to mount it with the **mount** button.

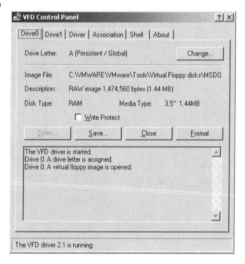

Figure 7.3: VFD is a very cool utility for mounting virtual floppies in Windows.

 Tip: if you need boot disks for your VMware environment or for any other reason, there are two very good locations on the web for all kinds of boot disks:

- Bart's boot disk via www.nu2.nu
- www.bootdisk.com

7.2 Sharing a Common Base Disk between Virtual Machines

This is a tip that will save you valuable disk space. For example, if you have multiple Windows workstations on your host PC that only have a slightly different configuration they will still take up maybe 1 or 2 GB each.

 Note: This only works with VMware Workstation version 4.x and VMware GSX Server 3.x. With VMware Workstation version 5 there is default support for multiple snapshots, which breaks this type of setup. Using multiple snapshots is described in section 3.5.

If you follow the steps provided in this section, your virtual machines can access the same base disk file and they will use Snapshot REDO-files to save the differences to that base setup. Figure 7.4 illustrates three virtual machines using a common shared disk.

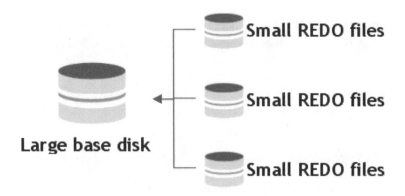

Figure 7.4: Three machines using a common base disk.

To create a setup with two virtual machines sharing a common disk, follow the steps outlined here:

1. Start out by creating a virtual machine with the operating system of your choice. This is an example of what your directory would look like:

nvram	9 KB	File
Windows 2000 Professional.vmdk	1 KB	VMware virtual disk file
Windows 2000 Professional.vmx	2 KB	VMware Configuration File
Windows 2000 Professional-s001.vmdk	1.592.064 KB	VMware virtual disk file
Windows 2000 Professional-s002.vmdk	320 KB	VMware virtual disk file
Windows 2000 Professional-s003.vmdk	64 KB	VMware virtual disk file

---

2. Power the virtual machine off and create a snapshot while the machine is in the power off state. Do not power the machine on at this point. Close the VMware application.

3. Now move the .VMDK disk files to a location where your master disk will reside. This includes all .vmdk files as well as the –s001, etc. files. Mark the virtual disk files as read-only, so they can not be changed by any of your VM's.

   I have created a directory structure in `c:\vmware` which I will use for the example paths:

   ```
   c:\vmware
   c:\vmware\windows2000master
   c:\vmware\windows2000vm1
   c:\vmware\windows2000vm2
   ```

4. Create a directory for your first virtual machine and move the remaining (.vmx .sav and nvram, etc.) files into that directory. The original directory is now empty.

5. Now open the .vmx file for the first virtual machine with an editor and locate the line where you virtual disk is specified. In my example, this is the IDE0:0 disk:

   ```
   ide0:0.fileName = "Windows 2000 Professional.vmdk"
   ```

   Edit this line with the full path to your master VMDK file.

   ```
   ide0:0.fileName                              =
   "c:\vmware\windows2000master\Windows
                                   2000
                        Professional.vmdk"
   ```

6. Open VMware with the .vmx configuration file of the first virtual machine. In the virtual machine settings, lock the snapshot for this virtual machine.

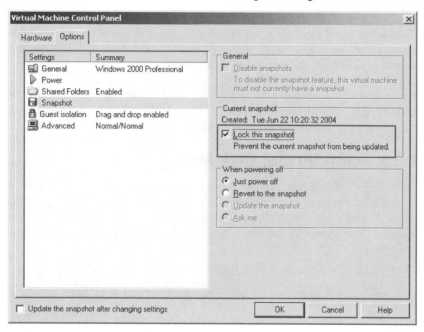

Figure 7.5: Locking a snapshot is only available in Workstation version 4.x and GSX Server 3.x.

7. Copy the .vmx file (and if important for your configuration, also the nvram bios file) to the directory for the second virtual machine.

8. You can now power both virtual machines on. They will both read from the shared master disk, but all changes to the disk will go into .REDO files which you will find in the virtual machine directory for each machine. This happens because the .REDO files do not have an absolute path; instead, they are stored in a path relative to the machine (the VM directory itself).

```
ide0:0.redo=".\Windows 2000 Professional.vmdk.REDO_a03292"
```

Tip: If you use the configuration with a separate swap disk for your guest operating system (as described in section 9.1: "Performance tips") in combination with this shared disk setup, then assign every virtual machine a separate swap disk and set the disk to be an independent. Keep the swap disk .vmdk file in the directory with the virtual machine configuration files. This way, the swap disk will not be affected by the snapshot. There is no need to keep the page file contents consistent between pre and post Snapshot configurations.

Tip: Copying the virtual machines will make exact copies of everything in the operating system, including the identity, SID, computer name, IP address, etc. All these settings can be re-configured to allow the virtual machines to work simultaneously. If there is no need for the machines to interact with each other (the network, or the host), leave the configuration in place and set the network interfaces to different host-only networks.

For example, you can run a virtual machine on VMnet5 without having to set up VMnet5 in your host operating system. This configuration procedure is explained in section: 11.2 "Configure host-only and bridged networking".

7.3 Using Virtual Disk Manager

This utility enables you to work with virtual disks outside of the VMware Workstation environment. Typically only your guest virtual machines have access to the virtual disks. With this program you can access them directly from the command line. Some of the main features of the VMware Virtual Disk Manager utility are:

- Expanding the size of virtual disks.

- Converting virtual disks from dynamically growing to fixed size and vice versa.

- Create, modify, and defragment virtual disks from a command line utility which you can use to script virtual disk operations.

The Virtual Disk Manager used to be only available for Windows hosts but it is now also available for Linux. On Windows, the utility (vmware-vdiskmanager.exe) is installed with VMware Workstation version 5. The default location is:

C:\Program Files\VMware\VMware Workstation.

For Linux, the executable is called vmware-vdiskmanager and it is located in /usr/bin.

In this section, I will cover some of the basic features that you might need for your environment. The online documentation covers the full set of features for this utility.

The command line format is as follows:

vmware-vdiskmanager OPTIONS diskName | drive-letter:

⚠ **Note:** The drive letter option is only useable if a disk is first mounted with the VMware Disk Mount Utility and it is only available on a Windows host.

Table 7.1: Available options for VMware Virtual Disk Manager.

Option	Description
-c	Create disk. The -a, -s and -t options must also be specified.
-d	Defragment the specified virtual disk.
-k	Shrink the specified virtual disk (Windows host only).
-n <source disk>	Rename the virtual disk; need to specify destination disk-type with the –t parameter.
-p	Prepare the mounted virtual disk specified by the drive-letter for shrinking (Windows host only).
-q	Do not log messages.
-r <source-disk>	Convert the specified disk; need to specify destination disk-type with the –t parameter.
-x <new-capacity>	Expand the disk to the specified capacity.
Additional options for create and convert:	
-a <adapter>	Adapter type (ide, buslogic or lsilogic).
-s <size>	Capacity of the virtual disk. The capacity can be specified in sectors, KB, MB, or GB. The capacity range for IDE adapters is from 100 MB to 128 GB. For SCSI disks this number ranges from 100 MB to 256 GB.
-t <disk-type>	Disk type id. You can specify the following disk types: 0: single growable virtual disk 1: growable virtual disk, split in 2 GB files 2: pre-allocated virtual disk 3: pre-allocated virtual disk, split in 2 GB files

The following are a few usage examples for using the Virtual Disk Manager:

1. Create a new virtual disk

To create a new virtual IDE disk with a capacity of 10 GB that is fixed sized, and is split into 2 GB files, enter the following command:

```
vmware-vdiskmanager -c -t 3 -s 10Gb -a ide
idedisk.vmdk
```

2. Increasing the size of an existing disk

To increase the size of an existing disk to 10 GB, enter the following command:

```
vmware-vdiskmanager -x 10gb diskfile.vmdk
```

Tip: Expanding the size of a disk does not modify the partitions of your guest operating system installation. You can use the newly created space to create new partitions or use a partition manager inside the virtual machine to resize the partition.

3. Converting a virtual disk

To convert a pre-allocated disk to a dynamically growing disk which is not split into 2 GB files, you enter the following command:

```
vmware-vdiskmanager -r fixeddisk.vmdk -t 0
dyndisk.vmdk
```

You must delete the original disk from the virtual machine and add the new converted disk manually, from the VMware Workstation virtual machine configuration.

7.4 Using the DiskMount Utility

Have you ever needed to get a file from a virtual machine which was on your computer? Or, have you had to put a file into the virtual machine? You have to start the virtual machine, log in to it, and then either drag and drop the file, or use Shared Folders (or a networking connection) to copy files back and forth between the guest and the host. And what do you do when Windows does not start any more in your virtual machine and you need to replace a DLL, or want to save a crucial file from the machine? The answers to these questions are covered next for Windows and Linux operating systems.

Windows

You can now also use the DiskMount Utility to access virtual disk files from outside the virtual machine. The utility mounts a virtual disk as a drive letter in your Windows environment, so that you can access it for read and write access from Windows Explorer or any other application directly. The VMware DiskMount Utility supports virtual disk files created with VMware Workstation, VMware GSX Server 2.5.1 and 3.x, and VMware ESX Server 2. Also, it can be installed on Windows 2000/2003 and XP.

Linux

The DiskMount utility itself is only available for Windows. VMware Workstation for Linux comes with a Perl script named vmware-mount.pl. With this script, virtual disk files can be mounted on a Linux host.

 Note: The VMware DiskMount utility is provided without support from VMware.

The utility is available for download via www.vmware.com/download. This download location also contains a PDF manual with the full documentation to this software.

After downloading and installing the utility on Windows, you can access the utility (vmware-mount.exe) from its installation directory. By default, this is C:\Program Files\VMware\VMware DiskMount Utility.

Run vmware-mount.exe /h to get a list of all the options that are available. On Linux, you run the utility with the vmware-mount.pl script located in /usr/bin.

To use the utility, follow the guidelines hereafter for Windows and Linux.

Windows configuration

```
vmware-mount [driveletter:] [path-to-virtual-disk] [options]
```

Table 7.2: Available options for the vmware-mount utility on Windows.

Option	Description
/d	Deletes the mapping to a virtual drive volume.
/f	Forcibly deletes the mapping to a virtual drive volume.
/v:n	Mounts volume N of a virtual disk.
/p	Displays the partitions (volumes) on a virtual disk.
/y	Opens the virtual disk whether or not a snapshot is in effect.
/n	Does not open the virtual disk if a snapshot is in effect.

The most simple usage scenario is to start the utility with a drive letter and a path to a virtual disk file, as in the following example that mounts a disk to the K drive:

```
vmware-mount.exe K: "C:\VMWARE\W2K Workstation\W2K Prof.vmdk"
```

 Note: Use quotes around the path to the virtual disk file if the path contains spaces.

Running the executable without any options displays a list of active disk mounts:

```
vmware-mount.exe
K:\  =>  C:\VMWARE\W2K Workstation\W2K Prof.vmdk
```

You can dismount a virtual disk with the /d option as in the following example:

```
vmware-mount.exe K: /d
```

 Tip: When you can not dismount a disk and one of the following messages appears, the disk is probably still in use.

```
Unable to dismount volume.
To forcibly dismount the volume, use the /f option.
```

For example, these messages can occur in Windows when Explorer still points to that directory or when a Linux application or terminal window has that directory as its present working directory. In that case, point explorer, or any other application using the drive letter to a different drive and try again.

Linux configuration

`vmware-mount.pl [option] <disk> <partition> <mount point>`

Table 7.3: Available options for the vmware-mount.pl script on Linux.

Option	Description
-p	Prints the partition table.
disk	Name of the virtual hard disk file.
partition	Partition number to mount.
mount point	Directory where the partition will be mounted.
-t type	Partition type.
-o options	Partition mount options.

Figure 7.6 shows an example of a virtual disk file that is mounted on a Linux host. When the partition is mounted, another terminal window or a file manager can be used to access the files in the mount point. When you are finished with accessing the virtual disk, press Ctrl-C. The script will then unmount the partition.

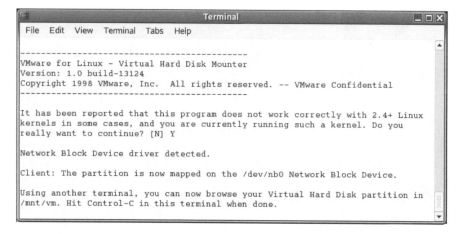

Figure 7.6: Mounting virtual disk files feature is now also available for Linux.

 Tip: When you can not dismount a disk and one of the following messages appears, the disk is probably still in use.

```
Unable to unmount the Network Block Device on the /mnt/vm
mount point. Please make sure that no process uses /mnt/vm
as its current directory or is accessing a file under this
directory.
```

DiskMount limitations
There are a few limitations you need to be aware of when using the VMware Disk Mount Utility:

- You can mount volumes within virtual disks on a Windows host only if they are formatted with the FAT (32) or NTFS file system.
- If you mount a virtual disk that has a snapshot all changes you make will be deleted if you revert to the snapshot.
- You can not mount a virtual disk if any of the .vmdk files are compressed or flagged as read-only.
- You can not use a virtual disk that is already in use by a running virtual machine or from a suspended virtual machine.

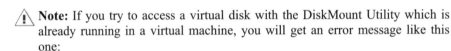 **Note:** If you try to access a virtual disk with the DiskMount Utility which is already running in a virtual machine, you will get an error message like this one:

```
Unable to mount the virtual disk. The disk
may be in use by a virtual machine or
mounted under another drive letter. If
not, verify that the disk is a virtual
disk file, and that the disk file has not
been corrupted.
```

You could actually access a disk that is in use if you had started the virtual machine with the parameter disk.locking = "false" in the .vmx file. However, this is even less supported than the use of the VMware Dismount Utility itself ☺.

Tip: There is a utility available from Ken Kato in Japan which can also mount virtual hard disk files. It is not supported, of course, but it might be interesting to keep an eye out for his project: chitchat.at.infoseek.co.jp/vmware.

7.5   Using RAW Disk Partitions

Virtual disk files are very convenient for many reasons. You can have as many of them as you want on your host's file system and they can be copied from one machine to another, and so on. So, why use a raw disk partition? First let's take a look at what it is.

A hard disk contains at least one partition. That is where all the data is stored after the partition is formatted by the operating system. You can however have multiple partitions. Reasons to create more than one partition are: to split data from the operating system, to create a dual boot system, or any other reason why the data should not be stored in the same partition. An example of this is to compress or encrypt one partition while leaving another untouched by these processes. Virtual machines can be given access to partitions on the physical hard disk. This means that all data access to and from the physical disk is directly written and read. It is not like a virtual disk where everything is stored in a single file.

A partition can be added to a virtual machine from the Add Hardware Wizard.

1. Open the virtual machine configuration utility via the Settings control panel, and click the **Add** button to open the wizard. The first selection that you must make is the disk type. Select **Use a physical disk (for advanced users)** to add an existing partition to the virtual machine.

2. In the next screen, select the physical disk where the partition resides, and select whether you want to use the entire disk or individual partitions. Selecting to **Use individual partitions** will open the next screen with a list of partitions.

3. In Figure 7.7, two partitions are selected from a Linux installation which is also available on that computer in a dual boot configuration.

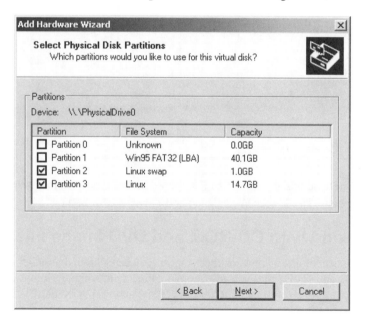

Figure 7.7: Individual partitions can be assigned to a virtual machine.

4. Click **Next** to go to the last step of this configuration. Provide a name for the control file that will be created for this physical disk.

7.6   Changing the SCSI Bus Adapter Type

VMware Workstation supports two types of SCSI adapters: LSI Logic and Buslogic. Once you have configured the machine for one of these adapters, all consecutive disks will be created for this type of adapter.

In VMware Workstation and VMware GSX Server, the SCSI bus type can be changed in the .VMX configuration file for the virtual machine. If the machine is configured with an SCSI adapter, one of these lines can be found inside the file:

```
scsi0.virtualDev = "lsilogic"
```

or

```
scsi0.virtualDev = "buslogic"
```

When you change the bus type for the virtual machine from LSI Logic to Buslogic or vice versa, then the virtual disk files must also be modified. VMware Workstation and VMware GSX Server both detect such a change automatically. As shown in Figure 7.8, it will ask you whether you want to change the disk type for your virtual disks or not.

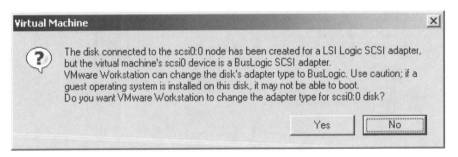

Figure 7.8:   When the adapter type changes, the virtual disks can automatically be updated by VMware Workstation and VMware GSX Server.

7.7   Working with CD-ROM and DVD Image Files

Do you sometimes feel like a "disk jockey"? Or, do you carry around a binder with all possible CDs and DVDs that you might need someday at some customer site? Are you afraid of not having that Windows NT Workstation 4 bootable CD with you when you need it?

Then look into using CD-ROM ISO files. Not only can they be used directly with virtual machines, they can also be burned on a CD whenever you need them. An external 60 GB laptop hard disk in a small USB 2 enclosure costs you about USD

200. And it will hold somewhere between 50 to 80 operating system CD-ROM or DVD ISO files, depending on the OS and the size of the files.

Many operating system manufacturers make their operating system CD-ROMs available for download via the Internet, with or without integrated service packs. These so called overlay CDs, will make it even simpler to install new machines, because they include the service pack. This is done so you do not have to update the server immediately after installation.

You can also create your own ISO files for archiving or for use with VMware. The easiest way is to create an ISO file directly from the original CD-ROM or DVD. This can be done with any of the popular CD/DVD softwares such as Nero and EasyCD Creator, or with many of the ISO utilities that are available on the Internet. This software category also allows you to create your own ISO files for use with your virtual machines.

Check out the following websites for ISO utilities:

- IsoBuster   www.isobuster.com
- WinISO   www.winiso.com
- Turtleblast ISO Commander   www.turtleblast.com
- Undisker   www.undisker.com
- Alex Feinman ISO Recorder   isorecorder.alexfeinman.com
- Daemon Tools   www.daemon-tools.cc

7.8 My Virtual Machine Does not Boot from CD-ROM

After installing your operating system, and when your virtual machine boots with an empty hard disk, you may encounter this error message: **No bootable CD. Floppy or hard disk was detected**.

If you did assign an operating CD-ROM to install from, check the BIOS of your virtual machine. Most likely your CD-ROM is not listed before your hard drive in the boot-order. Press F2 while booting the virtual machine to enter the setup. In BIOS, go to the Boot menu option, and use the + and − keys to change the boot order of your CD-ROM device.

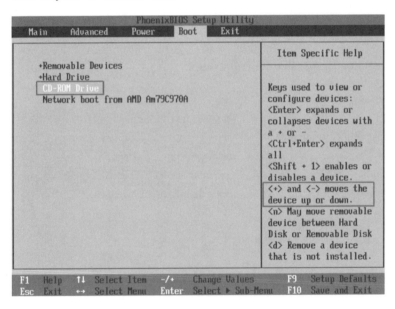

Figure 7.9: Set the CD-ROM drive in the BIOS to be the first boot device.

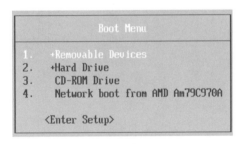

Another method is pressing the **Escape** key during the boot sequence to enter the Boot Menu. This opens a one time menu where you can select the device to boot from.

Figure 7.10: Select CD-ROM as a boot device at system startup by pressing Esc.

8 Performance Tuning and Optimization

Optimizing the performance of virtual machines is a subject that is discussed very often. This is very understandable because with multiple computers sharing the same hardware, it is easy to create bottlenecks. All your virtual machines are using the same disk channel, and they are all fighting to use the RAM in your machine. This chapter covers configuration settings and tips that will help you get the most out of your virtual machine environment. It will also show you how you can monitor the performance and behavior of your virtual machines.

Section 9.1 "Performance tips" also contains some very useful tips for users getting started with VMware.

8.1 Optimizing the Memory Used by your Virtual Machines

Virtual machines use physical memory from your host PC. Your physical memory is one of the limitations that you face when running multiple virtual machines. In GSX Server or ESX Server, you have to make sure that all your virtual machines have enough memory available. This is especially important with servers in a production environment, where you need enough RAM to make sure that the servers perform well.

 Note: Older versions of VMware Workstation could only use a maximum of 1 GB of RAM to run the virtual machines. Starting with version 4.5, the maximum amount of RAM that can be used by your running virtual machines is 4 GB. The maximum amount of RAM for an individual virtual machine is now 3.6 GB. On computers with a file system that can not hold files larger than 2 GB the maximum amount of RAM is 2 GB.

If you are the only user of the virtual machines in VMware Workstation, and you want to run multiple virtual machines that normally take more RAM than you have available, these tips might help:

1. Decrease the amount of reserved RAM for a virtual machine

If you install a Windows or NetWare server the installation process expects a large amount of RAM in your server (virtual machine in this case). If not enough memory is available, the installation procedure will issue a warning or maybe even stop. If you create a virtual machine, a default amount of RAM is assigned to it. But if the guest operating system is installed and fully configured, you can decrease the amount of RAM that is assigned to the virtual machine.

 Tip: Do not set the amount of RAM too low. Check the actual memory usage of the guest operating system, to see how much RAM it uses. If you do not allocate enough RAM, the guest operating system will start using Virtual Memory (swapping) and that will decrease the performance dramatically.

2. Allow virtual machine memory to be swapped

The memory that your virtual machines are using, could reach the maximum amount of RAM that is available to your virtual machines. Starting a new virtual machine will result in the error message displayed in Figure 8.1.

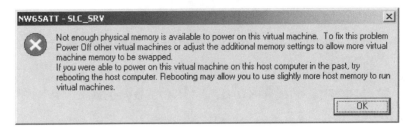

Figure 8.1: Trying to start too many machines results in an error message.

You can set the Memory Preferences from the **VM** menu under **Settings** (see Figure 8.2) to run virtual machines with more RAM than is really available.

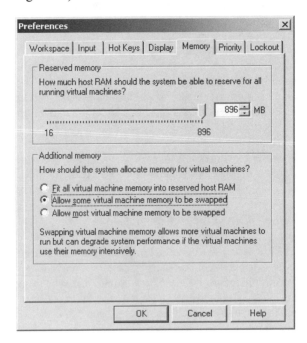

Figure 8.2: VMware Workstation memory configuration.

⚠ **Note:** You can configure your system to **Allow most virtual machine memory to be swapped**. Be careful when doing this, because it could decrease performance dramatically, depending on your host PC hardware specifications. You can start virtual machines with a total amount of RAM that exceeds the physical amount of RAM in your host PC.

If you enable this setting, the warning message displayed in Figure 8.3 will pop up each time you start a virtual machine.

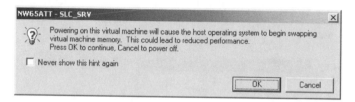

Figure 8.3: A warning is displayed when starting a virtual machine would result in swapping memory to disk.

It could reduce performance of course, but it could also be a solution, if you need to run three or more virtual machines on your host, with only 1 GB of RAM.

8.2 Monitor Virtual Machine Performance (Windows host only)

Have you ever wanted to know which of your virtual machines is slowing your host down? Or, do you need statistics on how much network traffic one of your guests is creating? You can now find all of these answers in the Windows Performance Monitor. This section explains how to do this with the Windows default utility, and how you can get other detailed information with an excellent freeware utility. To monitor your virtual machines, open **Performance** from the Administrative tools menu.

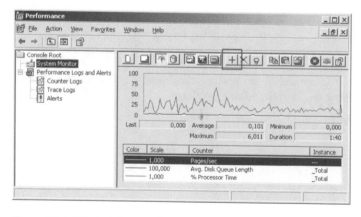

Figure 8.4: Workstation performance can be monitored on a Windows host.

In the performance window, click the plus sign in the toolbar (see Figure 8.4) to add counters to your monitoring environment. The **Add Counters** window (Figure 8.5) appears.

Note: The performance counters are not available in the 64-bit version of Windows. If you want to monitor performance on a 64 bit platform, you need to use the 32 bit version of the utility (C:\Windows\SysWOW64\perfmon.exe).

From the **Performance object** drop down list select VMware. Next, select one or all of the counters that you want to monitor. An overview of counters is listed in Table 8.1, later in this section.

Select which virtual machine(s) you want to monitor. You can select more then one machine by pressing the Ctrl-key while clicking the machine names.

Or, select the **All instances** radio button to monitor all current virtual machines. If you open new virtual machines, they will not be automatically added when you have chosen **All instances**.

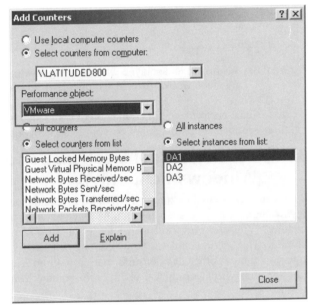

Figure 8.5: Individual counters can be selected for performance monitor.

When selecting a counter, you can click the **Explain** button to get more info on what the counter will show you in the performance monitor. The following table contains a list of available counters and their explanation.

Table 8.1: Performance Counters for Windows.

Counter	Explanation
Guest Locked Memory Bytes	The number of bytes of simulated physical memory that is locked by the guest OS.
Guest Virtual Physical Memory Bytes	The number of bytes of simulated physical memory in the virtual machine.
Network Bytes Received/sec	The number of bytes received by the guest OS over the network.
Network Bytes Sent/sec	The number of bytes sent by the guest OS over the network.
Network Bytes Transferred/sec	The number of bytes sent or received by the guest OS over the network.
Network Packets Received/sec	The number of network packets received by the guest OS.
Network Packets Sent/sec	The number of network packets sent by the guest OS.
Network Receive Errors/sec	The number of network errors from receiving packets by the guest OS.
Network Send Errors/sec	The number of network errors from sending packets by the guest OS.
Network Transfer Errors/sec	The number of network errors from sending or receiving packets by the guest OS.
Network Transfers/sec	The number of network operations performed by the guest OS.
Percent Guest Physical Memory Touched	The percentage of simulated physical memory used recently by the guest OS.
Virtual Disk Bytes Read/sec	The number of bytes transferred for disk read operations performed by the guest OS.
Virtual Disk Bytes Transferred/sec	The number of bytes transferred for disk operations performed by the guest OS.
Virtual Disk Bytes Written/sec	The number of bytes transferred for disk write operations performed by the guest OS.
Virtual Disk Reads/sec	The number of disk read operations performed by the guest OS.
Virtual Disk Transfers/sec	The number of disk operations performed by the guest OS.
Virtual Disk Writes/sec	The number of disk write operations performed by the guest OS.

Freeware Process Explorer

Another great tool to monitor what your virtual machines are doing is the Process Explorer from Sysinternals. It is a freeware utility that you can download from their website at www.sysinternals.com. You can use this utility for several purposes to analyze what you virtual machines are doing. If you right click a VMware virtual machine process (vmware-vmx.exe) and select properties you can retrieve a lot of information about your virtual machine. Figure 8.6 shows an example where you can see some of the statistics about memory usage and I/O.

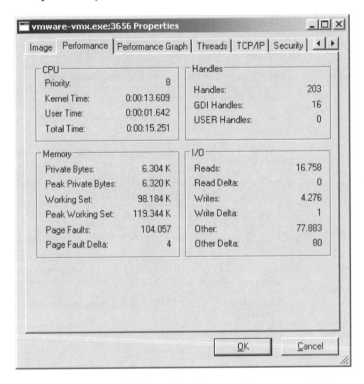

Figure 8.6: Process Explorer also shows performance statistics.

In the Process Explorer you can also see what files are being used by a virtual machine. To see this, select **View → Lower Pane View → Handles** to see what file system and registry entries are being used by the machine.

In the unlikely event that a virtual machine stops responding, the Process Explorer can also help you identify which vmware-vmx.exe process belongs to what file set. This will enable you to kill that individual process instead of the entire VMware environment.

---

9 Optimizing your Virtual Machine Environment

This chapter contains useful tips for optimizing the performance of your virtual machine, and to make your virtual environment easier to work with.

9.1 Performance Tips

A few basic tips can help you experience better performance in your virtual machines. First, make sure that you always install the VMware tools (especially for Windows), because together with the SVGA display driver, the performance with using the guest operating system is much better.

- **Disconnect the CD-ROM device**

If your guest operating system is trying to access the CD-ROM or DVD player, (either because you inserted a CD-ROM, or because the OS or an application is trying to read data from a CD-ROM that is not there), that process could slow down the host and guest.

When your virtual machine is completely configured and the OS is installed, go to the virtual machine settings and set the CD-ROM device not to **Connect at power on**.

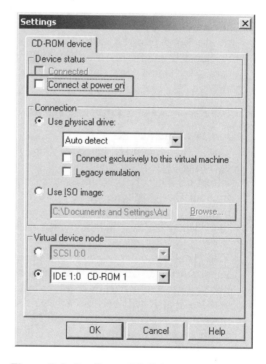

Figure 9.1: Configure CD-ROMs as not connected by default.

- **Run in full screen mode**

In Windows, but especially in a Linux host working in the graphical environment is much faster if you run your virtual machine in full screen mode.

- **Disable visual effects and other unneeded features**

  Windows contains a lot of features that enhance the user's experience. But all of that costs in performance level and uses resources from the display environment. Turn off this functionality (if you can do without it) in your virtual machine. You can find these effects in the **Display Control Panel**.

- **Remove hardware that you don't need**

  It will not increase your performance dramatically; however, if you remove devices that you do not need from your virtual machine, such as the sound adapter and the USB bus, it will prevent your guest from playing sounds that will be processed by the host's sound card. Also, it will not attach USB devices to the virtual machine that it will start to access.

- **Use a second hard drive in your host**

  If you will be running multiple virtual machines on your host system, you can increase the performance by using multiple hard disks. Remember from the VMware introduction that both the host and the guest are accessing their data on the same physical disk. Therefore, splitting them up or running virtual machines from different hard disks will increase performance, especially in the case of running disk intensive applications within your guest operating systems.

- **Use a separate disk for your swap files**

  Just as with a real PC, it is a good idea to have a separate swap partition for your OS. Of course, the best thing is to prevent swapping in the guest operating system as much as you can, by assigning enough memory to the virtual machine. This is an advanced topic that you might want to investigate for your specific environment; however, if for example the guest needs virtual memory (swap space) you could create a fixed sized disk that holds the swap file. Also, make sure that the file is not defragmented on your host system.

  There is also another reason to use a separate swap file disk that I find is more important for efficient use than for performance. If you assign a virtual disk that will grow dynamically to your virtual machine for use as a swap disk, you will see that it will become a large file. If you want to archive the virtual machine, this swap file space can be easily reduced by replacing it with an empty disk. To prepare this, I have created a swap file on an NTFS partitioned virtual disk, which I have copied to a safe location on my hard disk. If I am going to archive the virtual machine in a ZIP-file or if I need to burn it on a CD-ROM or DVD, I replace the used swap disk with this empty one. This way it does not take up space in the archive copy.

  This method also keeps the virtual disk smaller which makes it more efficient to shrink your disks.

9.2   Shrinking your Virtual Disks

Owners of multiple 400 GB hard disks in their PCs can skip this paragraph. Others, for whom hard disk space is limited, must read on to find out how they can save valuable disk space.

Your virtual hard disk files will grow dynamically. They start with a few megabytes but could become very large. After installing an operating system, your hard disk could be well over 2 GB, even if the OS you have installed only takes 1 GB of disk space. There are several reasons why your virtual disk will grow more than you would expect. During installation, for example, temporary files are copied to the hard disk, some times being unzipped locally. After that they are copied to the correct location on your hard drive and your temporary files are deleted again.

The installations of service packs, patches, and software applications will also work with temporary files on your virtual hard disk, causing your virtual disk to grow larger and larger. Dynamically growing disks are not automatically shrunk in size. Your virtual machine will re-use space available in the virtual disk file, but in the end your virtual disk file will grow larger than you need it to be.

The shrink process itself should start preferably from the VMware tools Properties window in your guest operating system.

Figure 9.2 is from a Windows guest, but the same window and options are available for NetWare and Linux.

Select the disks that you want to prepare and click Prepare to shrink. This process will take from a few minutes to half an hour depending on the size of your virtual disk, and of course the performance capability of your host's hard disk.

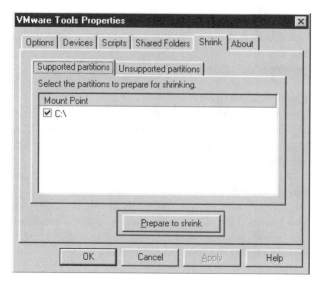

Figure 9.2: Virtual disks must be prepared for shrinking.

 Tip: You can shrink your disks from the command line with the Virtual Disk Manager. This is discussed in section 7.3: "Using Virtual Disk Manager".

When the **prepare for shrinking** process is complete, you are asked if you want to run the shrink operation at that point. If you click yes, VMware will start to create a temporary file that it will use during the shrink process. You will need to have at least as much hard disk space available as what your virtual disk is using on your hard disk, before the shrink operation is complete.

 Tip: For all operating systems it is a good idea to remove unnecessary files from the guest operating system's hard disk. Remove large files, temporary files, etc. Specific tips on Windows and NetWare can be found in chapter 9.

9.3   Archiving your Virtual Machines

Working with VMware is very efficient, because you do not need extra PCs and a new PC with a new operating system is up and running in less than an hour. If you are working with new PCs with the same operating system repeatedly, you will find that it is useful to have a working copy of a virtual machine with that OS, which you can start with. This section will provide you with a few tips to work even more efficiently with VMware.

Archiving virtual machines is not only about storing them on a safe location to use them later, but also to have a copy that you can use as your starting point for future projects. The method described here also helps you save your virtual machine on one or more CD-ROMs or DVDs.

 Tip: For virtual machines that will contain a large amount of data use virtual disk files that are split up in 2 GB parts. That will make it easier to archive the files on multiple CD-ROMs (zipped per file) or DVDs.

Remove snapshots
Before archiving your virtual machine, remove the snapshot you have taken. The original .vmdk file will be untouched and extra s###.vmdk files are created. Together, they will take up more disk space than actually in use by the guest operating system.

Shrink your disks
Use the shrink process described in the previous paragraph to decrease the size of your virtual disk. If you have chosen to use a separate disk for the swap file for your guest operating system, you can now also replace that .vmdk file (with an original smaller one) and save it in a safe location.

Power off your virtual machine
Do not copy or ZIP your virtual machine in a suspended state. It would work if you resume the virtual machine on the same PC with the same version of VMware. Resuming the virtual machine on another PC, with a different CPU in the future or with a newer version of VMware, will most likely result in error messages. Also, you have to discard the saved memory state file (VMSS) anyhow.

Exit VMware

When you copy your virtual machine or create a ZIP file, do not do that when the machine is still open in VMware. There will be lock files in your archive and that does not look nice or clean.

Delete any unnecessary files

You can delete the .log file and vmware-core dump file (if it exists) to clean up your virtual machine directory before you archive or ZIP it.

10 Transferring Data To and From a Virtual Machine

Your virtual environment will not be a static environment. You will probably have to install applications in your virtual machines or you may have created data inside of your virtual machine that you need to store on another computer. This chapter describes several ways in which you can do that with the VMware built-in functionality and by using other methods.

To install software inside a virtual machine, you can do it the same way you would normally do on a physical computer. You can attach a CD-ROM drive, floppy drive, or USB storage device to your machine to install the software from a removable device. But if the installation source resides on your host computer, you can also directly access it. There are many ways to transfer not only software but also data to and from a virtual machine. Let's see how.

There is also an advanced method available with the VMware DiskMount utility. Section 7.4: "Using the DiskMount Utility" explains how to use this utility in detail.

10.1 Using the Clipboard (Windows only)

Windows contains a clipboard which can hold all sorts of data, such as text files, images, and so on.

VMware Workstation supports transferring text fragments (no images) between the host and the guest or between two guests.

The contents of the clipboard is accessible via the default keys (Ctrl-C Ctrl-X Ctrl-V) and viewable with the ClipBook viewer (CLIPBRD.EXE)

This feature is turned on by default and can be turned off via **Edit** → **Preferences** → **Input** tab (see Figure 10.1). Disable the checkbox to disable this feature if needed.

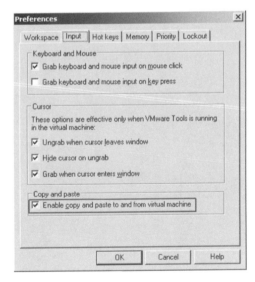

Figure 10.1: Easy copy and paste via the Windows clipboard.

10.2 Using Drag and Drop (Windows only)

The Drag and Drop feature allows you to pick a file or folder from the host and drag it into the guest or vice versa. To use this feature, you must have installed the VMware tools in your Windows guest operating system.

The procedure works in the same way as dragging and dropping files or folders in the host or inside the guest operating system. The files will be dropped at the location where you point your mouse pointer and release the mouse button. The file will be stored in a temporary location in the virtual machine or the host (%TEMP%\VMwareDnD). From there, it is transferred to the application where you dropped the file such as Windows Explorer, the desktop, or any other application that you have running which supports files being dropped into it.

This feature is enabled by default. To disable this feature, open the Virtual Machine Settings and select the **Guest Isolation** entry in the **Options** tab (see Figure 10.2). Enable the checkbox to Disable drag and drop to and from the host and the virtual machine.

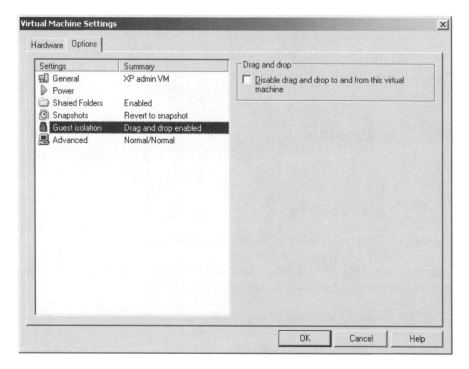

Figure 10.2: Drag and drop is enabled by default on Windows.

10.3 Using Shared Folders (Windows and Linux)

Transferring data to and from a virtual machine became very simple when VMware introduced this feature into VMware Workstation with version 4. You can easily assign a folder on your host operating system which will become visible in your virtual machine. You must have the VMware tools installed for this feature to be available.

For both Windows (NT/2000/2003/XP) and Linux (Kernel 2.4 and higher), enable this feature from the Virtual Machine Settings. Shared Folders can be configured and enabled, even when the virtual machine is running. The Shared Folders functionality is enabled by default, but no folder sharing will be configured. In the Shared Folder window, click the Add button to specify a host folder to be attached to your virtual machine. This will start the Shared Folder Wizard.

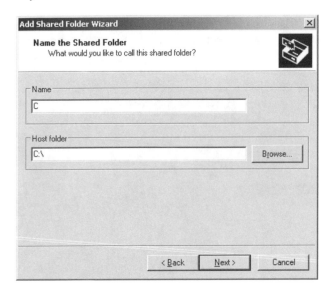

Figure 10.3: Creating a shared folder for a virtual machine.

Specify a name for this shared folder which will be used inside your guest operating system (for Linux this is case sensitive).

Click Next to specify additional settings for this Shared Folder:

- Enable this share (checked by default)
  The share will be available immediately after closing the wizard.

- Read only
  Only read-access is allowed to the host disk folder. Other operations to the host file system are restricted by the user account that you use to run the virtual machine.

- Disable after this session
  The share will be removed when you power the virtual machine off.

You work with the Shared Folder in the same way as you do with a network share. In Windows, the folder is available as drive Z: in Windows Explorer or via the following UNC path:

`\\.host\Shared Folders\<name>`   (use quotes when using it on the command line)

In Linux, the Shared Folder is accessible via the mount directory at:

`/mnt/hgfs/<name>`

Note: Consider the Shared Folder option as a feature to transfer files to and from the guest and host and, for example, as a means to install software in your guest operating system. Running applications with data from the guest, and accidentally accessing the same data from the host, could lead to data loss or corruption.

10.4 Use Virtual or Removable Devices

For situations where you do not have direct access to the virtual machine, you can also work with virtual devices such as floppy disks, or CD-ROM ISO-files. You can also attach external USB devices (hard disks, memory keys, ZIP-drives) to a virtual machine to transfer data.

Using virtual media is described in chapter 7: "Virtual disks, floppies and CD-ROMs"

10.5 Use Operating System Specific Networking (all platforms)

The methods described previously are not available for all platforms. However, there is one thing that every operating system nowadays has: networking capabilities. Consult the operating system's manuals to find all information on how to use these features.

Windows
Use normal Windows workgroup or domain networking to create network shares between the host and the guest

Linux

You can use Samba (smbclient) to attach a Linux workstation to a Windows host, or a Samba server to attach a Windows workstation to a Linux host. Another method is to use SSH and specifically Secure Copy (SCP), which is available as open source for Linux and Windows.

NetWare

When you install the NetWare client in your Windows host, you can login to the server. Or, you can use Native File Access (CIFS) to use normal Windows networking. For Linux hosts, you can use NFS to mount a NetWare server's volume.

11 Networking Configurations

A lot of people have been asking me questions such as how to access virtual machines from a LAN, or how to set up routing within a host to route between multiple virtual networks. In this chapter, I will discuss a few common scenarios that will give you a feel for what the possibilities are. I will start out with the basics on host-only and bridged networking to make sure everyone understands what networking options VMware has to offer.

11.1 Network Adapters in VMware

First of all, you need to understand the correct terminology. A bridged adapter is a physical network adapter in your host PC which allows your virtual machines to communicate with the physical Ethernet Network. A host-only adapter is a virtual adapter, that shows up in the list of adapters in Network Settings but it does not have any relationship with any of the physical adapters in your computer. The default setup of a VMware Workstation installation is that you have VMnet1 for a normal host-only network and VMnet8 for a host-only network, using NAT to access the physical LAN. Figure 11.1 shows a typical network environment on a Windows host PC.

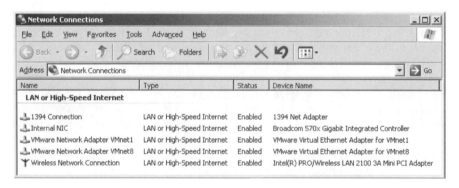

Figure 11.1: VMware adds two network adapters, VMnet1, and VMbet8 by default.

11.2 Configure Host-Only and Bridged Networking

Bridged networking is set up by default. You can view or edit the bridged networking settings by selecting **Edit → Virtual Network Settings**. This opens the Virtual Network Editor. In the summary screen you get an overview of the configured VMware networks. By default, the checkbox **Automatically choose an available physical network adapter to bridge to VMnet0** is enabled.

You find this on the **Automatic Bridging** tab. Click the **Host Virtual Network Mapping** tab (see Figure 11.2) to set up a network configuration manually.

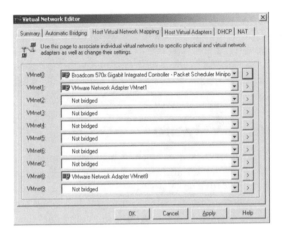

Figure 11.2:   Bridged networking is set up by default.

Selecting a Bridged Network adapter will manually disable the automatic bridging process. With VMware workstation, you can bridge more than one physical adapter and assign them to different machines with the VMet networks. An example of this is that when I deliver trainings, I use my built-in network adapter in my laptop to connect to the classroom network with a classroom virtual server, and I use a PC-card adapter to connect the other virtual machines to the Internet.

 Tip: Physical adapters that were not enabled on the host PC when the VMware application was loaded are not displayed in the Virtual Network Editor. If for example, the wireless network adapter was not enabled, it would not show up in the list of available adapters. This is the case even after enabling it when VMware is already running. After enabling an adapter, close VMware and open it again to display the adapter in the Available Network Adapters drop down list.

Setup extra host-only network adapters
With the Virtual Network Editor, you can modify the configuration of your virtual host-only networks. It allows you to add network adapters to you host PC in the Host Virtual Adapters tab. You need this extra adapter if your host operating system needs to communicate with the guest. When two guests will communicate via a host-only network (let's say VMnet6) without the host being involved, then no virtual network adapter in the host PC is required.

11.3 Host-Only Network DHCP Configuration

The host-only adapter in your PC and the virtual machines that are assigned to the host-only network (VMnet1 by default) communicate via this virtual network inside your host PC. The virtual machines can be configured with static IP addresses, or via the DHCP service available for the host-only network.

To configure the DHCP Service on a Windows host, select **Edit** → **Virtual Network Settings** and select the **DHCP** tab (see Figure 11.3)

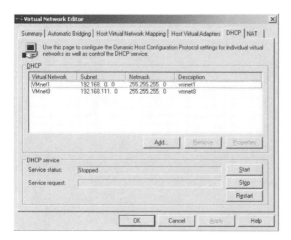

Configured DHCP ranges for the host-only network adapters, as well as the status of the DHCP service are displayed. Click the **Add new** button to create a new address range for a virtual host-only network. This will not automatically create the virtual network adapter in the host PC. Creating a new adapter, however, will create a DHCP range.

Figure 11.3: DHCP can be configured for host-only adapters.

The properties page of a DHCP address range allows you to modify the addresses being used for your virtual machines. By default, the address range starts at address .128 and ends with .254:

In the properties page, you can also set up the lease duration for your virtual machines. The default is set to 30 minutes with a maximum lease time of 2 hours.

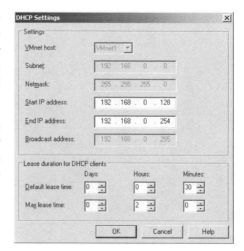

Figure 11.4: Default DHCP address range and lease duration.

On a Windows host, the DHCP configuration is stored in a text file called vmnetdhcp.conf located at C:\Documents and Settings\All Users\Application Data\VMware. DHCP leases are stored in a file in the same directory with the name vmnetdhcp.leases. On a Linux host, the configuration is stored in a file called dhcpd.conf which is located in a subdirectory dhcpd in the virtual network adapter configuration directory in /etc/vmware. For a default installation, this is /etc/vmware/vmnet1/dhcpd. For a Linux host, the host-only DHCP configuration can be modified by editing this file.

 Note: Before modifying a configuration file, always make a backup copy.

11.4 Using NAT to Connect Virtual Machines to the Network

Bridged networking is one of the simplest methods to connect virtual machines to the network. However, sometimes you can not use this method because you do not have enough addresses available on the network or because security issues do not allow you to connect new PCs directly to the network. In that case, you can use Network Address Translation to connect your virtual machines to the network.

What is NAT?
With NAT, your virtual machine will send its TCP/IP packets to the NAT service on the host PC. This service will change the source IP address into its own IP address which it uses on the local network, and sends out the packets to the destination. When the packets are received back from the destination, the NAT service will use its translation table to send the TCP/IP packet to the correct virtual machine. This way, your virtual machines can all use their own IP addresses internally and all the traffic they send onto the network looks as if it comes from the host PC.

Configuring NAT
To set up NAT for your virtual machines, open the Virtual Network Editor via **Edit** → **Preferences** and click on the NAT tab.

If the service is disabled, the **VMnet host** drop down box will show Disabled. Set this to the host-only network where you want to enable NAT. The default virtual network for this is VMnet8.

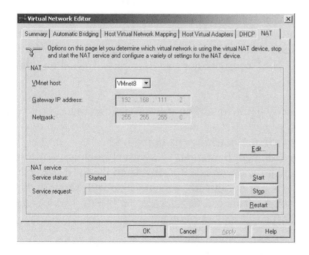

Figure 11.5: Nat is configured on VMnet8 by default.

Enabling NAT does not automatically start the VMware NAT Service. This service is started when you click Apply or Ok to activate the NAT configuration.

This is the easiest way to set up NAT because you don't have to configure IP addresses on your virtual machines. The NAT DHCP configuration is accessible from the DHCP configuration tab. DHCP is discussed in the previous paragraph.

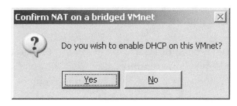

Figure 11.6: DHCP can be enabled for the NAT configuration.

 Note: Using DHCP is not practical when using port mappings, which is discussed later. It is not required, but having fixed addresses guarantees mapping the same virtual machine every time.

After enabling NAT, point your virtual machine's network interface to the NAT networking configuration, or to the custom NAT network that you have configured (something other than VMnet8). Your machines will now be able to access the network via the NAT service on your host computer. They will use that host as a DNS server. The NAT service works as a DNS proxy for DNS requests from within the guest operating system.

On a Windows host, the configuration of the NAT service is stored in a text file called vmnetnat.conf located at C:\Documents and Settings\All Users\Application Data\VMware. On a Linux host, the NAT configuration is stored in a file called nat.conf which is located in a subdirectory nat in the virtual network adapter configuration directory in /etc/vmware. For a default installation, this is /etc/vmware/vmnetb/nat. For a Linux host, the host-only NAT configuration can be modified by editing this file.

 Note: Always make a backup copy before modifying a configuration file.

Using port mappings to access virtual machines from the LAN
With a Network Address Translation configuration, your virtual machines will use an internal IP address within the host, which is not available on the local network. This means that PCs on the LAN can not directly communicate with services that are running in your virtual machine. This can be all kinds of TCP/IP services, or other services such as Windows file sharing or printing.

PCs on the local network can only send packets to the host PC's IP address, because that is the address used for all virtual machines behind the NAT configuration. In the example shown in Figure 11.7, a PC sends packets to the host's IP address (to port 80) to access a Web Server, but the host is not running a

Web Server. Therefore, the sender will receive a message informing him or her that service is not available.

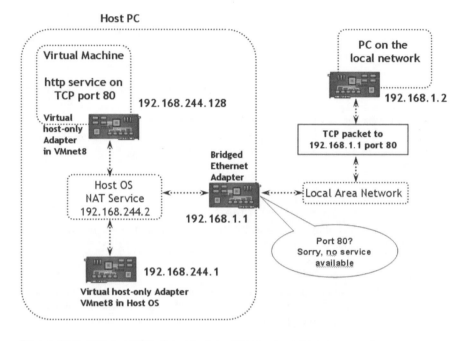

Figure 11.7: Without NAT, the virtual machines can not be accessed.

With port mappings, you can build a configuration where the packets received for a specific port can be sent to the correct virtual machine when they are received on the host's 'outside' network adapter. In the previous example, configuring the NAT service to forward all incoming traffic at address 192.168.1.1 for port 80 to 192.168.244.128 effectively let's the PC on the local network communicate with the http service running on the virtual machine. The sender could think that the web server is at address 192.168.1.1, while it is actually on the virtual machine's address at 192.168.244.128.

Figure 11.7 also shows the host-only network adapter for VMnet8. This adapter is being used by the host operating system to communicate with the guest operating system, in much the same way as you would normally use a host-only network.

To set up this configuration on a Windows host, click the **Edit** button on the **NAT** tab of the Virtual Network Editor. In the NAT Settings window, click the Port Forwarding button to define port mappings.

You can choose between TCP or UDP port mappings. Make sure to set up the correct type of traffic for your service. In the **Port forwarding** screen, click **Add** in the TCP or UDP chapter.

This will bring up a mapping configuration dialog box. In the example in Figure 11.8, all incoming traffic for port TCP 80 is forwarded to address 192.168.244.128.

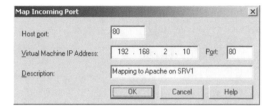

Figure 11.8: Individual ports can be forwarded.

For a Linux host, port forwarding must be configured in the `nat.conf` file in `/etc/vmware/vmnet8/nat`. Here is an example of how to map incoming TCP port 80 to a virtual machine with IP address 192.168.2.10:

```
[incomingtcp]
80 = 192.168.2.10:80
```

For a UDP port mapping, enter the configuration entry under the [incomingudp] header.

Use static addresses, no DHCP
With these port mappings, you have to specify an IP address where the packets need to be sent. It is better to use statically assigned IP addresses for your virtual machines, instead of dynamically assigned ones via DHCP. If the addresses change the port mapping will point to the wrong or a non-existent server.

With many DHCP servers, you could still assign an IP address based on the MAC address of the machine. You can not do this with the VMware DHCP service.

11.5 Routing to and from the LAN

If you are running your virtual machine in a bridged mode, there is no routing involved to access the LAN. They are part of the network, just as any other real PC with their own MAC-address and IP address. Your host and guests are able to communicate with each other, and any PC on the network can access your virtual machine. This is the easiest setup used to access virtual machines from the real world.

If you want to set up routing, for example because you need another subnet for your virtual environment, or if you just want to test routed configurations, you have various options. You can do that by using a Windows 2000 Server, Windows Server 2003, or a Linux host PC to create a router between the LAN and the virtual environment.

 Note: Only do this after consulting your network administrator, if you are taking part of a larger network where adding routers could have serious implications. Also be ware that any domain controllers etc. that you run in your virtual environment will show up on the LAN, depending on how you configure your router. This could cause unwanted results for other administrators or users of the network.

Figure 11.9 shows an example of a routing configuration, where the host PC's operating system contains routing software to route from the Local Area Network into the virtual host-only network.

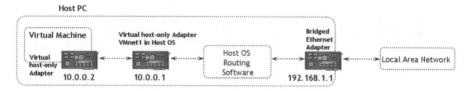

Figure 11.9: A configuration with routing set up on the host PC.

The IP addresses in this example are chosen for two private networks (192.168.1.0 and 10.0.0.0). For your configuration, you can choose the networks that are available in your environment.

 Tip: I have seen a lot of people having problems with accessing virtual machines and the LAN, when they started configuring their physical and virtual adapters. It is very important to make sure that all adapters (physical, including wireless, VMnet1 and VMnet8) are in different IP subnets. A real PC with two network adapters on different Ethernet segments but with the same IP subnet used on both LAN's, would not know where to send its packets.

Compare it to a junction with two signs pointing to Paris. You would also be confused about what direction to choose; unless they both point to Rome, of course, since as everyone knows, all roads lead to Rome!, A PC with a physical adapter and/or more virtual adapters that would be configured for the same subnet will have the same problem and will prevent you from accessing hosts on either the physical or virtual network.

11.6 Routing Between Virtual Machines

In the previous section, I discussed how to set up routing from the LAN to your virtual machines. One scenario in which to use that is when you want to test access from machines in your production network into a virtual test environment. There may also be scenarios where it is unwanted or not needed to have an extra router on the physical network. This is why it is useful to create a set of virtual networks that can communicate only within the host where the network traffic never leaves the host machine.

You can build this scenario to be as complex as you want. You can run a router within the host operating system which routes between two virtual networks. Or, you can run a router in a virtual machine that will take care of the routing between the virtual networks. For both configurations, you will need extra host-only network adapters. But first, let's take a look at what these configurations look like. Again, I have chosen IP addresses in private network ranges which you will need to change to the appropriate addresses in your own environment.

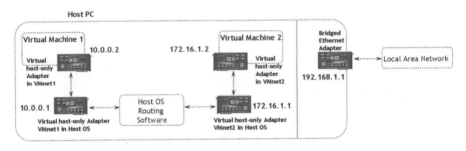

Figure 11.10: Routing between virtual networks with host-OS routing.

First, let's take a look at the simplest approach in Figure 11.10. This is where the host operating system uses two virtual network adapters, and each virtual machine is in a different host-only subnet. You can see that I have configured three subnets in this example. The physical network adapter is part of the Local Area Network, but it is not used by any of the virtual machines. So, there is no traffic going to the physical network which can interfere with anything. And there will be no extra routers showing up on the network either.

In this example, I am still using the host operating system to do the routing (Windows Server or Linux). This router forwards the packets between the 10.0.0.0 and 172.16.0.0 subnets. For this to work, you must add a second VMnet2 host-only adapter. The next section explains how to do this.

Also, don't forget to assign the second VMnet2 host-only adapter to virtual machine 2 (as it is called in Figure 11.10). You can do that by entering the virtual machines configuration: **VM → Settings**. Select the NIC and select a Custom network to be used in this virtual machine.

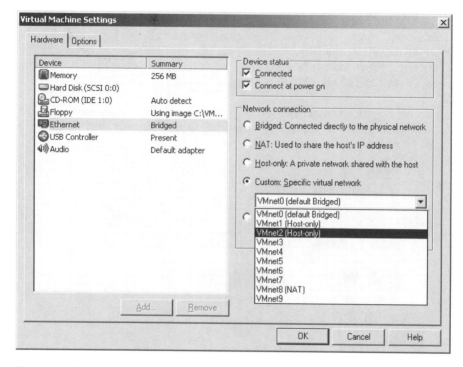

Figure 11.11: Configuring the custom adapter to VMnet2.

Now, let's take a look at another possible scenario to set up routing between two virtual machines. Take some time to absorb Figure 11.12.

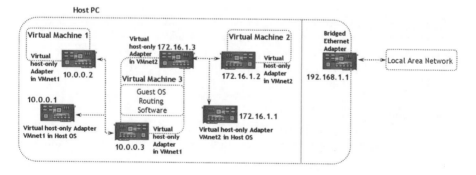

Figure 11.12: Routing with guest-OS routing software.

In this example, I have added a third virtual machine to the host PC. The host operating system again has a physical adapter which is not being used and two virtual host-only adapters (VMnet1 and VMnet2). The host operating system can still access the two virtual networks. But there is no routing software loaded on the host.

This time the routing is performed by the new virtual machine. The guest OS in this machine (Windows, NetWare, or Linux) has two network adapters that are both in a different virtual host-only network. The guest OS takes care of the routing between the 10.0.0.0 and 172.16.0.0 subnets.

Is this not complex enough for you? If you answered "No", take a look at Figure 11.13 and use your imagination as to what is happening there, and how far you could go with a maximum of nine virtual host-only networks.

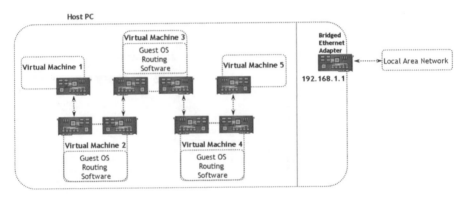

Figure 11.13: A routing configuration can be as complex as you want it to be.

Adding a second host-only adapter
If you want to set up one of the two routing examples explained here, you need to add a second host-only network adapter to you host-PC.

 Tip: If there is no need for your host operating system to interact with the host-only virtual machines, then you don't have to add a second virtual host-only adapter to your host. In other words, your virtual machines can both be configured to operate on VMnet6 and communicate with each other without adding a VMnet6 network adapter to your host PC.

On a Windows host
To add an adapter to your host PC in VMware Workstation, open **Edit → Virtual Network Settings.** Select the **Host Virtual Adapters** tab. Click the **Add new adapter** button.

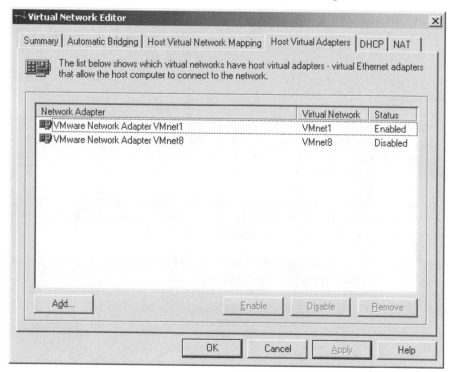

Figure 11.14: Virtual adapters can be added by using the Virtual Network Editor.

Select the virtual host-only network that you want to use ranging from VMnet2 to VMnet9. Notice that VMnet8 is not listed because it is used by default by NAT networking for VMware.

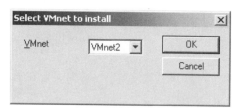

Figure 11.15: Select the new virtual network.

A New Device will now show up in the list of Host Virtual Adapters. Click OK to save this configuration and close the Virtual Network Editor. Now open **Network Connections** from the **Control Panel** on the host operating system. A new adapter, Local Area Connection # was added to your PC. For your convenience, rename this adapter to VMware Network Adapter VMnet2 to make it easier for you to distinguish the adapter that you are configuring. At this time, also assign an IP address in the subnet range to the adapter which you will be using for this second virtual network.

On a Linux host

To modify the networking configuration for your VMware environment on a Linux host, you must run the vmware-config.pl script. This script will run through the same wizard-like questions that you have seen during your initial VMware Workstation configuration. The script allows you to configure bridged networking, host-only networking, and NAT.

Setting up a virtual machine with two host-only adapters

If you are going to create the setup where the guest operating system (virtual machine 3 in Figure 11.13) takes care of the routing, you must set up that machine with two virtual host-only network adapters.

 Tip: In your guest operating system, rename the network adapter (Windows) or identify the adapter by its configuration to be able to distinguish between this already existing adapter and the new adapter that you will be adding here.

Open the configuration of your virtual machine **VM → Settings**. Click Add to add a new Ethernet Adapter to your virtual machine.

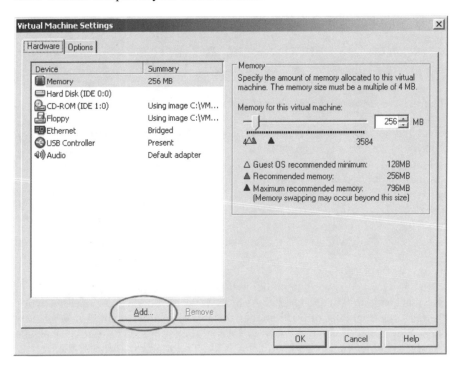

Figure 11.16: Adding a second network adapter to a virtual machine.

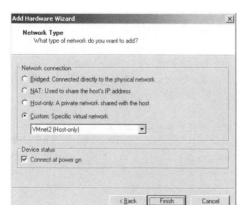

In the **Add Hardware Wizard**, select Custom network connection and select the virtual host-only network that you will be using in this virtual machine.

If you reboot the virtual machine now, a new adapter will be found by your guest operating system. Rename this adapter (in Windows), to distinguish easily between the two adapters in the different networks. This will make it easier to configure the routing for these adapters.

Figure 11.17: Add a second adapter to the virtual machine on VMnet2.

11.7 Configuring MAC Addresses for your Virtual Machines

Every network adapter in the world has (or should have) a unique Media Access Control (MAC) address. This is also the case for your virtual machine. This section explains how MAC addresses are assigned and how to configure them manually.

First, we will look into what MAC addresses are. From the technical point of view, they are 6 byte identifiers that uniquely identify each network adapter. The first three octets are reserved for the manufacturer's identification code, and the last three octets form a unique identifier for every network adapter that the manufacturer ships.

You can find the MAC address of your network adapter by using the following commands in the three guest operating systems that this book covers:

- Windows   ipconfig /all

- Linux   ifconfig

- NetWare   config

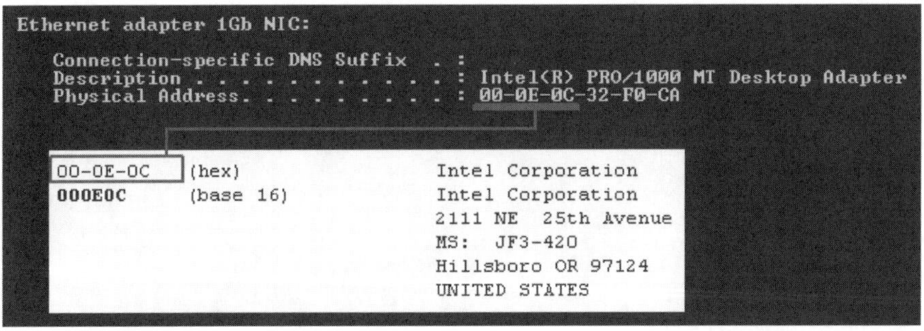

```
Ethernet adapter 1Gb NIC:

    Connection-specific DNS Suffix  . :
    Description . . . . . . . . . . . : Intel(R) PRO/1000 MT Desktop Adapter
    Physical Address. . . . . . . . . : 00-0E-0C-32-F0-CA


    00-0E-0C    (hex)              Intel Corporation
    000E0C      (base 16)          Intel Corporation
                                   2111 NE  25th Avenue
                                   MS:  JF3-420
                                   Hillsboro OR 97124
                                   UNITED STATES
```

Figure 11.18: An example of a MAC address and a manufacturer identifier.

The manufacturer identifiers are registered in a public registry. They are called Organizationally Unique Identifiers (OUI) and they are managed by the Registration Authority of the Institute of Electrical and Electronics Engineers (IEEE). Manufacturers can be searched for, based on the first three bytes of the MAC address or by name. Point your browser to the following URL to perform a search:

standards.ieee.org/regauth/oui/index.shtml.

A search on the keyword "VMware" tells us that three possible ranges of MAC addresses are registered by VMware: 00-05-69, 00-0C-29 and 00-50-56. The last one is the one used by all current VMware software. The virtual host-only adapters in the host computer and the Ethernet adapters in the guests will use this `00-50-56` prefix. For the host-only adapters, the last octet in the MAC address is 01 for VMnet 1, 02 for VMnet 2, and so on.

Automatically generated MAC addresses
There is no need to worry about MAC addresses being unique for your virtual machines because in almost every case, they are unique. VMware assigns unique MAC addresses to your virtual machines. There is no guarantee that all the MAC addresses on all your virtual machines, maybe on multiple computers, are unique. If you ever encounter problems, they can be manually created. Manually generated MAC addresses are discussed later in this section.

The .vmx parameters which specify that the MAC addresses will be automatically generated are:

```
ethernet0.addressType = "generated"
ethernet0.generatedAddress = "00:0c:29:7a:39:41"
ethernet0.generatedAddressOffset = "0"
```

First, you have to know something about the way that VMware creates the MAC addresses. We will start out with something else first: the Unique Identifier that every virtual machine gets. This 16 byte value is assigned to every virtual machine to identify it uniquely. It is listed in the .vmx configuration file in the `uuid.location` and `uuid.bios` parameters.

```
uuid.location = "56 4d 2d d3 cc 9d a2 39-7c 4d 26 f0 1f 76 c1 80"
uuid.bios = "56 4d 2d d3 cc 9d a2 39-7c 4d 26 f0 1f 76 c1 80"
```

The last three bytes of this value are used as the three byte MAC address part for the virtual machine network adapter. Using the example value above, the MAC address of the virtual Ethernet adapter will be:

```
00-50-56-76-c1-80
```

 Note: With multiple adapters, the last byte is increased by 10 decimal (0A hex) for every adapter. Two new adapters will get the following addresses: `00-50-56-76-c1-8A` and `00-50-56-76-c1-94`. There is a .vmx parameter called ethernet0.generatedAddressOffset = "0" for the first adapter, which will have a value of "10" and "20" in the previous example for the two other adapters.

The virtual machine's unique identifier will not normally change. When you move the virtual machine's files to a different location, or modify the name of the .vmx file, VMware will ask you whether you want to create a new identifier or to keep the old one.

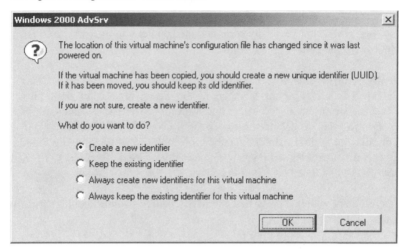

Figure 11.19: After moving or copying a virtual machine create a new unique identifier or keep the old one.

If you keep the existing identifier, nothing changes and the MAC address remains unchanged. Creating a new identifier does change the `uuid.bios` and `uuid.location` values and therefore creates a new MAC address.

 Note: You can configure the behavior of a virtual machine to always keep the UUID or to always create a new one after copying a virtual machine. Use one of these settings in the .vmx file:

```
uuid.action = "create"
```

or

```
uuid.action = "keep"
```

 Note: If you image a PC that holds virtual machines (such as in an education environment) and the virtual machines will communicate via the Local Area Network, you will end up with duplicate MAC addresses. In this scenario, either rename the directories on your destination computers and create new identifiers, or manually assign MAC addresses.

Manually assign MAC addresses
Manually assigning MAC addresses needs to be done from the .vmx configuration file by removing and adding parameters. Make sure that the .vmx file is not opened by VMware if you manually edit the file.

First, remove the lines that take care of the automatic generation:

```
ethernet0.addressType
ethernet0.generatedAddress
ethernet0.generatedAddressOffset
```

(or for any other number of Ethernet adapters that are specified in the .vmx file)

Add the following line to specify the MAC address to be used by your adapter:

```
Ethernet0.address = 00:50:56:XX:YY:ZZ
```

(or for any other number of Ethernet adapters that are specified in the .vmx file)

The first three bytes are reserved for the VMware manufacturer's identifier and the last three bytes need to be provided manually.

Construct these three octets with the following rules:

- XX must be a valid hexadecimal number between 00 and 3F
- YY and ZZ must be valid hexadecimal numbers between 00 and FF

⚠ **Note:** It is very important to use unique MAC addresses on your network. When working with multiple virtual machines on more than one VMware server with manually assigned addresses, make sure that a mechanism is in place to register the MAC addresses that are used in your organization. This is as you would normally do with IP addresses being documented.

11.8 Sniffing the Virtual Network

VMware Workstation comes with a utility called vnetsniffer. It is very basic, but it can help you out when monitoring if and when network traffic is generated on your virtual networks. The utility is located in the VMware program directory:

```
usage: vnetsniffer [/e] VMnet?
```

Load the program with the name of the network VMnet0 to VMnet9. It will display lines in your command line window with all the source addresses and destination addresses, and the type of packets being transferred. Adding the /e parameter will display enhanced information; from what I have gathered, the extra information is only the MAC address of the source and the destination of the packets.

Using Ethereal to analyze the network
The virtual network adapter on a Windows host supports the so called promiscuous mode which allows it to read all the packets that are transferred to be analyzed off

---

line. This can be done with any of the commercially available network analyzers. But life is expensive enough, so let's take a look at a freeware alternative.

Ethereal is an Ethernet packet analyzer which can analyze many protocols that are transferred via your network. It uses another freeware, Packet Capture Architecture for Windows. To work with Ethereal on your Windows host, you will have to install this WinPcap software and the Ethereal software. Both are available from the Ethereal download webpage:

```
Ethereal    www.ethereal.com
WinPcap     winpcap.polito.it
```

11.9 Using the Wireless Network from your Virtual Machines

With older versions of VMware Workstation (prior to version 4) it was not possible to access the wireless network directly by using bridged networking. However, starting with VMware workstation version 4, you can now bridge your virtual machine to the wireless network directly. But sometimes it does not work to get the wireless bridging to work. That is why I also explain the other methods.

Using bridged networking
From the **Edit** menu, select **Virtual Network Settings** to change the bridged networking mode. You can edit the Host Virtual Network Mapping manually to change the default bridged adapter VMnet0, to use your wireless adapter.

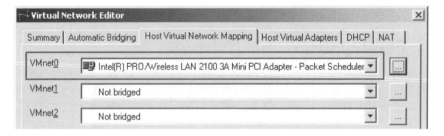

Figure 11.20: Bridged networking can also be assigned to the wireless network.

By selecting the wireless adapter, your default bridged mode is now using the wireless network. There is no need to configure anything about the wireless LAN like ESSID or WEP keys inside your virtual machine. It will just see the network as a normal Ethernet network.

Using Internet Connection Sharing
If bridging to the wireless network does not work for you, one of the other options is to use the Virtual Host Only network, and Windows Internet Connection Sharing

(ICS), to share the wireless network adapter. You could also use VMware's NAT adapter, but I think ICS is easier and sufficient for most users.

To configure Internet Connection Sharing on your Wireless adapter, go to the properties of your adapter and select the **Advanced** tab.

In the ICS frame, enable the check box to **Allow other network users to connect through this computer's Internet connection**.

As the adapter for your Home networking connection, you select a Virtual host-only adapter, by default this would be VMnet1. If you click OK to save this setup, you will receive a message which informs you that your network adapter for the Home Network (VMnet1) will be set up with IP address 192.168.0.1. The subnet mask for that adapter is set to 24 bits (255.255.255.0).

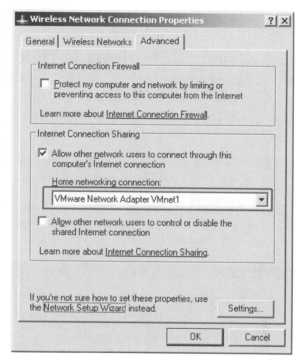

Figure 11.21: Internet Connection Sharing can also be used to provide access to the network.

You can verify this in the IP properties of your host-only network adapter.

To use the Internet from your virtual machine, you configure it to use the Virtual host-only network. Configure your guest operating system to use an address in the range from 192.168.0.2 to 192.168.0.254. Set the gateway and DNS server to 192.168.0.1.

You can now use the Internet from the host-only adapter being routed to the wireless network via ICS.

 Tip: This method is also a workaround to use virtual machines on a Token-Ring network. Just enable the Internet Connection Sharing on your Token-Ring adapter, and you can access the network based on TCP/IP communications.

12 VMware Tips for Windows

The tips in this chapter are for your Windows guest operating systems, which are independent of the host operating system that you run VMware on: Windows or Linux. Some of the tips are not really VMware related, but because of the usage scenarios for VMware, they are important to understand when you are getting started with Windows and VMware.

12.1 Using SCSI Drivers in Windows Virtual Machines

If you are running VMware Workstation or VMware GSX/ESX Server, and you select the LSI Logic or BusLogic SCSI adapter during installation, your SCSI disks will be automatically detected and used by Windows 2000.

When installing Windows XP or Windows Server 2003, you will have to download the special Windows SCSI Driver available at: www.vmware.com/download.

Starting a virtual machine with SCSI devices will display the warning message displayed in Figure 12.1. This message will tell you that you have such a disk and will guide you about what to do.

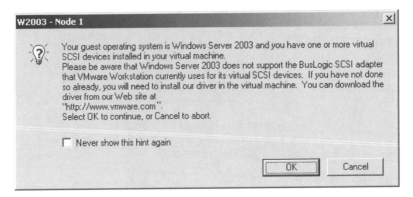

Figure 12.1: Warning message when using SCSI disks in Windows XP and 2003.

The SCSI driver download comes as a virtual floppy image (VMware-BusLogic-SCSIDriver-1.2.0.0.flp). This is very convenient, because you can directly add this floppy to your virtual machine, and use it during Windows installation.

If you need access to the floppy, you can get access via a Windows virtual machine which is already up and running. Do this by connecting the virtual floppy file to the machine. You can also use WinImage or the virtual floppy driver to access the contents of the floppy. This is described in detail in section 7.1: "Working with Virtual Floppy disks".

Assign the floppy to your virtual machine, and press F6 when the appropriate message appears at the bottom of the installation screen. Consult the Microsoft Windows documentation for more information on adding drivers during installation.

12.2 How to Disable CD-ROM Autorun

The VMware setup program disables autorun for your CD-ROM player during installation. You can change this manually after the installation, or you can change this setting within your Windows guest, by modifying a registry value. The correct method to do this is described in Microsoft Knowledge base article 155217: "How to Enable or Disable Automatically Running CD-ROMs".

There is no option to enable or disable automatically running CD-ROMs in the user interface. To enable or disable automatically running CD-ROMs, you must edit the registry by using the following steps:

1. Click **Start**, click **Run**, type **regedit** in the **Open** box, and then press ENTER.

2. Locate and click the following registry key:

   ```
   HKEY_LOCAL_MACHINE\System\
                   CurrentControlSet\Services\CDRom
   ```

3. To disable automatically running CD-ROMs, change the **Autorun** value to 0 (zero). To enable automatically running CD-ROMs, change the **Autorun** value to 1.

4. Restart your computer.

12.3 Shrinking your Windows Disks

How to shrink your disks is described in section 9.2: "Shrinking your virtual disks". For every operating system, there a few extra steps that you can take to prepare your virtual machine for shrinking. The most important one is to remove unnecessary files.

- Search for all files on the virtual hard disk in the guest that are larger than 1 MB. From this list sort based on file size and analyze the largest files in the list. It is guaranteed that you can remove over 50MB of files. Be careful with what you delete: do not delete .DLL of .EXE. Files you can delete are media files, bitmaps, etc.
- Delete driver files when your virtual machine is completely configured. Windows stores a local copy of the most important drivers on the hard disk. These files (located in C:\Windows\Driver Cache) can take up over 50MB of

data space. These files are useful when adding hardware, but consider the likeliness of needing them and decide if you can delete them.

- Clear up temporary directories. Do not only remove files from the Windows temporary directory in C:\Windows\Temp but also check the Local Settings\Temp directory for all users in C:\documents and settings.
- Also, do not forget any temporary Internet files. Delete them from the **General** tab in **Tools → Internet Options** in Internet Explorer.
- Check the root of your C: drive and your C:\windows directory because Windows updates and other applications sometimes create temporary files there. They should be cleaned up after installation. They should, but they not always are so make sure to check that yourself.

The amount of disk space used inside your virtual disk can be decreased by using these tips. This makes archiving your virtual machine more efficient. One last tip is for Windows XP and ME.

Turn off System Restore
Another important thing to keep in mind is to turn off the System Restore function in Windows XP and ME, if you can do without it. This function keeps track of changes within the operating system. It saves restore points, which can be used to restore your system to a certain point in time (where drivers and applications where working correctly). Saving these restore points will use hard disk space. The amount of hard disk space depends on the settings of the System Restore function. However, depending on what you will be using the virtual machine, for you may as well turn off the entire feature.

To turn off System Restore, open the **System Properties** in **Control Panel** and select the **System Restore** tab. You can configure the amount of disk space to be used by this function, and you can disable the function here.

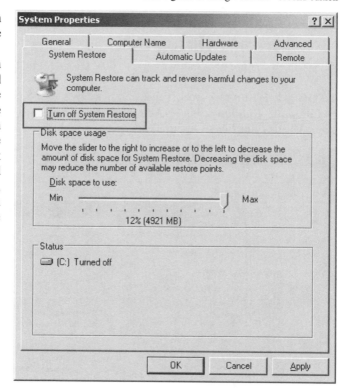

Figure 12.2: Turn off system restore in Windows XP.

12.4 Generating New SIDs

Working with Security Identifiers (SIDs) is not something that is related specifically to virtual machines. However, it is very likely that you will copy virtual machines, in order to use them multiple times. By doing so, you can end up in the situation where two machines have the same SID. This situation will cause problems, especially when working with NT or Active Directory domains.

One method for creating unique identities is to use the SYSPREP utility from Microsoft. This will remove all identification information from the machine and shut it down. It can be copied or imaged, and when the copy and/or the original are started, a mini setup wizard will start and will ask for a computer name, domain name, or a workgroup to join. This will also create a new SID for your machine.

There are also tools available on the Internet which can help you generate new SIDs. One freeware tool is NewSID which is available from Sysinternals. The tool is available via their website at www.sysinternals.com.

12.5 Disable the "why do you shutdown your server?" Dialog Box

This is a new feature of Windows Server 2003. Disable it by following these steps:

Go to **Start → Run** type gpedit.msc Click **OK**. Go to **Local Computer Policy → Computer Configuration → Administrative Templates → System**.
Select **Display Shutdown Event Tracker** and disable it.

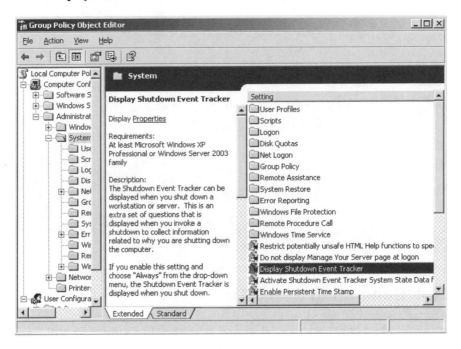

Figure 12.3 Disable the Shutdown Event Tracker.

13 VMware Tips for Linux

The tips in this chapter are for your Linux guest operating systems, which are independent of the host operating system that you run VMware on: Windows or Linux. Some of the tips are not really VMware related, but because of the usage scenarios for VMware, they are important to know when getting started with Windows and VMware.

13.1 Keep the Kernel and Kernel Source at the Same Patch Level

When you install VMware Workstation for Linux or when you install the VMware Tools inside a Linux guest operating system, on many occasions you need to compile modules for your product. One example of such a module is vmmon. The installation script will check the kernel version that you are running and will try to compile the modules for your kernel. In addition, it also accesses the kernel source files. If you install these kernel source files from a CD-ROM when you need them, then you most likely will install another version than is currently on your system. If you ran an update for your operating system, the kernel could very well be updated to a kernel patch level and since you did not install the kernel source files during initial installation the kernel is patched but the sources are not. Figure 13.1 shows an example where the usr/src/linux directory for the current kernel level (found with the uname -r command) is not correct.

```
linux:/usr/src/linux # uname -r
2.6.5-7.151-default
linux:/usr/src # ll
total 1
drwxr-xr-x    6 root root 248 Sep  5 16:35 .
drwxr-xr-x   12 root root 344 Apr  3 20:14 ..
lrwxrwxrwx    1 root root  17 Sep  5 16:35 linux -> linux-2.6.5-7.111
drwxr-xr-x    3 root root  96 Sep  5 16:31 linux-2.6.5-7.111
drwxr-xr-x   20 root root 712 Apr  3 20:33 linux-2.6.5-7.151
drwxr-xr-x    3 root root  72 Mar 18 18:06 linux-2.6.5-7.151-obj
lrwxrwxrwx    1 root root  21 Apr  3 20:34 linux-obj -> linux-2.6.5-7.151-obj
drwxr-xr-x    7 root root 168 Mar 23 14:15 packages
linux:/usr/src #
```

Figure 13.1: An example of a Linux installation with a mismatched kernel source.

If you run into a problem, such as when the running kernel and the sources are not identical, then the easiest option is to use your distributions installation directory to re-install the kernel sources package and have them updated automatically.

If you know how to download and install the correct courses manually, then you can find them at the following URL: ww.kernel.org.

When it was necessary to build the vmmon module, it could have displayed a message saying: Module.symvers is missing' modules will have no modversions and Unable to build the vmmon module.

If that is the case, run the following commands from the Linux source directory. First make that directory the present working directory:

```
cd /usr/src/Linux

make cloneconfig
make modules_prepare
```

13.2 Graphical Installation Problems

Some Linux distributions have problems with showing the correct graphics during installation. One of the problems that you may have come across is the one displayed in Figure 13.2, where the SuSE Linux installation is scrambled across four small screens.

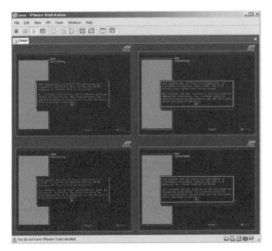

If you encounter a problem such as the one shown here, there are two options in general that let you work around the problem. The first option is to use a text-based installation, and the other option is to use VNC to remotely access the installation procedure.

It depends on your Linux distribution if the feature works exactly the way I describe here. For example, some parameters could be different.

Figure 13.2: An example of a graphical installation problem in SuSE Linux.

 Tip: This problem has been fixed in the latest SuSE 10 release.

Running a text based installation
The actions that you need to take to run a text based installation depend on the Linux distribution that you want to install. In Figure 13.3, you see an example of SuSE Linux installation.

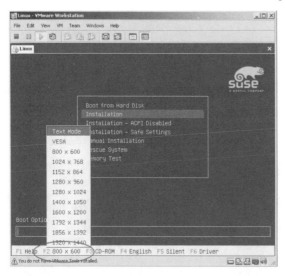

In the example shown here, a SuSE Linux installation is being configured to run a text-based installation. To do this, press F2 when the boot loader displays the boot options.

From the list of available screen resolutions, select the top most option called **Text Mode** to run a non-graphical installation.

Figure 13.3: In SuSE Linux, select Text Mode to work around any graphical installation problems.

Using a VNC based installation

Another option to work around graphical installation problems is to access the installation remotely through a VNC connection. When the boot loader is activated from your installation source, enter the VNC parameters to activate this feature.

In the example in Figure 13.4 the parameters have been added to a SuSE Linux installation. The sample command is printed below. The vncpassword parameter is optional. If you leave it out, you will be prompted for a password. The hostip and netmask parameters are also optional. If you leave them out, you will be asked if you want to use DHCP or to specify IP settings manually.

Figure 13.4: Specify VNC parameters to access the installation process remotely.

The parameters that can be entered in the boot loader for a VNC installation are:

```
vnc=1 vncpassword=<pw> hostip=<ip> netmask=<ip> gateway=<ip>
```

The hostip and netmask parameters are optional, but when you leave them out you will be prompted to select either DHCP or to manually enter the static IP information. The gateway parameter is always optional. If the computer that is used for the remote installation is on the same subnet as the virtual machine you are installing, then they will be able to communicate without a gateway address.

```
Loading data into RAM disk... (58000 kB).............................
creating device nodes ... done
integrating the shared objects of the installation system...
starting syslog (messages are logged to /dev/tty4)...
starting klogd ...
integrating kernel modules of the installation system...
starting slpd to anounce VNC...
starting yast...
OK

starting VNC server...
a log can be found in /tmp/vncserver.log ...

***
***             You can connect to 192.168.2.150, display :1 now with vncviewer
***             Or use a Java capable browser on  http://192.168.2.150:5801/
***

(When YaST2 is finished, close your VNC viewer and return to this window.)
```

Figure 13.5:   An example of a Suse Linux installation that is listening for VNC connections.

The installation procedure will start and it will display a message about the IP configuration and how to access the VNC server to continue the installation.

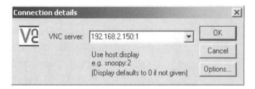

On your remote computer, start a VNC client and access the VNC server on its IP address and screen number.   For   example, 192.168.2.150:1 as shown in Figure 13.6.

Figure 13.6: Access the installation from a client with the IP address and screen number.

14 VMware Tips for NetWare

The tips in this chapter are for the NetWare operating system. They apply to all versions, from NetWare 4.x to Open Enterprise Server, unless otherwise stated.

14.1 Available Options for the VMware Tools

Starting with VMware Workstation v3.2, the VMware Tools for NetWare became available. You can see available commands by using the help command:

```
VMWTOOL Help
```

Table 14.1: Available commands for the VMware Tools for NetWare.

Command	Description
help	Displays commands and options.
partitionlist	Displays a list of all disk partitions in the virtual disk and whether or not a partition can be shrunk.
shrink <partition>	Shrinks the listed partitions. If no partitions are specified, then all partitions in the virtual disk are shrunk. The status of the shrink process appears at the bottom of the system console.
devicelist	Lists each removable device in the virtual machine, as well as its device ID, and whether the device is enabled or disabled. Removable devices include the virtual network adapter, CD-ROM, and floppy drives.
disabledevice or enabledevice <device name>	Disables or enables the specified device or devices in the virtual machine. If no device is specified, then all removable devices in the virtual machine are disabled or enabled.
synctime on or off	Turn the time synchronization with time on the host operating system. on or off. By default, time synchronization is turned off. Use this command without any options to view the current time synchronization status. **Tip:** You can synchronize the time in the guest operating system, with time on the host

	operating system, only when the time in the guest operating system is set earlier than the time set in the host, it must not be in the future.
idle on or off	It allows you to turn the CPU idler on or off. By default, the idler is turned on. The CPU idler program is included in VMware Tools for NetWare guests. **Tip:** Do not use the older commonly used NW-IDLE NLMs. Using those NLMs can cause the performance to degrade instead of improve.

14.2 Network Adapter for NetWare

It is not obvious what adapter you should use for your NetWare server. When installing NetWare in VMware, two or three options are presented, depending on your version of NetWare: the CNEAMD.LAN driver, or the CPCNTNW.LAN and PCNTNW.LAN drivers.

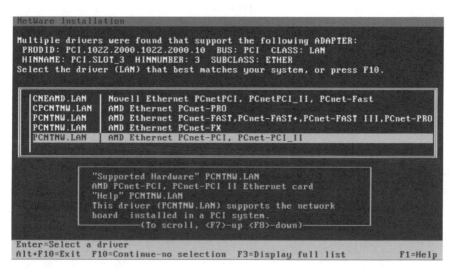

Figure 14.2: Choose the PCNTNW.LAN driver for a NetWare guest installation.

My preference is to use PCNTNW.LAN

Why? There are a few reasons that build my case for this choice:

- Virtual machines contain the AMD am79C970A Ethernet adapter. The PCNTNW driver is created by AMD and the CNEAMD driver is a compatible driver from Novell.

- The PCNTNW driver is from 2000, the CNEAMD driver from 1998

- The PCNTNW driver compared to the CPCNTNW and CNEAMD drivers is written in Assembly while the other two are written in C language. This gives a slight advantage for the ones written in the C language. The CPCNTNW.LAN driver is newer however (2002), and is not available in all versions of NetWare and is not used in the Yes Tested and Approved program. I still prefer PCNTNW over the other two.

By the way, all three drivers work and PCNTNW and CNEAMD are both used in the Yes Tested and Approved program by Novell. You can search this database via the following URL: `http://developer.novell.com/nss`.

14.3 Shrinking your NetWare Disks

How to shrink your disks is described in section 9.2: "Shrinking your virtual disks". For every operating system, there a few extra steps that you can take to prepare your virtual machine for shrinking. The most important is to remove unnecessary files.

First, you must prepare your volumes. Follow these steps to shrink your disk really small:

Delete unused files

There will be many files on your NetWare file system that you perhaps are not going to use. Be selective with what you install in the first place. Do you really need the exteNd Application Server? Or iPrint with a 200MB driver set?

Files you can delete from the server without any problems:
- ConsoleOne (sys:\public\mgmt) (Use this from a workstation or even better use iManager)
- DNS/DHCP management console (sys:\public\dnsdhcp)
- sys:\public\winnt & win95
- CD-ROM index files in SYS:\CDROM$$.ROM
- SYS:\PVSW (Pervasive SQL)

Even after a new server installation, the file system is packed with salvageable files (the installer unzips many temporary files to SYS). So, make sure that you purge your volumes before shrinking. Purging is available from a client, but with

NetWare 6.5 service pack 1 there is a new command available on the server to perform this task.

`PURGEVOLUME SYS` (or any other volume name for your server)
(output from the purge process is printed to the Logger Screen)

You can shrink the disk from the VMware tools menu in the GUI. The tools are started with the `VMWTOOLJ.NCF` command. Alternatively, you can use FILLZERO.NLM to fill all unused blocks with zeroes. The file is available from the tools section on the author's website at the following URL: `www.robbastiaansen.nl`.

14.4 Use the Snapshot Feature of VMware During Installation

During installation, and mainly in the GUI part of it, there have been some occasions when the installation screen would freeze and stop working. Starting the installation over and over again becomes annoying and time consuming. By using the new Snapshot feature, you can revert back to a previous point in the installation.

Based on my experience, you should create a snapshot every time you successfully reach one of the following steps in the installation:

- When the GUI installation starts.
- After the files for the installation are copied.
- After making all the selections for products (the NetStorage screen is the last one; while in that screen, make a snapshot before it starts creating eDirectory objects).

14.5 Remove the Platform Support Module from STARTUP.NCF

It depends on your hardware, but you may have to remove the Multiprocessor Platform Support module (MPS14.PSM) which is added during installation. With this module loaded, I frequently had "FOUND SPINLOCK TO BE BUSY WITH SINGLE PROCESSOR ACTIVE" Abends.

More information about this is available in the following Technical Information Document: "Single processor server abending often." TID10067515

14.6 My NetWare Server Keeps Losing Time Synchronization

Running multiple servers in VMware asks for time synchronization between your NetWare servers. You can set this up with the normal Timesync mechanism. It happens frequently that NetWare virtual machine configurations lose their time synchronization. If your NetWare servers keep losing their time synchronization, then change the synchronization parameters as follows:

- Set the Polling Interval to 3600
- Set the Short Interval to 600

The TID that explains these parameters is located at the end of this paragraph.

⚠ **Note:** Do not use NTP for time synchronization with NetWare and VMware. The normal Timesync synchronization (also via TCP/IP) that NetWare uses is sufficient for most configurations.

⚠ **Note:** After setting up time synchronization between the NetWare servers, do not enable the time synchronization that VMware offers between the host and the guest. Check this status in the VMware tools in the GUI or with the command VMWTOOL SYNCTIME.

The parameters described here only work with Timesync. On older versions of NetWare, you can use MONITOR.NLM (with !h switch to show hidden parameters). But in NetWare 5.1 and 6.x, you can use Remote Manager to show the hidden parameters and set them accordingly.

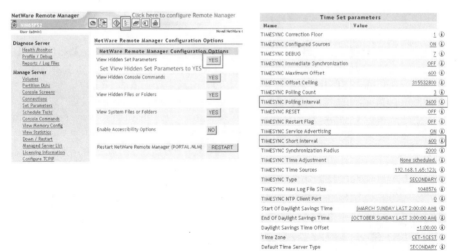

Figure 14.3: NetWare time synchronization parameters.

TIMESYNC SET Parameters Reference - TID10011517

The parameters described in this section are explained in detail in TID 10011517. You can access this Technical Information Document via support.novell.com. For the three parameters listed, a short abstract is printed below.

Table 14.2: TIMESYNC SET Parameters.

Parameter	Description
Short Interval (SI) Default = 10 seconds Hidden Parameter	Whenever a server is not synchronized to network time, polling occurs at the short polling interval. After synchronization is achieved, the polling interval gradually increases until it reaches PI.
Polling Interval (PI) Default = 600 seconds	This is the time between polling intervals when time is synchronized on the network. If time gets out of sync, the polling interval changes to SI.
Polling Count (PC) Default = 3 Upper limit = 1000, Lower limit = 1	The number of "Time Packets" to exchange during a polling cycle.

14.7 Using SCSI Drivers in older NetWare Servers

Virtual machines in VMware Workstation, GSX Server, or ESX Server contain either LSI logic LSI53C10xx Ultra 160 I/O Controller or a Mylex (Buslogic) BT-985 compatible host bus adapter. Based on my experience, the LSI Logic driver is the best one to choose. If you install a NetWare version prior to version 6.5 with either an LSI Logic or Buslogic adapter, you will see that it is not found by the installation program. You can add the drivers manually.

 Note: For NetWare 6.5 and Open Enterprise Server, just select LSI Logic as the SCSI controller type. The adapter will automatically be detected and the LSIMPTNW.NLM will be loaded. The description that follows is for NetWare 5.1 and NetWare 6.

Once the servers are up and running, we will add the Buslogic SCSI driver and activate the SCSI hard disk driver.

You need the BLMM3.HAM driver. You can download it from Buslogic (Mylex nowadays), or you can download a virtual floppy called NetWare Tools Floppy from http://www.robbastiaansen.nl containing the Buslogic driver.

The easiest way to insert the driver into the server is to add the driver to a virtual floppy, or to use the one mentioned above and connect it to the server. In NetWare 6, you can add new hardware on the server console with the HDETECT.NLM.

1. In the first screen that lists the Platform Specific Module, choose **Continue**

2. At the Device Driver screen select **Modify**.

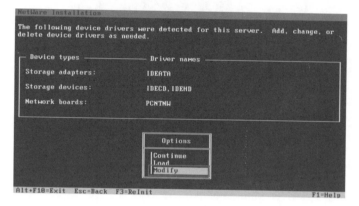

Figure 14.4

3. Press **Enter** in the Storage Adapter field and click **Modify** in the driver overview screen.

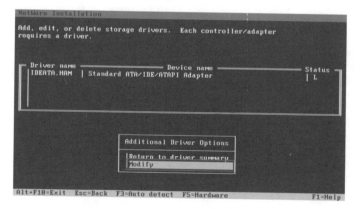

Figure 14.5

4. Press **Insert** to add a driver and in the Driver List press insert again to add an unlisted driver. The default path that will be scanned for the driver is A:\. If you have connected the virtual floppy with the driver, then press **Enter** to let NetWare do a search on the floppy. Otherwise use F3 to select a different path.

5. The BLMM3.HAM driver will be listed. Press **Enter** to select this driver and select **Return to driver summary** in the next screen.

Figure 14.6

6. Select **Return to Driver Summary** to return to the Device Driver screen. The Buslogic driver will now be listed. In the field with Storage Devices, the IDEHD and IDECD will be listed. Select modify to add the SCSIHD.CDM driver in the same way that you did for the storage adapter. The SCSIHD.CDM driver is listed in the default driver list.

Figure 14.7

7. Select the driver and return to the Device Driver screen. Both the Storage adapter and the SCSI hard disk are now listed. If you select continue, the drivers will be loaded.

8. Select continue on the remaining screens and HTDETECT will be unloaded.

Prepare for Cluster Services installation
When you are adding the drivers to prepare your servers for Cluster Services installation, perform the steps described in this chapter on both servers.

When the drivers are loaded on both servers, issue the list devices command on the two servers and make sure that both servers show the extra disk that was added. The following image shows the shared SCSI-disk which was added to both servers.

```
DA1:list devices
0x0002: [V025-A1-D1:0] NECVMWar VMware IDE CDR10 1.00 [CD]
0x0004: [V024-A2-D1:0] Legacy Floppy [FLOPPY]
0x0006: [V380-A3-D0:0] VMware, VMware Virtual S rev:1.0 [HDD]
0x0008: [V025-A0-D0:0] VMware Virtual IDE Hard Drive [HDD]

DA2:list devices
0x0001: [V024-A0-D1:0] Legacy Floppy [FLOPPY]
0x0005: [V025-A2-D1:0] SAMSUNG CDRW/DVD SN-324B U102 [CD]
0x0007: [V025-A1-D0:0] VMware Virtual IDE Hard Drive [HDD]
0x000C: [V380-A3-D0:0] VMware, VMware Virtual S rev:1.0 [HDD]
```

Figure 14.8

Part 3

Physical to Virtual Conversion

REBELLIOUS YOUNG SERVERS OFTEN RESIST THE CONVERSION PROCESS.

15 Introduction to Physical to Virtual Conversion

In this chapter, I will introduce the fine art of physical to virtual conversion (P2V). Where VMware software impresses people who use it, P2V really astonishes them. The day starts out with 10 servers lined up in the server room and ends with only one machine neatly stacked in a rack. Or, their five server production environment is copied into a one hardware box virtual machine setup in one evening.

This chapter introduces P2V in general. The next chapters will go into more detail on how to perform conversions with several different products and for several different operating systems.

15.1 P2V Conversion Usage Scenarios

Working with virtual machines makes it very simple to test new software for your environment. Whether it is a new version of an end-user application or a service pack for your server, you can test it in a virtual machine before you put it into production. But would it not be nice if you could test all of this on an exact copy of your production environment? Of course you can create a traditional test environment on physical hardware and restore servers from tape, or copy the files during a nightly operation. With the process of physical to virtual conversion, this becomes much easier. Basically, you will copy your machines into virtual machines on one box, and you will have exactly the same environment and test results as you would have in your production environment.

 Note: There are two limitations to this. When hardware specific applications are involved, the software will operate differently with the hardware in the virtual machine. And when you want to test the performance with a new application, it could also behave differently in VMware.

Other uses of VMware technology include consolidating servers into one single hardware box running VMware GSX Server or ESX Server. To get to this point, you can also use physical to virtual conversion. You move your machines into VMware and power off your old hardware. It is as simple as that.

But how do you get there? What is the easiest way to copy all the data from a real computer to a virtual computer? The next section describes what methods are available. The rest of this section explains how to use low cost tools that you may even already own, to convert physical machines into virtual machines.

15.2 Methods for Physical to Virtual Conversion

There are applications available that can perform the physical to virtual conversion for you. The methods they provide are very simple, and reduce a lot of the complexity from converting operating systems across hardware.

VMware itself has a P2V tool that works with VMware ESX Server. It converts Windows PCs into virtual machines. The current version at the time of writing this book is version 2. With P2V Assistant, physical machines can be converted into virtual machines for VMware Workstation, GSX Server, and ESX Server. It can also be used for migrating virtual machines to other virtual machines. As an example, it can be used to transfer a machine with an IDE drive to a new one with a SCSI drive.

VMware P2V Assistant   `www.vmware.com/products/vtools`

There are two, third party vendors that also have a P2V solution:

Leostream   `www.leostream.com`

Platespin   `www.platespin.com`

So, as you can see, there are tools available that can make the job easier. Why bother going through the process of converting machines manually with the solutions described in this book? It is simple. This part has been created to get you started with low cost tools, because the tools described before are not really low cost.

It all depends on your physical to virtual conversion requirements. When you have to perform multiple conversions on a regular basis, you are always better off with any of the supported tools that you can buy.

Converting the occasional server or workstation into a virtual machine is something that you can do with the methods described in the next parts. Another reason for this is that you may need to convert a non-supported operating system in any of the tools to a virtual machine. NetWare is an example that is discussed later, because it is not supported by any vendor at the time of writing this book.

Some vendors support Linux but not all of its distributions. Platespin, for example, is the only one that supports Linux at this time but it only supports RedHat Linux. By following the procedures explained in the next chapters, you can convert Linux machines without buying any additional software or by using generally available imaging software.

15.3 The Low Cost Approach of P2V Conversion

During the last few years, I have performed many conversions to move physical machines into virtual machines. The actual technique is simple, but the complexity is in the operating system. Windows is especially not an operating system that can easily be transferred from one hardware platform to another.

Imaging software
The software that I will introduce in this part for P2V conversion is regular imaging software that you may already own. I will also use tools and commands that are standard in all Linux distributions. The skills that you need for P2V, especially with Windows, are the skills that you would also need to have for normal imaging operations between different hardware platforms.

With imaging software, you copy a hard disk to another hard disk (mostly in another PC) directly via the network or via an image file to create a copy of a PC. This is a very common technology that is being used for deploying new PCs. The problem with imaging is mainly the difference in hardware on the source PC and the destination PC. Different network and video drivers, another hard disk type (IDE or SCSI), as well as many other differences in hardware can result in you not being able to load the imaged operating system on the destination PC. And not surprisingly, all available PCs contain other hardware than those on your virtual machines.

Whether you encounter problems with your P2V conversion depends on the operating system that you are converting. NetWare, for example, is a very imaging-friendly operating system. This is because it starts the kernel and if the configured hardware (storage adapter or ACPI support) is not found, it just does not load the driver. It stops at the server console, and allows you to copy the correct drivers to the server, and adds them to the server startup files. For Windows, the process is more complex, because if the Hardware Abstraction Layer is different, Windows generates a stop-error and ends with a blue screen. This is also something we can overcome. You will learn how to do this in chapter 21.

There are two methods to be used: P2V via an image file or P2V via the network. They both have their advantages and disadvantages.

P2V via an image file
To use this method, you need to create an image file from your PC and store it somewhere. From that location, you should add the file into a virtual hard disk file and restore the image inside your virtual machine. The advantage is that it works with all imaging software because they all support image files. However, they do not all support imaging via the network. The disadvantage is that you may need a lot of disk space if your PC contains a lot of data. Storing a 50 GB image file, copying it into a virtual hard disk, and restoring it to another virtual destination hard disk requires 150 GB of available storage. This is three times the amount that you have available on your physical machine.

P2V across the network

With this method, a PC sends its data directly into a virtual machine via TCP/IP, where it is restored to the destination hard disk. There is no need for temporary storage with this method. Another advantage to this method is that it saves time because you do not have to take an image first and restore it later. It all happens at the same time. The disadvantage is that not all imaging applications support this kind of so called peer-to-peer or multicast operations. Symantec Ghost supports this peer-to-peer feature as does Portlock Storage Manager, but the latter is only available for NetWare.

General tip on P2V conversions

Whatever method you will be using, it may be useful to split any partitions that you have on the physical computer, into partitions that are divided into separate virtual disk files in your virtual machine. I have added Figure 15.1 to clarify this.

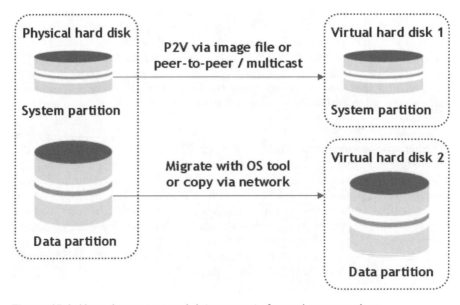

Figure 15.1: Keep the system and data separate for easier conversions.

In this example the system partition, which is not too large, is imaged with a P2V tool. This makes the P2V process fast and simple. The data could be copied via the network later, depending on the OS you are running, and whether you can have both servers up and running in the same network.

 Tip: Another benefit of this approach is that the data is now on a separate disk. This makes it more flexible; for example, by updating the operating system with a service pack it will not affect the data. It also allows you to use the Snapshot feature to revert to a previous version, without doing that for the data disk which you can set to independent mode.

Where to go from here

The remaining section will discuss several methods of performing physical to virtual conversions.

Methods that work via the network are described in the following chapters:

- Chapter 16: "Symantec Ghost's Peer-to-Peer imaging"

- Chapter 17: "Other peer-to-peer or multicast networking solutions"

- Chapter 18: "Using Acronis True Image file based imaging via the network"

- Chapter 20: "Imaging the Really Cheap Way"

A method of using disk access only is described in chapter 19: "Create a virtual disk from an image file (for any imaging application)".

Whatever method you choose to copy the data and whatever operating system you transfer, you will have to make modifications to your destination virtual machine. This is described for Windows, Linux and NetWare in chapter 21: "Modify your restored operating system to work with VMware".

Tip: Virtual to Physical and Virtual to Virtual conversions
All the methods described here are not only useable for P2V conversions. Transferring an operating system running in a virtual machine to a physical machine, or from one virtual machine into another virtual machine, can be done with the same procedures described in this part of the book.

16 Symantec Ghost's Peer-to-Peer Imaging

The simplest and fastest approach is to send the image directly from the source PC to the destination virtual machine or from one virtual machine into another virtual machine. This direct approach requires no extra storage for image files. This is extremely useful when imaging large hard disks into VMware. And, you can also use it to migrate a virtual machine from VMware Workstation into a VMware ESX Server virtual machine.

 Note: If you own a copy of the first edition of my VMware guide, you may remember reading that I sometimes experienced problems with CPU hogging and network packet loss, while using Norton Ghost inside a virtual machine. I am happy to report that this is no longer an issue with VMware Workstation version 5. However, you can still run into performance problems with VMware Workstation 4.x.

16.1 Creating the Ghost Boot Disk for VMware

You will need to start your virtual machine that you want to use as a target with a Ghost boot floppy. Using Ghost 2003, you need to follow this procedure to create the boot floppy that holds the AMD network adapter that VMware uses. It is based on the default Ghost procedure. If you want to create your own boot disks, use the web sites listed in section 7.1: "Working with Virtual Floppy disks".

1. The first step is to create a virtual floppy:

    - You can create a physical floppy which you can also connect to your virtual machine. This will work if you have installed Ghost on your Windows Host PC. If you want to create a virtual floppy image from your physical disk to use with your virtual machine, you can do that with WinImage as described in section 7.1: "Working with Virtual Floppy disks".

    - Another method is to use the Virtual Floppy Driver, which allows you to mount a virtual floppy in Windows. You can create the Norton Ghost boot disk directly into the mounted virtual floppy. How to use this tool is described in section 7.1: "Working with Virtual Floppy disks".

    - You can also run Ghost from a Windows virtual machine, and directly create the virtual floppy from the version of Ghost installed in that machine. In that case, you either need to create a virtual floppy yourself from a virtual machine or download `VirtualFloppy.zip` from `www.robbastiaansen.nl`.

2. In Norton Ghost 2003, select the **Ghost Utilities** and click **Norton Ghost Boot Wizard**

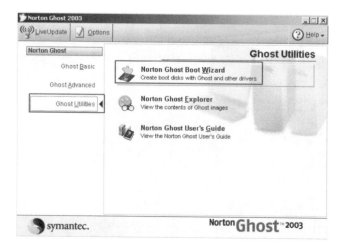

Figure 16.1: Create a boot floppy with the Norton Ghost Boot Wizard.

3. From the Norton Ghost Boot Wizard, select the **Peer-to-Peer Network Boot Disk**.

4. In the list of Network Interface Cards, select the **AMD PCNet Family** adapter and click **Next**.

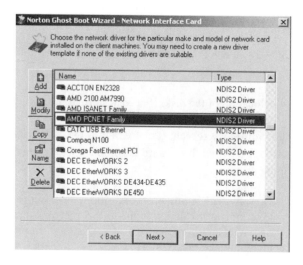

Figure 16.2: Select the correct network adapter for your computer or select the AMD PCnet adapter for use within a virtual machine.

5. In the next screen, select the DOS-version that you want to use. Just choose the PC-DOS which is listed by default.

6. The Wizard now asks you for the location of the GHOST.EXE file. You can also specify extra parameters here which will be used when Ghost starts. You can specify the –TCPS parameter which starts a TCP/IP Peer-to-Peer session automatically.

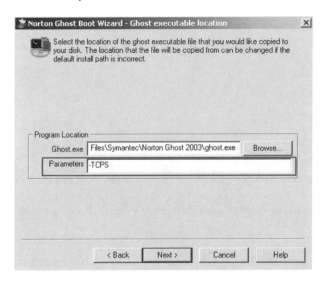

Figure 16.3: Add the -TCPS parameter to automatically start the Peer-to-Peer session.

7. In the Network Settings screen, enter an IP address or leave the default setting to use DHCP.

8. You now can specify the location of the disk. If needed, format the floppy.

9. You can now review the **Summary screen**. If everything is OK, you can click **Next** to create the boot floppy. When the Wizard is complete, close Ghost and continue with the imaging process.

At this point you have created a physical floppy or virtual floppy disk image with the Ghost boot files. You need to assign this floppy to the virtual machine that will be the slave for your peer-to-peer imaging operation. The next step is to prepare your master PC and start the imaging operation.

Physical to Virtual Conversion

16.2 Starting the Master Computer

The computer that holds your current operating system which you want to image to a virtual machine, can be started with the same kind of floppy disk that you have created in the previous paragraph. The difference with your slave floppy is that your master PC will most likely have a different network adapter. However, you can also start Ghost automatically without creating a boot floppy. You can do this by selecting Peer-to-Peer from the Ghost Advanced Menu option.

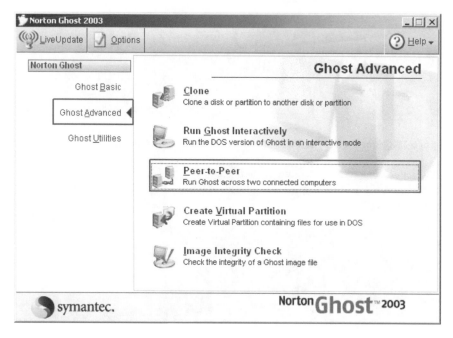

Figure 16.4: Ghost can be started without a floppy for the master computer.

The information that you need to provide is similar to those which you used when you created the boot disk for your slave. Therefore, I am assuming that you do not need any additional instructions.

 Tip: If your network adapter is not automatically detected and it is not listed, you can add the driver for your NIC from the Network Interface Card selection screen. Make sure that you download the NDIS2 driver for your network card to add it to the list. Also, make sure that you enter the correct parameters for the PROTOCOL.INI to the parameters window, while adding your custom driver.

16.3 Performing the Imaging Operation

When you reboot the master PC into ghost, and you have booted the VMware guest with the Ghost boot disk, you can start the peer-to-peer session. If the TCP/IP stack is successfully initialized, the peer-to-peer menu option will be available. Select **Peer-to-peer → TCP/IP → Slave** to start the session on the slave computer.

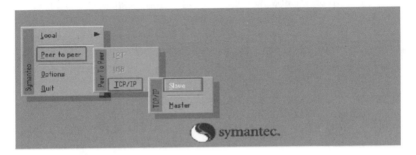

Figure 16.5: Start a Peer-to-Peer operation on the slave computer.

The slave will start connecting to a master. In the **Slave Connect** screen, the TCP/IP address of this slave is displayed. You must specify this address in the master computer.

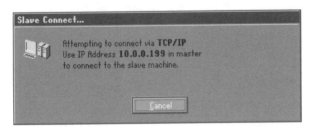

Figure 16.6: The slave will display a message with
its IP address to be specified in the master.

On the master computer, select **Peer-to-peer → TCP/IP → Master** to start the imaging session. You will be asked for the slave's IP address. When the master connects to the slave, the slave computer will display a message that it is connected. The master will return to the original menu where you can select your imaging operation (disk to disk, or a single partition). The easiest conversion can be accomplished by selecting the disk-to-disk option to copy the entire PC into the virtual machine. However, you can also do this on a partition level.

Where to go from here
Depending on the operating system you are restoring, you may need to modify drivers, etc. This is explained in detail in chapter 21: "Modify your restored operating system to work with VMware".

17 Other Peer-to-Peer or Multicast Networking Solutions

Norton Ghost is a widely available imaging tool which I have selected to discuss this topic in the previous chapter. There are other products available that I would like to briefly mention.

Portlock Storage Manager
This application is very often used in NetWare environments, but it is multi functional. Storage Manager supports NetWare's NSS file system but it also supports FAT, NTFS, EXT2, EXT3, and ReiserFS. The application supports local imaging operations from hard disks and removable media, such as writable CDs and DVDs, as well as networking imaging operations via TCP/IP networking.

For the NetWare environment, this is the best tool to use because it supports the NSS file system, which allows it to image specific volumes from your server. Another benefit is that it uses the normal LAN and storage drivers from NetWare, because the application runs as an NLM. For your virtual machine target, you will have to use a DOS floppy with the NetWare TCP/IP stack. A virtual floppy disk with DOS, LAN drivers and TCP/IP stack is available for download at: www.robbastiaansen.nl.

More information on Portlock Storage Manager is available at: www.portlocksoftware.com

Novell ZENworks imaging
Many users with a Novell NetWare environment also own the Novell ZENworks for desktop products. It contains an imaging component which supports the Windows file systems. It can be used for imaging operations to and from an imaging server, but you can also perform peer-to-peer imaging, by setting one workstation as a multicast master, and another one as a multicast slave.

Altiris Client Management Suite
This management suite is very popular for workstation management and also contains peer-to-peer imaging functionality.

18 Using Acronis True Image File Based Imaging via the Network

The Symantec Ghost peer-to-peer option described in the previous chapter is the easiest one to use because it sends the image to another computer directly. This solution will not always work, either because of limitations of Ghost which I have explained in the peer-to-peer section or because of limitations in the network bandwidth. However, you can, store an image file directly on a server volume or another PC with Acronis True Image. This allows you to restore that image file from that location, or you can copy the image to another location. An advantage of this approach is that you can use the image file multiple times, where the peer-to-peer imaging operation is a one time action.

I have decided to use the True Image software from Acronis, because this software can create images from within Windows and they also provide a very powerful restore CD.

Note: For Windows Server products, you will need a server version of Acronis True Image. The server version is more expensive than the regular workstation version. It is not only Acronis that has a special server version. Symantec also sells a specific server version of their DriveImage software. For Linux, you will need the True Image Server for Linux software if you want to run the imaging software on a running Linux box. With the restore CD, you can create images of any machine when you reboot it with that CD.

There are two approaches for creating an image with True Image. The first one is to install the full Acronis application in your Windows or Linux environment. The second is to boot the machine with the True Image rescue CD in order to perform the operation from outside the regular operating system.

When you use the first option, you actually create an image from the running operating system. That contradicts with all other approaches to imaging up until now, when we needed to create an image of a machine with a shut down operating system. So, is it safe to execute an imaging operation on a running server?

I have added the following piece of text from the Acronis support pages to shed some light on this issue:

I have complex applications such as Microsoft SQL Server, Oracle or Microsoft Exchange running on my server. I plan to create an image, but I'm not sure if these applications can be running during the imaging process. What should I do?

Although Acronis True Image 8.0 Server for Windows takes care of hard disk and filesystem-level consistency via snapshot technology, it could not guarantee application-level consistency. We recommend you to suspend complex servers such as Microsoft SQL, Oracle or Microsoft Exchange before pressing the Proceed button on the last page of the Acronis True Image 8.0 Server for Windows Create Image wizard, or before starting a scheduled task. Once the imaging process starts, you can resume server operations. It is not necessary to suspend the applications for the duration of the imaging process.

As you can read in the previous text, it is safe to execute an imaging operation from a running Windows host. But is it wise? What will happen to the disk and network performance when all regular tasks are running and you pull an image off the server? It all depends on the load of your server, but I suggest that you create the image when no other users are working with the server or at least during off-peak hours.

 Note: Running the imaging operation with no users attached, is especially important if you are migrating a server into a virtual environment permanently. Once the imaging has been completed, nothing that goes into the physical machine will ever be added to the virtual machine.

18.1 Creating the Image

You can start the imaging in two ways, as explained earlier. You can either start with the True Image rescue CD or install the application on your Windows or Linux host. When you install the application, you will be prompted to create the Rescue Media (see Figure 18.1). With that CD-ROM or a set of floppies, you can boot your PCs or virtual machines to create images or restore them.

 Tip: To use the rescue CD-ROM inside a virtual machine, it is best to use an ISO-file. How to create an ISO file form a CD-ROM is explained in detail in chapter 7.

To create the image, start the application or boot your computer with the Rescue Media. Once you see the main application screen with the option **Create Image**, all the steps are identical to what follows, no matter how you get to this point.

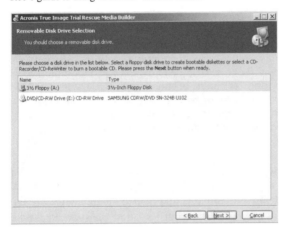

The Acronis software lets you create the Rescue Media during installation or after that, when you select **Tools → Create Bootable Rescue Media**. It depends on the hardware you have installed what write options you have available. Using floppies requires 6 floppy disks so I really recommend using a CD-ROM instead.

Figure 18.1: Create the Bootable Rescue Media during installation or later from the application.

Creating the image is wizard based. You can go through the selection of which hard disk and which partitions you want to restore. Once you have selected your source, it is time to select the destination. You can store the image on a local hard disk but the cool thing about Acronis True Image is that you can store the image directly on a network location. With the Windows version, as well as with the Rescue Media this can be another Windows machine.

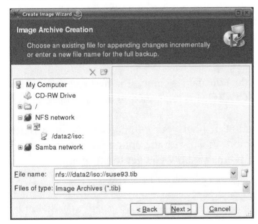

In the Linux version, you can also use Windows shares by selecting the **Samba Network** option. However, it is also possible to directly access NFS network resources. But both options and all other types of destinations will work, if you mount them to a local directory and use that as the destination.

Figure 18.2: True Image allows you to store the image on a networked destination directly.

Acronis True Image allows you the option to add a password to the image file and a description, where you can add information about the machine where the image was created from, the date, and other information that might be relevant at restore time.

Physical to Virtual Conversion

18.2 Restoring the Image

What can I say? If you have read the previous section on how to create the image, then there is not much more to say about restoring the image. You can also boot with the Rescue Media and browse the network to select the source image file. Then you can select the destination hard disk and partition and restore the image to the machine.

There is one tip that I would like to give you when restoring images. Make sure the destination drive is large enough to contain the source partition. If it is too small, the Restore Image Wizard will not show that disk as a destination for your restore. This should of course never be a problem with restoring inside a virtual machine where adding a large enough hard disk is just a matter of a few mouse clicks.

Figure 18.3: Select a destination that is large enough to contain the image to be restored.

Where to go from here

Depending on the operating system that you are restoring, you may need to modify drivers, etc. This is explained in detail in chapter 21: "Modify your restored operating system to work with VMware".

19 Create a Virtual Disk from an Image File (for any imaging application)

With the imaging operations described in the previous parts for peer-to-peer imaging and imaging to network destinations, you rely on a network connection being available. In addition, you rely on network drivers that are operating correctly. This is not always the case, and therefore, I also describe another approach where only disks are involved. Therefore, this procedure is supported by all operating systems and with all imaging applications.

To restore an image of a physical machine into a virtual machine, with this method, you need to first create an image file by using the method which works best for you (with your favorite imaging application). Then you need to create a virtual machine, and restore the image inside the virtual machine. Of course, you still have to edit your restored operating system to work with the virtual machine hardware as described in chapter 21: "Modify your restored operating system to work with VMware".

The short description of the method that is described here is that we create a virtual machine with two disks. One will hold the image file, and the other will be the destination disk. You then boot with your boot-medium from your imaging solution and restore the local disk file.

1.   At this point I am assuming that you have already created the image file with the imaging application of your choice.

2.   Create a virtual machine with the settings that reflect your destination operating system (Windows, NetWare, etc.). Create a disk that is the same type as your original disk from the physical PC (IDE or SCSI), and make it large enough to receive the restored image file.

3.   Next, you will need to add a disk that will hold the image file. There are two approaches to this; first I will discuss the one for the gui-users:

   •   Use a Windows or Linux virtual machine with a second disk to format the disk, and copy the image file into that separate virtual disk via either the network or by a Host-to-Guest shared folder.

   Next, I will discuss the one for those who are into the command line stuff:

   •   Create a virtual disk with a FAT file system (or download an empty disk Empty1999mbFATdiskv4.zip or Empty1999mbFATdiskv5.zip from the tools section at www.robbastiaansen.nl).

- Mount the empty disk with the DiskMount utility (described in section 7.4: "Using the DiskMount Utility".

  `vmware-mount k: Empty1999mbFATdisk.vmdk`

- Copy the image file into the virtual disk.

- Dismount the disk file and attach it to the virtual machine, where you will be restoring the image.

4. At this point, you have a virtual machine with an empty disk (disk 1) and a disk containing the image file.

5. Start your virtual machine now, with the boot media from your imaging solution. This can be a (virtual) boot floppy or CD-ROM created for Ghost, DriveImage, or any other solution. In addition, if you own ZENworks for Desktops, you can use the CD-ROM iso file to boot the virtual machine.

Tip: If you are using Ghost, then you can find the procedures for creating a virtual boot floppy in section 16.1: "Creating the Ghost boot disk for VMware"

Tip: If you use Novell ZENworks imaging with the bootcd.iso which comes with ZENworks for desktops, you should mount the second disk in the system (that holds the image file) with the following command: `mount -t msdos /dev/hdb1 /mnt/harddisk`. You should then restore the local image with the following command: `img rl /mnt/harddisk/<imagefile.zmg>`.

6. You can now restore the local image file with your imaging solution. Depending on the operating system that you are restoring, you may need to modify drivers, etc. This is explained in detail in chapter 21: "Modify your restored operating system to work with VMware".

20 Imaging the Really Cheap Way

If you have read the previous chapters, then you can see that one part of physical to virtual conversion is getting your data from one machine to another. The second part is modifying your operating system to work on the new hardware. This chapter will explain how to perform the second part.

There are no tools involved for which you have to pay. That was not so for the imaging solutions we have just looked into in the previous chapter. If you really do not want to spend any money on software for this process, or if you need a solution that is as low level and basic as possible, then this chapter will help you with that.

The solutions which I explain in this chapter use freely available tools and commands that are standard and are available in Linux. But before you stop reading: you do not have to install Linux, as you will see how later. The two methods that I will describe are using a free utility called g4u and standard Linux commands.

20.1 Imaging with g4u

Creating an image is really just dumping your disk into a file. If you do that with any of the available commercial programs, they offer you the feature of working with individual partitions to image and restore them. They also offer features to manipulate partitions, such as to increase them while you restore them to a destination hard disk. But sometimes you do not need these features and you just want to copy an entire hard disk or entire partitions from one hard disk to another. This is exactly what g4u will do for you.

The application is called Ghost for Unix. It is named after the commercial product which was one of the first to offer imaging solutions. The utility is available as a free download from the programmer's website: www.feyrer.de/g4u. The program can be downloaded as a floppy image or CD-ROM image. The source is also available from the website.

What the program does is simple: it creates an image, which reads sectors from the hard disk and sends the data via ftp to a file on another computer. To restore an image, the file is read via ftp and is written into the local hard disk or partition. Performing these operations on local disks to clone them is also supported.

The software download is available as a CD-ROM image, which is my preference because it is the easiest way and many PCs do not have a floppy drive anymore. You can burn the ISO file to a CD-ROM or attach it directly to a virtual machine if you want to image one of those.

The requirements for the utility are as follows:

- A DHCP server
- An FTP server with enough space to store the image file

Tip: Almost all Linux distributions come with an FTP server or you can easily add one of the many freely available ones. For Windows, if you need a free FTP server, you may want to take a look at FreeFTPd. You can download it from the following URL: www.freeftpd.com.

After booting the CD-ROM, a small help menu is displayed which shows the available commands. Figure 20.1 shows the welcome screen with the available commands.

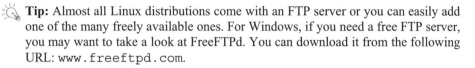

```
Reading disklabels: wd0 wd1 wd2 wd3 sd0 sd1 sd2 sd3.
-------------------------------------------------------------------------
 Welcome to g4u Harddisk Image Cloning V2.1!

Commands:
  * Upload disk-image to FTP:      [GZIP=1] uploaddisk serverIP [image] [disk]
  * Upload partition to FTP:       [GZIP=1] uploadpart serverIP [image] [disk+part]
  * Install harddisk from FTP:              slurpdisk  serverIP [image] [disk]
  * Install partition from FTP:             slurppart  serverIP [image] [disk+part]
  * Copy disks locally:                     copydisk disk0 disk1
  * Copy partitions locally:                copypart disk+part0 disk+part1
  * List all disks:                         disks
  * List partitions:                        parts disk
  * See all devices:                        dmesg
  * This screen:                            help

 [disk] defaults to wd0 for first IDE disk, [disk+part] defaults to wd0d for
 the whole first IDE disk. Use wd1 for second IDE disk, sd0 for first SCSI
 disk, etc. Default image for slurpdisk is 'rwd0d.gz'.

 Enjoy!                                     Send comments to hubert@feyrer.de
                                            Donate at paypal@feyrer.de !
                                            http://www.feyrer.de/g4u/
-------------------------------------------------------------------------
g4u>
```

Figure 20.1: gu4 offers a simple but effective imaging solution.

Uploading a disk image to an FTP server is performed with this command:

```
uploaddisk [user@]<server-ip-address> [imagefilename] [disk]
```

The only mandatory parameter is the server's IP address. If you do not specify anything else, the program will login to the server as user install and create a file of your first hard disk with a default name, for which it will use your hard disk identifier.

To restore a disk image from an FTP server, use the following command:

```
slurpdisk [user@]<server-ip-address> [imagefilename] [disk]
```

With the slurpdisk command, the same rules apply as for creating the file; without any parameters, it logs into the FTP server and downloads a file named after your first disk's identifier and downloads it.

As you can see in Figure 20.1, individual partitions can be specified as well as local hard disk cloning. To identify your hard disks and partitions, you can use the command disks and parts <disk>, where <disk> is the disk identifier that you found with the disks command.

Where to go from here

Depending on the operating system that you are restoring, you may need to modify drivers, etc. This is explained in detail in chapter 21: "Modify your restored operating system to work with VMware".

20.2 File Based Imaging with Standard Linux Commands

Linux commands are very powerful. This section proves this fact again. With only a few simple commands, you can dump the contents of your hard disk into a file and restore it on another computer. You do not need any tools, such as the g4u utility which was discussed earlier. The only thing you do need is a running Linux environment on your computer. But that does not mean that you have to install Linux on your PC. You can run one of the many live CDs that are freely available. The one I always use is Knoppix. Simply download the ISO file from the website at www.knoppix.com and burn it to a CD-ROM. Or, use the ISO to boot your virtual machine directly if you are imaging a virtual machine.

 Tip: The description in this paragraph is based on an original publication at www.okmoore.com. If have comprehended the information and clarified it for those readers that are no Linux gurus (yet).

What you need to make this work is to access another host via a networking protocol such as NFS, Samba, or as I use in this example SSH. The remote host needs to have enough available disk space to store a file with the size of the entire original hard disk. When you have booted the computer with Linux, you become root with the su command and perform the following command to create the image file.

```
dd if=/dev/hda | ssh user@remotehost /bin/dd of=/tmp/hda.img
```

With this command line the dd command reads file input directly from the first hard disk (or it uses another identifier for your computer and hard disk). It pipes the output to the remote computer through an ssh connection, where the remotely executed dd command outputs the incoming stream into a file called hda.img.

To restore, execute the following command on the host where you want to dump the image file to the local hard disk:

```
ssh user@remotehost cat /tmp/hda.img | dd of=/dev/hda
```

The restore operation performs the reversed operation. It uses the `cat` command (concatenate) on the remote host through an ssh connection to output the contents of the `hda.img` file to the first local IDE hard disk.

Where to go from here
Depending on the operating system that you are restoring, you may need to modify drivers, etc. This is explained in detail in chapter 21: "Modify your restored operating system to work with VMware".

20.3 Peer-to-Peer Imaging with Standard Linux Commands

In the previous section, you learned how to create an image file from a machine with standard Linux commands. The advantage of creating a file is that you can use it more than once. The disadvantage is that it takes more time because you will first have to create the file and restore it later. When you just want to create a copy of a physical machine into a virtual machine or if you want to copy a virtual machine into another virtual machine on another VMware product then peer-to-peer imaging is a faster solution. And it can also be done with default Linux commands to clone Linux and Windows machines.

The only requirement is that you are running a Linux environment on your computer. But that does not mean that you have to install Linux on your PC. You can run one of the many live CDs that are freely available. The one I always use is Knoppix. Simply download the ISO file from the website at `www.knoppix.com` and burn it to a CD-ROM. Or, use the ISO to boot your virtual machine directly, if you are imaging a virtual machine.

You can use the default `netcat` command to set the sending computer to a listening mode where it will send the output of the `dd` command to the computer that plugs into the listening port. On the destination computer, you need to start `netcat` and connect to the source computer and everything that is received on standard input will be sent to the `dd` command through a pipe.

In this example, I dump a hard disk that is located on /dev/hda (the first IDE hard disk) inside a virtual machine on hard disk /dev/sda (the first SCSI disk):

Set the source computer to listen on port 2000:

```
dd if=/dev/hda | netcat -l -p 2000
```

Start the destination computer to connect to the source IP and port:

```
netcat 192.168.1.10 2000 | dd of=/dev/sda
```

The only disadvantage of this procedure is that you will not see what is happening. However, from the disk and network activity on your computer or inside your virtual machine you will be able to tell that the process is sending the disk information from source to destination.

Where to go from here
Depending on the operating system that you are restoring, you may need to modify drivers, etc. This is explained in detail in chapter 21: "Modify your restored operating system to work with VMware".

20.4 Preparing your Computer for Smaller Images

When you create a hard disk image with an imaging utility such as g4u or the dd command which just reads blocks from the hard disk and stores them in a file, that file by default becomes the same size as your hard disk. Even when g4u performs compression on the file it creates, it depends on you hard disk whether the compression is efficient. Blocks on the hard disk may seem empty, but they are not. And gu4 does not contain drivers for all file systems, so it is not aware of the way that your hard disk is being used. Therefore, it is a good idea to prepare your hard disk from within the operating system. You do this by filling all the blocks that are not used with bytes which contain the same value: zero.

There are tools and commands available for this for every operating system. I have listed the most common ones here:

Unix/Linux
Use the default dd command to create the file and delete it afterwards:

```
dd if=/dev/zero of=/zerofile bs=1m
rm /zerofile
```

The first command uses the if parameter to specify the special /dev/zero device, and it sends the output to the file specified with the of parameter. The bs parameter specifies that every write cycle to the file is written in 1 MB chunks. The second command then removes the file. You must do this for every partition that you will be imaging.

Windows
For Windows, one of the freely available tools, available under the GNU General Public License is **Eraser**. It is available from the following URL: sourceforge.net/projects/eraser.

NetWare
On a NetWare server, use the FILLZERO.NLM to fill all unused blocks with zeros. The file is available from the tools section on the author's website at the following URL: www.robbastiaansen.nl.

---

21 Modify your Restored Operating System to Work with VMware

Once you have restored an image to a virtual machine, you will need to modify the operating system to load the correct drivers for the hardware that is used in VMware. This section will explain how to do that for Windows, Linux, and NetWare operating systems.

21.1 Windows 9x Operating Systems

Windows 95, 98 and ME are the simplest of all Windows versions to image to different hardware compared to what the source computer is running. They do not have anything such as Hardware Abstraction Layer that you need to take care of after imaging. It is my experience, that the Plug and Play capabilities of these versions of Windows find all the hardware in your virtual machine.

21.2 Windows NT/2000/XP/2003 Operating Systems

These versions of Windows have a so called Hardware Abstraction Layer module which is installed on a PC during installation. If you move a disk into other hardware (whether physically or when restoring to a virtual machine), you will have to manually modify this HAL.DLL to the one needed for Windows in VMware.

Furthermore, you need to add the correct drivers to your virtual machine for your video adapter, sound adapter, network adapter, etc. Also, you should keep in mind that by default the mass storage drivers are not replaced. Therefore, you need to make sure that you image from a computer with an IDE disk to a virtual machine with an IDE disk and from a computer with an SCSI disk to a virtual machine with an SCSI disk. At the end of this section I have added detailed information on how to image a Windows machine from an IDE disk to a SCSI disk.

 Note: Imaging Windows PCs is something that falls outside the scope of this book. Microsoft's official position is that you need to use the SYSPREP utility to prepare a Windows machine, and there are many items to take care of. An example of this is the Security Identifier (SID), which is especially important when a workstation is part of a domain.

The following links to SYSPREP information by Microsoft will help you get started if you want to use this utility:

```
msdn.microsoft.com/library/default.asp?url=/library/en-
us/dnw2kmag00/html/sysprep.asp
```

```
www.microsoft.com/technet/prodtechnol/windows2000pro/de
ploy/depopt/sysprep.mspx
```

```
www.microsoft.com/resources/documentation/Windows/XP/al
l/reskit/en-us/prbc_cai_vnve.asp
```

The steps that I will describe below do not require the use of SYSPREP. Be aware that it is not guaranteed that it will work in your environment.

To replace the HAL.DLL with the one you need for VMware, one of the possible methods is described here:

1. Find out what the HAL.DLL is; you will need it for your specific version of Windows and the installed service pack. The easiest approach is to install the same version of Windows and service pack into a virtual machine, and copy the HAL.DLL to your host PC.

2. When you have the correct HAL.DLL, you need to add it to the restored machine. You could have copied it to the original PC, before taking an image, but you can also add it to the newly restored disk by mounting it with the VMware DiskMount utility as explained in section 7.4: "Using the DiskMount Utility"

3. When you have loaded the Windows operating system, and you now have the correct Hardware Abstraction Layer, it will start detecting the hardware in your virtual machine. It is a good idea to make sure that you have the driver files available in the virtual disk file or in an ISO file which you can attach to the virtual machine.

Tip: It might also be convenient to add the i386 directory from the Windows installation CD-ROM or the Service Pack source files, into the virtual disk when you have it mounted with the VMware DiskMount utility. That way if files are needed, they are easily available.

4. When all the hardware is detected and all the matching drivers are found, do not forget to install the VMware tools.

Microsoft Product Activation

When imaging Windows XP or Windows 2003, depending on the type of license being used, you may have to activate Windows again. Make sure that the machine is completely configured with all the new hardware before activating Windows.

Figure 21.1: After a restore Windows might need to be activated.

Imaging from IDE to SCSI

It is possible to restore an image of a computer with an IDE device into a virtual machine with an SCSI device. An example of this is when you restore into an ESX Server virtual machine, since that server only supports SCSI virtual disks. The trick is to install the VMware SCSI driver into the machine, before creating the image. Prepare for this configuration by downloading the Windows SCSI drivers from the following URL: www.vmware.com/download. The download is a virtual floppy. You can extract it with Winimage or mount it with the Virtual Floppy Driver. This is explained in chapter 7.

You do this from the **Add Hardware Wizard**. You need to start the wizard from the **System Properties** window in the **Control Panel**. Perform the following steps when the wizard runs (this example is based on Windows XP):

1. The wizard asks you if you have already installed the hardware in the computer. Select yes here, even when there is no VMware SCSI disk present.

2. At the bottom of the installed hardware list, select **Add a new hardware device** and select **Next**.

3. In the next window, select the option to manually select the hardware that is installed.

4. When a list of hardware categories to install from is displayed, select the top item called **Show all devices**.

5. In the device driver selection window, click the button **Have Disk**.

6. Browse to the vmscsi.inf file and click **Ok**.

---

7. The wizard will now show an overview of drivers available in the `.inf` file. Select the VMware SCSI Controller and click **Next**.

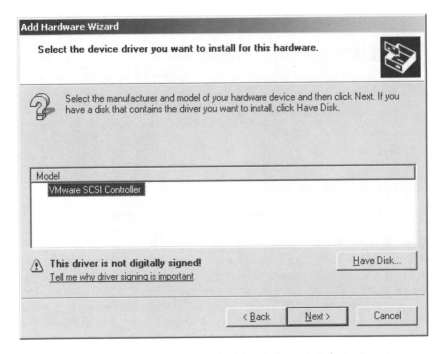

Figure 21.2: Install the VMware SCSI driver before starting the imaging process.

8. In the summary window, click **Next**.

9. You will see a message that the driver has not passed Windows Logo testing by Microsoft. Select **Continue anyway** to install the driver.

You have now successfully installed the SCSI driver on your Windows machine. You can start the imaging process and restore this image inside a virtual machine later, by using a virtual SCSI disk.

Tip: If partitions change during the imaging process, you will have a problem with booting the Windows guest. Modify the `boot.ini` file to reflect the new partition layout. You can do that with the Rescue Console from the Windows installation CD-ROM, but you can also modify this file before the imaging process when you already know what the new layout will be. Do not forget to create a backup of the original `boot.ini` file and to restore the original file when the imaging process is complete.

21.3 Linux Operating Systems

After restoring a Linux operating system into a virtual machine, it depends on the distribution you are running whether it automatically finds the virtual machine's hardware. Most current distributions such as SuSE and Red Hat do a great job on this.

What you might need to change yourself are the boot loader and the specification of the partitions that must be loaded.

Boot Loader Configuration

Generally, there are two boot loaders being used for Linux systems: LILO and GRUB. I hope that there will be no readers that are religious about their boot loader because I have decided to only discuss GRUB.

When your image is restored inside a virtual machine, and it does not boot with error messages in the boot loader, then the problem is most likely that it tries to start the operating system from the wrong hard disk and partition. It is possible that you have changed the partition order or you may have created an image of an IDE hard disk and restored it within a virtual machine with an SCSI hard disk.

The files that you need to modify on a Linux host for the GRUB boot loader are /boot/grub/device.map and /boot/grub/menu.1st.

This is an example of a device.map file:

```
(hd0)   /dev/hda
(fd0)   /dev/fd0
```

In this file, you need to change the entry that specifies the hard disk to boot from. That can be disk 1 (hd0), disk 2, (hd1) etc. For every disk, you need to specify what partition is used to boot from. In this example, it is the first IDE disk (/dev/hda) but it can also be the SCSI disk (/dev/sda).

This is a partial example of a menu.1st file:

```
color white/blue black/light-gray
default 0
timeout 8
gfxmenu (hd0,0)/message

title Linux
kernel (hd0,0)/vmlinuz root=/dev/hda3
initrd (hd0,0)/initrd

title Floppy
    root (fd0)
    chainloader +1

title Failsafe
```

```
kernel (hd0,0)/vmlinuz root=/dev/hda3 ide=nodma apm=off acpi=off
initrd (hd0,0)/initrd
```

In this file, all references to the hard disk identifier (hd0) must be specified and the partition number on that hard disk must be modified, when the partition order has changed. In this example, the kernel is located in /dev/hda1 (hd0,0) and the root partition is located in the third partition /dev/hda3 (hd0,2).

Modifying Partition Information

After changing the boot loader configuration, you need to edit the file that specifies what partitions must be mounted when the system boots. This is defined in /etc/fstab. Here is a partial example of this configuration file:

```
/dev/hda3    /         reiserfs   acl,user_xattr   1 1
/dev/hda1    /boot     reiserfs   acl,user_xattr   1 2
/dev/hda2    swap      swap       pri=42           0 0
/dev/hdc1    /data1    reiserfs   acl,user_xattr   1 2
/dev/hdd1    /data2    reiserfs   acl,user_xattr   1 2
```

In this file, the references to the partitions need to be modified to reflect the restored configuration. For example, when you restore the original image that was on an IDE hard disk and the destination is an SCSI disk, the partitions that are now mounted from /dev/hda need to be mounted from /dev/sda.

21.4 NetWare Operating System

NetWare is a very friendly operating system to restore to different hardware, and to modify it to work within VMware.

NetWare includes a DOS partition that boots DR-DOS, or a Novell proprietary OS (if you have selected that with a Service Pack 1 overlay installation) with the **Do not boot into DOS option**. Whatever method you have chosen, it will always boot the OS and will try to load the drivers. If it fails to load the correct drivers that are listed in the configuration files, it just does not load them and leaves you with the command prompt where you can edit the files manually.

You can also suppress loading the operating system altogether, by pressing F5 when the server comes up. On the DOS prompt, you can then start server.exe with the -ns switch to skip loading the startup.ncf file or -na to skip loading the autoexec.ncf.

The modifications that you need to make are to the storage adapters in the startup.ncf, and the network adapter in the autoexec.ncf, or via inetcfg.nlm.

For IDE disks, you can use the drivers that ship with any version of NetWare (IDEATA.HAM and IDEHD.CDM). For SCSI, you load the drivers as described in section 14.7: "Using SCSI drivers in NetWare servers".

Part 4

Clustering Virtual Machines

EDGAR TAKES HIS WORK HOME WITH HIM.

22 Introduction to Clustering in VMware

This chapter describes how to set up a cluster in a VMware environment. It will start out with the description of a cluster in VMware Workstation, followed by a cluster in VMware GSX Server and will conclude with the description of VMware ESX Server clustering. If you own a copy of the first edition of my VMware guide, then you realize that in that in the first edition I described how to install a cluster for NetWare and Windows in detail. This chapter does not contain that detailed information any longer. Information on operating system specific clustering installation is available in the documentation that is available from all operating system vendors. I will, however, provide you a few instructions on how to get started with clustering for NetWare and Windows.

Clustering Requirements
When computers are being configured for clustering, one required item is a common disk that can be used to access the same data and to enable the computers to communicate with each other for clustering housekeeping purposes. This latter part of the shared disk is called a Quorum disk in Windows or a Split Brain Detector disk in Open Enterprise Server.

 Note: If you have read the first edition of this book, you may remember that clustering with a shared disk stopped working with VMware Workstation version 4.5. Even though it was never supported in VMware Workstation, it used to work fine nevertheless. With some of the performance enhancements that were included in version 4.5, the caching by cluster nodes caused corruption of the shared disks. In this chapter you will learn that a new parameter to disable caching allows us to create a true shared disk cluster with VMware Workstation again.

Clustering is supported in VMware GSX Server and VMware ESX Server. The VMware documentation explains how to configure clusters for these products. In the next chapters you will find a comprehensive guide to creating clusters in both server products. However, I will also explain how to build a cluster with VMware Workstation.

22.1 Using Fixed Sized (Plain) Disks

The first thing that you need to know is that you should use virtual disks that have a preconfigured size. Normal virtual disks will grow dynamically, from a few bytes at the time of creation, to the maximum number of gigabytes that you have specified for that disk.

If you start sharing a regular disk between two virtual machines, you will encounter problems with disk corruption. This is because they will both try to grow the disk dynamically when data is added to the shared disk.

To prevent this from happening, you must use virtual disks that are pre-allocated. These disks were known as "plain disks" with VMware version 2. In VMware Workstation 4 and 5 and VMware GSX Server 3.x, you can create fixed sized disks by selecting the check box **Allocate Disk Space Now**, when you create a virtual disk. This creates a disk file that is the same size as the number of megabytes or gigabytes that you specified when you created the disk. Therefore, make sure that you have enough space available on your hard disk when you create large shared disks.

For clustering purposes, it is OK to use a small disk (500 Mb), as the Quorum disk (Windows) or as the disk for the Split Brain Detector partition (Open Enterprise Server). You can then add other plain disks to your cluster, in order to store the actual data for your clustered applications.

22.2 How to Share a Disk

Clustering software uses a shared disk that two or more physical cluster nodes can access for storing data. The disk can be accessed by the physical servers via a shared disk channel (typically SCSI or Fibre Channel).

With a virtual machine we do not have a real Fibre channel or SCSI channel available, but we can use a shared virtual disk. However, it is important to realize that using a shared disk is only supported in VMware GSX Server and VMware ESX Server. These products contain a configuration for a shared disk with SCSI reservation. For VMware Workstation, you can use a shared disk but that is not supported by VMware. However, it does work fine in the workstation version when you follow the guidelines in this chapter.

Using a shared disk within VMware is a great solution for working with clustering software. There can still be some scenarios where you may want to cluster a virtual machine with a physical machine. Or, you may want to use storage that is available on a physical server.

iSCSI Considerations

As I described earlier, shared disks stopped working with VMware Workstation version 4.5. Disks became corrupted because of the caching that was performed by the virtual machines. In the first edition of my VMware guide I explained how to use iSCSI as a work around for this problem. By using this protocol which transports SCSI blocks via TCP/IP packets, it is possible to build a cluster with every possible combination of hardware and operating system. Your virtual machines only rely on networking to build a cluster; they no longer require exclusive SCSI or Fibre channel access to a shared disk. With VMware version 5 the shared disk works fine again and in both cases of GSX server and ESX server using a shared disk is supported.

However, there can still be a need to use iSCSI in your clustering scenarios. An example of this is when you want to build a cluster with virtual machines that are running on separate hardware boxes. Or, in case you want to build a cluster with virtual machines that use an iSCSI target outside the virtual environment. Another application could be if you want to build a cluster with nodes that are virtual machine and physical servers. All these types of combinations are possible by using iSCSI; the sky is the limit.

Because iSCSI has become a more commonly used technology, I have decided not to keep the detailed iSCSI manual for creating clusters inside this VMware guide.

⚠ **Note:** Be aware that when implementing iSCSI, your network adapter also becomes the adapter that is used to access your storage device. This could cause a bottle neck. Therefore, make sure that you investigate the network's load and storage traffic for your cluster nodes if you plan to configure them with iSCSI. You may want to add extra physical network adapters to assign separate adapters to the regular networking part and to the storage networking part.

22.3 Preparing for a VMware Cluster Installation

No matter what type of cluster you are going to build, there are a few preparatory steps that you will need to take before creating the actual cluster. You must create at least two virtual machines that will form the cluster and you must install an operating system inside the two machines.

The flow for creating your VMware cluster is as follows:

1. Create two or more virtual machines in VMware Workstation, GSX Server, or ESX Server as you normally would do. This is covered in the OS specific chapters that will follow.

2. Install the guest operating system on all the virtual machines that will take part in the cluster. Refer to one of these chapters for detailed instructions:

    Chapter 23: Windows
    Chapter 24: NetWare

3. Add a shared disk to your cluster nodes. This step is different for every VMware product. Refer to one of these chapters for detailed instructions:

    Chapter 25: VMware Workstation
    Chapter 26: VMware GSX Server
    Chapter 27: VMware ESX Server

4. Install the clustering software and configure the cluster inside your virtual machines. Refer to one of these chapters for detailed instructions:

    Chapter 28: NetWare
    Chapter 29: Windows

23 Preparing for a Windows Server 2003 Cluster

This chapter describes how to prepare for a cluster with two Windows Server 2003 servers and the Microsoft Cluster Server Software. This chapter provides general information for a cluster in VMware Workstation, or VMware GSX Server and ESX Server.

This chapter describes the system requirements for your Windows Server 2003 cluster, and explains the required preparation steps prior to getting started.

The instructions in this chapter are a summary of the Guide to Creating and Configuring a Server Cluster under Windows Server 2003. This official Microsoft publication is available on the web at:

```
www.microsoft.com/technet/prodtechnol/windowsserver2003
/technologies/clustering/default.mspx
```

Before Getting Started
The required software is Windows Server 2003 Enterprise Edition or Datacenter Edition. Because Enterprise Edition is easily available as an evaluation copy, this chapter only covers the Windows Server version.

23.1 Creating the Virtual Machines for your Windows Cluster

You can create your virtual machines for the Windows Server 2003 cluster in the normal way. You need to configure two virtual machines for your VMware product and install the Windows Server 2003 operating system.

 Tip: When you run VMware Workstation version 5 to create your cluster, you can use the new cloning feature to create a copy of your first machine so that you do not have to go through the entire installation twice.

Network Adapters
You must be aware that when you create your machines for Windows clustering, you will need more than one network adapter. Every server needs two network adapters; one for the public network and one for the private network. If you create your servers with two network adapters in the beginning, it will be very hard to distinguish which adapter is which. Therefore, we start out with one adapter in each virtual machine, and we will add a second adapter further on in this chapter.

The easiest solution is to use your bridged network adapter as the public adapter for the cluster nodes, and the host only adapter for the private network between the cluster nodes. This will be explained later on in this chapter. However, you could

---

also bridge a second network adapter, and use it so that the private and public networks are both bridged, or you can use a second host only network adapter so that the private and public adapters are both working host only. It is up to you to decide which option you prefer.

The first adapter that you assign to your virtual machines (at creation time) will become the public adapter in the setup that you create in this chapter. Therefore, assign your servers a fixed IP address (on the network adapter that is in another subnet to your private network) that you will use between your cluster nodes.

In this chapter I use the following setup:

Table 23.1: IP addressing for the Microsoft Cluster example.

	Node 1	Node 2	Cluster management
Public Network Adapter	192.168.1.101	192.168.1.102	192.168.1.150
Private Network Adapter	10.0.0.101	10.0.0.102	

23.2 Install Two Servers in a Single Domain

Cluster services require that all your cluster nodes are in the same Active Directory domain. DNS must be configured, and all the servers must be configured as member servers or domain controllers. If a server is configured as a member server, then it needs to have access to a domain controller in your network. Since we are going to create a two node cluster in this chapter, it is important to assign the role of domain controller to both servers, because we do not want to have a single point of failure.

23.3 Pre-Configuring the Servers

At this point you should have created your virtual machines and installed the two Windows Server 2003 servers in a single domain. Now we can start with the necessary preparations inside the server operating systems.

1. Rename the first network adapter.

   You have installed the servers with one network adapter each. This first network adapter will be your public network adapter. So, we are going to rename that adapter accordingly in order to be able to identify it easier later on. Go to **Control Panel** → **Network Connections** and rename the adapter to Public Network Adapter.

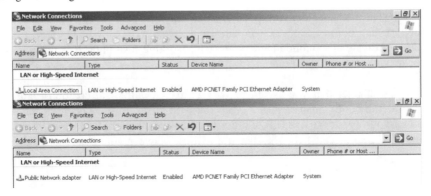

Figure 23.1: Renamed network adapter before and after.

2. Assign a second network adapter to the cluster nodes.

Power off your servers, and add a second network adapter to both servers. This additional adapter will become the adapter for the cluster's private network.

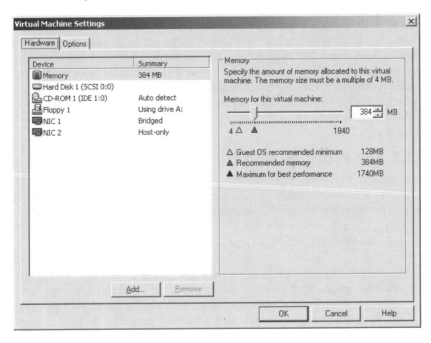

Figure 23.2: Windows servers must be configured with two network adapters.

Your configuration should look somewhat like the configuration screen shown in Figure 23.2. This screenshot is from VMware Workstation. For GSX Server and ESX Server, your configuration may look different but you probably get the idea about the two network adapters.

Disable the "why do you shutdown your server?" dialog box.

You are going to reboot your servers a few times during the entire setup. Therefore, you may want to turn off the feature that asks you (every time you shut down) why you are shutting down. To turn off this feature:

Go to **Start** → **Run** type gpedit.msc, and Click **OK**. Next, open **Local Computer Policy** → **Computer Configuration** → **Administrative Templates** → **System**. Select **Display Shutdown Event Tracker** and disable it.

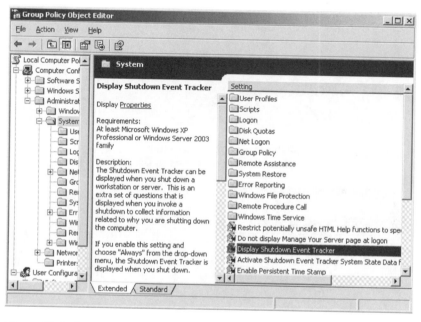

Figure 23.3: For your convenience, disable the Shutdown Event Tracker.

3. Rename and configure the second network adapter.

   After adding the second network adapter for the private network, rename the newly added adapter in your server to **Private Network Adapter**.

   Assign the IP Address that you have planned to use for the private network to this adapter.

⚠ **Note:** Make sure that no default gateway is added to this network adapter on both servers. We do not want the cluster nodes to route traffic via the private network.

Next, configure the network adapter's DNS and WINS configurations as displayed in Figures 23.4 and 23.5.

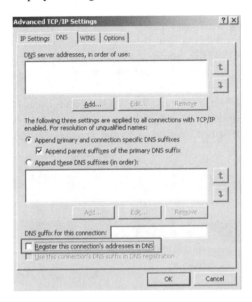

Figure 23.4: Disable the checkbox for **Register this connection's addresses in DNS**.

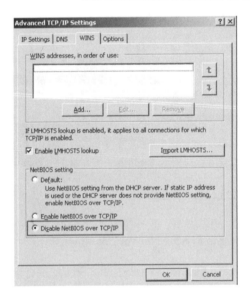

Figure 23.5: Disable NETBIOS traffic via the Private Network.

4. Create the cluster user account.

From the Active Directory Users and Computers application add a user to the Users container with the name of `cluster`.

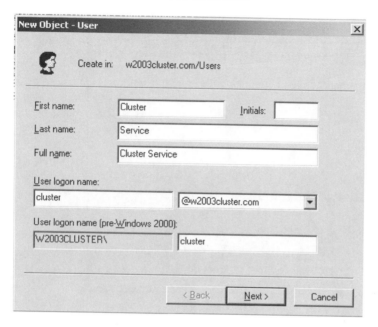

Figure 23.6: Add a user account to be used by the cluster software.

Click **Next** after entering the user information, and in the Password settings window select **User cannot change password** and **Password never expires**.

Assign a password to the user. The default requirements for passwords are:

- Is not based on the user's account name.
- Contains at least six characters.
- Contains characters from three of the following four categories:
    - Uppercase alphabet characters (A–Z)
    - Lowercase alphabet characters (a–z)
    - Arabic numerals (0–9)
    - Non-alphanumeric characters (for example, !$#,%)

5. Add the newly created user as a member of the built in group **Administrators**. This will make the user a member of the Local administrators group on every node in the cluster. It is not necessary to add this user to the **Domain Admins** group.

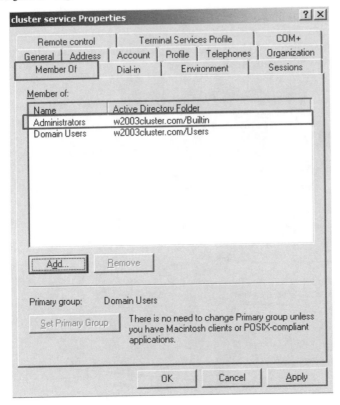

Figure 23.7: Add the cluster user to the Administrators group.

At this point you have prepared two servers in one domain to be used as cluster nodes in one of the three possible cluster scenarios.

 Tip: This may be a good time to secure these two servers by creating a ZIP file of them and storing them in a safe place. Or, you can just copy them to a safe location. As a minimum, you should create a snapshot of your virtual machines. This is not supported on VMware ESX Server, therefore you have to copy your configuration and virtual disk files to a safe location manually.

Where to go from here
If your servers are up and running, continue with one of the following chapters to prepare your VMware environment for your Windows Server 2003 cluster:

Chapter 25: VMware Workstation
Chapter 26: VMware GSX Server
Chapter 27: VMware ESX Server

24 Preparing for a NetWare 6.5 Cluster

This chapter describes how to prepare for a cluster with two NetWare 6.5 servers and Novell Clustering Services Software. In addition, it describes the system requirements for your NetWare 6.5 cluster as well as the preparations steps that are required before getting started.

 Note: Novell shipped Open Enterprise Server (OES) in early 2005 to replace NetWare. OES comes in a Linux version and a NetWare version. In this chapter you will learn about building a NetWare cluster. Technically speaking, NetWare 6.5 with service pack 3 is identical to OES NetWare. The difference is in three available services: iManager 2.5, Virtual Office 1.5 and QuickFinder. The clustering part is identical for both operating systems.

Before Getting Started

The software that you need to create the setup for any of the three clustering scenarios is of course VMware Workstation, VMware GSX Server, or VMware ESX Server. However, you will also need to have the NetWare 6.5 operating system. Your best option is to use the so called Service Pack Overlay CD-ROM, to install the server with an integrated Service Pack. You can find this software on the Novell Support website at http://support.novell.com by searching for NetWare Overlay in the Knowledge Base. You can also download the Open Enterprise Server NetWare ISO files. With these files you can install the same cluster as described here.

 Tip: You can download the ISO images and use them directly by assigning the ISO files to the virtual machines as the CD-ROM is to be used.

24.1 Creating the Virtual Machines for your Cluster

You can follow the normal procedures to create your virtual machines and install the NetWare Operating System. There are only a few things that you must change or be aware of in order to set up your cluster.

First, we are going to use SCSI as our disk type for the shared disk clustering. Buslogic was the best choice for older NetWare versions, because of the driver availability. With OES and NetWare 6.5 service pack 3, you can select the LSI Logic SCSI type.

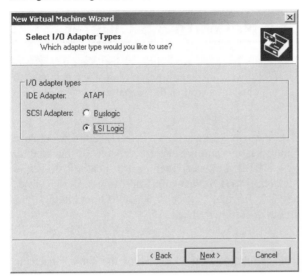

Figure 24.1: Select LSI Logic as the SCSI adapter type.

VMware workstation contains either an LSI logic LSI53C10xx Ultra320 I/O Controller, or a Mylex (Buslogic) BT-958 compatible host bus adapter. We will use the LSIMPTNW.HAM driver for the LSI Logic adapter and the SCSIHD.CDM driver for the hard disk later on in this chapter, to use this hardware in the NetWare server.

If you need to change the hardware platform for your SCSI adapter for existing virtual machines, you can edit the .vmx file for your disk and change the following lines accordingly:

```
scsi0.virtualDev = "lsilogic"

scsi0.virtualDev = "buslogic"
```

Once you turn the power on for your virtual machine after changing this parameter, you will be asked if you want to change your virtual disk files (.VMDK) to be configured for the new adapter type.

24.2 Install and Configure NetWare

After creating the two virtual machines, you will install two NetWare servers in a single tree. Follow the normal procedures to install NetWare as described in the Novell on-line documentation.

Make sure that your first server is fully installed, and that the security objects are created (Certificate Authority) before you add your second server to the tree.

　　　　　　　　　　　　　Clustering Virtual Machines

After you install your first server, the best thing to do is to reboot, and check that everything is up and running so that you can access Remote Manager and iManager. For NetWare 6.5 these are available via the Web Manager at `https://ipaddress:2200` or at the individual URLs at: `https://ipaddress:8009` and `http://ipaddress/nps/iManager`. (This last one is case-sensitive)

Before continuing with the shared disk and clustering installation, make sure that the two servers that you have installed are communicating with each other and that you have the VMware tools installed.

 Tip: This may be a good time to secure these two servers by creating a ZIP file of them and storing them in a safe place. Or, you can just copy them to a safe location. As a minimum, you should create a snapshot of your virtual machines. This is not supported on VMware ESX Server, therefore there you have to copy your configuration and virtual disk files to a safe location manually.

Where to go from here
When the two servers are up and running with NetWare 6.5, you can start preparing them for the shared disk access in one of the three following chapters:

Chapter 25: VMware Workstation
Chapter 26: VMware GSX Server
Chapter 27: VMware ESX Server

25 Shared Disk Cluster with VMware Workstation

This chapter covers the installation of two virtual machines with a shared SCSI disk. It is in preparation for the installation of Novell Clustering Services or Microsoft Cluster Services software. This part is generic for NetWare and Windows.

 Note: With VMware Workstation 4.5, clustering with a shared disk was not made an option. It was not documented in any way by VMware, because clustering is not supported in that product (it is only supported in GSX Server and ESX Server). That is also the reason that I moved to iSCSI for the first edition of my VMware guide. In this new edition, you can learn how to set up a cluster with VMware Workstation version 5.

25.1 Adding a Shared Disk to Virtual Machines

After installing two NetWare servers into a tree, and configuring them with the VMware tools, it is now time to add a shared disk that will be used for clustering.

 Tip: I prefer to use a separate disk as the Windows Quorum disk or for the NetWare Split Brain Detector partition, and a second shared disk for the data. With such a configuration, you have more flexibility to re-create the SBD partition, or to back up your VMware configuration.

First, power down both servers and close the VMware application. It is always a bad idea to manually edit the .VMX files while the application is running.

Open the .VMX files of both servers and add the following lines to the file:

```
disk.locking = "false"
diskLib.dataCacheMaxSize = "0"
diskLib.dataCacheMaxReadAheadSize = "0"
diskLib.dataCacheMinReadAheadSize = "0"
diskLib.dataCachePageSize = "4096"
diskLib.maxUnsyncedWrites = "0"
```

It does not matter where in the file you add these lines. Save the .VMX files and open the virtual machine software without powering the machines on.

On the first server, add a new virtual disk that will become the shared disk for clustering.

Follow these steps to perform this action:

1. Open the virtual machine settings and click **Add** to add a new device.

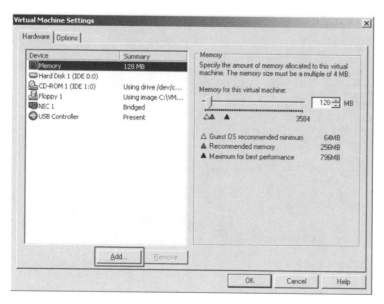

Figure 25.1: Add a new device to your virtual machine.

2. In the **Add Hardware Wizard** welcome screen, click **Next**.

3. Select **Hard Disk** as the type of device and click **Next**.

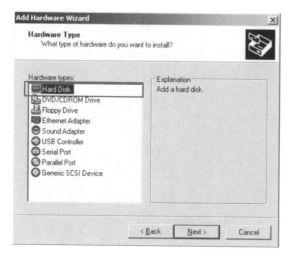

Figure 25.2: Select to add a hard disk.

4. In the Select a disk window select **Create a new virtual disk** and click **Next**.

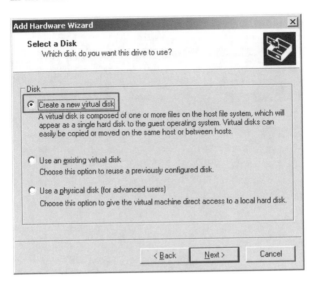

Figure 25.3: Create a new virtual disk.

5. Change the default setting to SCSI and click **Next** (I always use SCSI for the shared disk so that it looks most like a real world clustering example and to make it easier distinguish between the server-IDE disks and the shared-SCSI-disk).

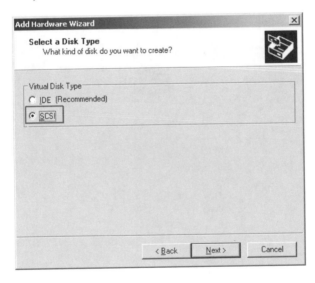

Figure 19.4: Select SCSI as the disk type.

Clustering Virtual Machines

6.   In the **Specify Disk Capacity** window select the proper disk size.

In the image below, you can see that I have selected a half gigabyte disk size. That is adequate for a small shared disk that can hold some data. Remember that we also have to enable the option **Allocate all disk space now**, so that a 500 Mb file will be created on your hard disk. Selecting a 10 Gb disk could take up excessive space on your workstation.

Whether you need to split the disk file in two gigabyte files depends on your file system. FAT32 only supports files up to four gigabytes and traditional FAT supports two gigabyte files. For both of them, you need to split the files into two gigabyte chunks.

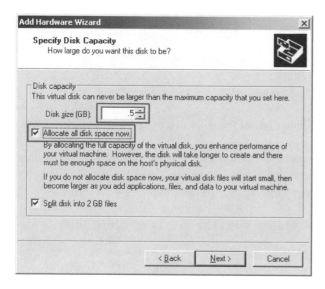

Figure 19.5: Create a fixed size disk.

7.   You will be warned that creating a pre-allocated disk may take a long time. If you are prepared to create the disk that you have selected, select **Yes**.

8.   You can create your server in one directory together with this shared disk; however, I prefer to keep the configuration on separate directories because it provides a better overview.

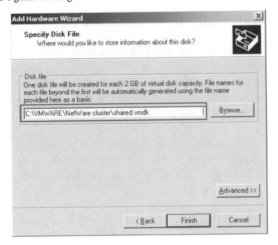

Figure 19.6: Give the disk a descriptive name.

9. Click **Finish**. The fixed sized disk will now be created.

10. Close the configuration Control Panel for this virtual machine.

11. Open the virtual machine configuration for your second server. Follow the same steps as the ones that you performed on your first server to start adding a new hard disk to your server (steps 1, 2, and 3).

12. In the **Select a Disk** window, select **Use an existing virtual disk**.

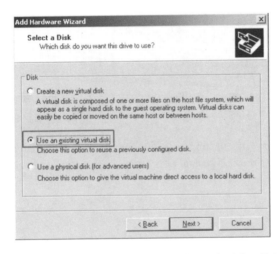

Figure 19.7: In the second machine select the disk you have just created.

Clustering Virtual Machines

13. Browse the shared disk file (this is **not** the file with the f001 suffix). Select the .vmdk file which you created in step 8.

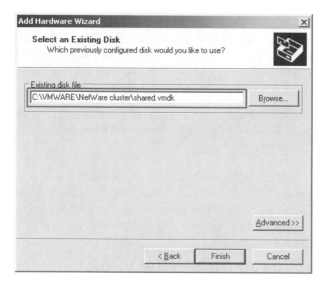

Figure 19.8: Select the existing shared disk.

14. Click **Finish** and close the virtual machine setting's Control Panel.

Where to go from here

For NetWare
When the servers are up and running you may need to activate the SCSI hard disk driver, depending on your version of NetWare. This is explained in detail in section 14.7 "Using SCSI drivers in older NetWare servers". After that, install the cluster services as described in chapter 28 "Installing Novell Cluster Services".

For Windows
Leave the servers powered off and continue with the configuration of Microsoft Cluster Services as described in chapter 29: "Configuring Microsoft Cluster Services Software".

26 Shared Disk Cluster with VMware GSX Server

This chapter covers the installation of two virtual machines with a shared SCSI disk, in order to prepare for the installation of Novell Clustering Services or Microsoft Cluster Services software. This part is generic for NetWare and Windows.

The technology for sharing disks in GSX Server is called SCSI Reservation. This is an SCSI technology, where the servers can send Reserve and Release commands to the disk to gain access to a shared disk.

By adding the `scsi1.sharedBus = "virtual"` command to the `.vmx` file, SCSI Reservation is activated in the GSX Server virtual machines. And the `disk.locking = "false"` command disables the file locking, so that a virtual machine can not lock the virtual disk file and prevent the other cluster servers from accessing the virtual disk file.

26.1 Adding a Shared Disk to the Virtual Machines

After installing two servers with Windows, Linux or NetWare, and configuring them with the VMware tools, it is now time to add a shared disk that will be used for clustering.

Make sure that you have taken all the necessary preparation steps described in chapter 23: "Preparing for a Windows Server 2003 Cluster" or chapter 24: "Preparing for a NetWare 6.5 Cluster".

 Tip: I prefer to use a separate disk as the Windows Quorum disk or for the NetWare Split Brain Detector partition, and a second shared disk for the data. With such a configuration you have more flexibility to re-create the SBD partition, or to back up your VMware configuration.

On the first server, add a new virtual disk that will become the shared disk for clustering. I have created this example from a VMware virtual machine console. You could add additional hardware from the Management Interface, but it is much more convenient from the remote console application.

Follow these steps to perform this action:

1. Open the virtual machine settings and click the **Add** button to add a new device.

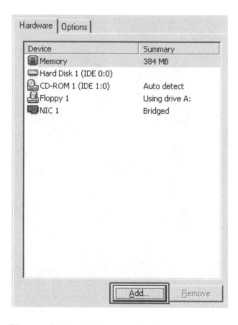

Figure 26.1: Add a new device.

2. In the **Add Hardware Wizard** welcome screen, click **Next**.

3. Select **Hard Disk** as the type of device and click **Next**.

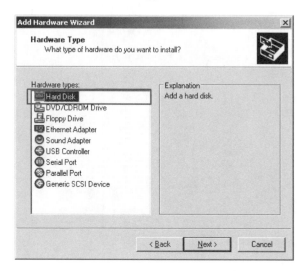

Figure 26.2: Select to add a hard disk.

4. In the Select a disk window, select **Create a new virtual disk** and click **Next**.

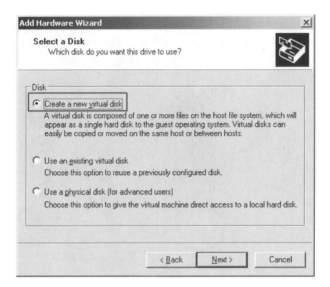

Figure 26.3: Create a new virtual disk.

5. Change the default setting to SCSI, and click **Next**. Whether the default is IDE or SCSI depends on the operating system that you have selected for the virtual machine.

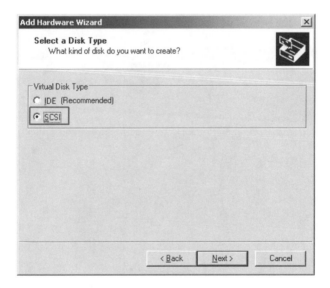

Figure 26.4: Select SCSI as the disk type.

6. In the **Specify Disk Capacity** window, select the proper disk size. In the following image you can see that I have selected a half gigabyte. That is an adequate disk size for a small shared disk that can hold some data, and will be used as the Quorum disk (Windows) or the disk for the Split Brain Detector (NetWare). You can add additional Fixed Sized disks to your cluster later, to store the data for your cluster application.

    Do not forget to enable the option **Allocate all disk space now** so that a 500 Mb file will be created on your hard disk. Selecting a 50 Gb disk could take up excessive space on your workstation.

    Whether you need to split the disk file into two gigabyte files, depends on your file system. FAT32 only supports files up to four gigabytes and the traditional FAT supports two gigabyte files. For both of them you need to split the files into two gigabyte chunks.

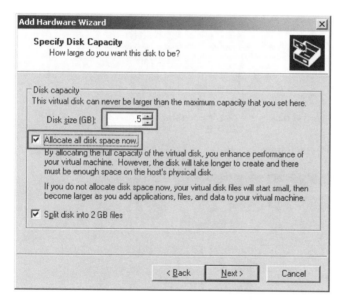

Figure 26.5: Create a fixed size disk.

7. You will be warned that creating a pre-allocated disk may take a long time. If you are prepared to create the disk you have selected, click **Yes**.

8. Specify a name for your disk, and select a location on your hard disk. The best choice is to save the file in a different directory than the server, and to provide the full path to the file. Normally relative paths are used for the virtual disk files, and they will be searched for in the server directory. This could work if

you store both of the servers in one directory, but I prefer to keep the configuration on separate directories because it provides a better overview.

After selecting the location of the disk file, click the Advanced button to specify the correct SCSI bus for your disk.

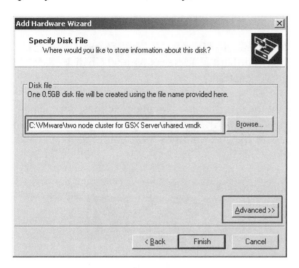

Figure 26.6: Give the disk file a descriptive name.

9.   In the **Advanced Selection** screen, select SCSI 1:0 for your SCSI disk.

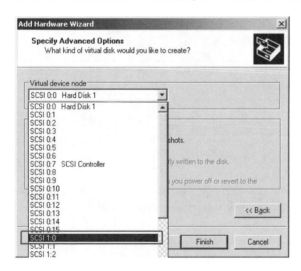

Figure 26.7: Select SCSI bus 1 for the new disk.

We will use this extra SCSI bus, which will be added to your virtual machines.

10. Click **Finish**. The fixed size disk will now be created.

11. Your disk configuration should now look something like this:

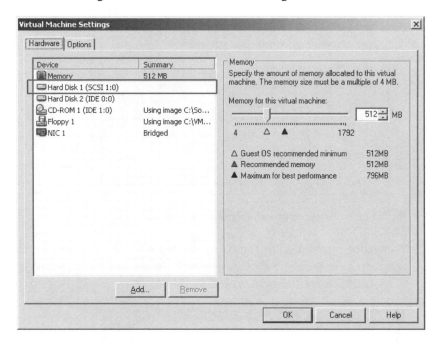

Figure 26.8: The disk is now configured for the first server.

12. Close the configuration Control Panel for this virtual machine.

13. Open the virtual machine configuration for your second server. Follow the same steps that you performed on your first server to add a new hard disk (steps 1, 2, and 3).

14. In the **Select a Disk** window, select **Use an existing virtual disk**.

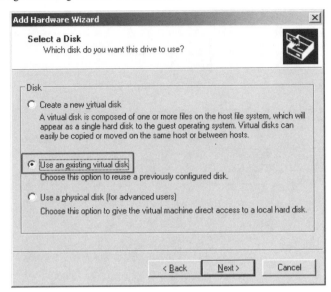

Figure 26.9: Select to use an existing virtual disk.

15. Browse the shared disk file (this is **not** the file with the `-flat` suffix) Select the `.vmdk` file which you created in step 8. Also select the Advanced button to select SCSI1:0 as the location of you disk.

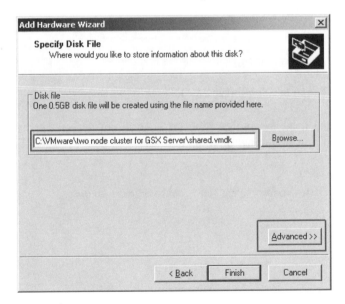

Figure 26.10: Select the previously created fixed size disk.

16. In the **Advanced Selection** screen, select the SCSI 1:0 location for your SCSI disk.

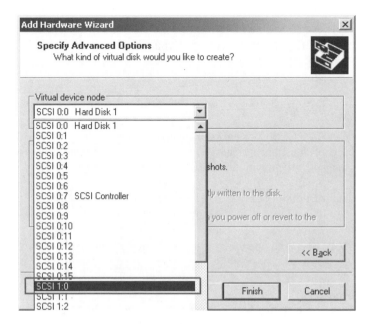

Figure 26.11: Select SCSI bus 1 for the new disk.

It is common practice to add your shared disk to a separate SCSI bus channel and not on the SCSI 0 bus. That bus is commonly used for a SCSI boot disk and you do not want to accidentally share your server's system boot disk.

17. Click **Finish** and close the virtual machine settings' Control Panel.

18. At this point the .vmx file for both virtual machines should contain the following lines:

```
scsi1.present = "true"        (Added to create a second SCSI bus)
scsi1:0.present = "true"
scsi1:0.fileName = "C:\<pathtodisk>\shared.vmdk"
scsi1:0.deviceType = "plainDisk"
```

19. To enable the SCSI Reservation on the SCSI Bus and to disable the disk locking, add the following lines to the .vmx files of both virtual machines. First, power down both the servers and close the VMware application. It is always a bad idea to manually edit the .VMX files while the application is running. It does not matter where in the file you add these lines.

```
disk.locking = "false"

scsi1.sharedBus = "virtual"
```

This setting enables SCSI sharing for the entire SCSI1 bus. If you do not want to share the entire bus, but instead you want to share individual disks on that bus, you can also configure an individual disk to be shared with the entry:

```
scsi1:1.shared = "true"    (1:1 specifies the second disk on
                            the second SCSI bus.)
```

20. Save the .VMX files, and open the virtual machine software without powering the machines on.

Where to go from here
At this time, if you have started both servers and configured the SCSI reservation correctly, then when the virtual machines are powered on, a file called <diskname>.vmdk.RESLCK will be created in the same directory as your shared disk.

For NetWare
Once the servers are up and running, we may need to activate the SCSI hard disk driver, depending on your version of NetWare. This is explained in section 14.7 "Using SCSI drivers in older NetWare servers". After that, install the cluster services as described in chapter 28 "Installing Novell Cluster Services".

For Windows
Leave the servers powered off and continue with the configuration of Microsoft Cluster Services as described in chapter 29: "Configuring Microsoft Cluster Services Software".

27 Shared Disk Cluster with VMware ESX Server

This chapter covers the installation of two virtual machines with a shared SCSI disk. It will help to prepare for the installation of Novell Clustering Services or Microsoft Cluster Services software. This part is generic for NetWare and Windows. At this point you should have created at least two virtual machines with an operating system (Windows, Linux or NetWare) and the VMware tools installed. Power both virtual machines off to start the clustering configuration.

 Note: The example in this chapter is based on the configuration with the Management Interface. All configuration steps can also be performed from VirtualCenter. If you have this software installed, it should not be too difficult to translate the configuration options for your virtual machines from the Management Interface to VirtualCenter.

1. In the Management Interface, click on the virtual machine name (hyperlink) to open the configuration window. Go to the **Hardware** tab or select **Configure Hardware** from the popup menu to go to that tab directly.

2. Click the link for **Add device** at the bottom of the hardware configuration tab. See Figure 27.1 for the location of this option.

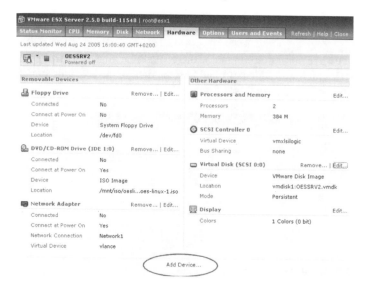

Figure 27.1: Add the shared virtual disk from the Management Interface.

3. Select Hard Disk as the device type to be added. This will start the virtual disk configuration wizard. In the wizard, select to create a blank virtual disk.

---

4. In the next configuration window, select the location and the size of the virtual disk file. 500 Mb is sufficient for the Quorum disk in Windows and the SBD disk in NetWare. Assign the disk to virtual SCSI adapter 1 (see Figure 27.2). Shared disks must be assigned to a separate controller. Leave the **Disk Mode** setting at the default setting of **Persistent**.

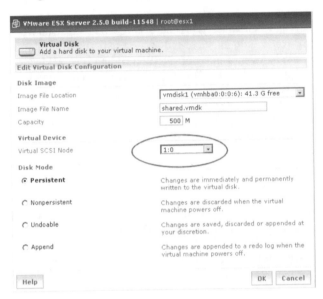

Figure 27.2: Assign the shared virtual disk to a separate SCSI adapter.

5. In the **Hardware** configuration tab of the virtual machine, select **edit** for SCSI Controller 1 which was added after adding the disk in the previous step. Set the Bus Sharing option to virtual (see Figure 27.3).

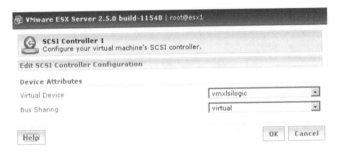

Figure 27.3: Set the Bus Sharing option to Virtual.

6. Open the hardware configuration tab for the second node in your cluster to add the shared disk to that node. Click the Add device link at the bottom of the configuration screen. Add a hard disk to the machine, but now choose an existing disk and point to the shared disk that you created in step 4. As you can

see in Figure 27.4, the disk must be assigned to an SCSI node 1:0, just as it was done for the other virtual machine.

Figure 27.4: Add the existing disk to node two on SCSI node 1:0.

7. Now configure the SCSI Controller 1 which was added to the second node by adding the virtual disk to this controller. Set the **Bus Sharing** setting to **virtual**, just as you did for the other node in step 5.

You have now configured the two nodes to share the virtual disk.

Where to go from here

For NetWare
Once the servers are up and running, you may need to add the LSI SCSI driver and activate the SCSI hard disk driver, depending on the version of NetWare you are running. This is explained in chapter 14.7 "Using SCSI drivers in older NetWare servers". After that, the cluster services will be installed as described in chapter 28 "Installing Novell Cluster Services".

For Windows
Leave the servers powered off and continue with the configuration of Microsoft Cluster Services as described in chapter 29: "Configuring Microsoft Cluster Services Software".

28 Installing Novell Cluster Services

After you have finished your installation of the virtual machines and the shared disk, and all servers can see the shared disk, you can start the installation of Novell Cluster Services. This chapter describes the normal procedure that can also be found in the Novell on-line documentation.

1. You can start the Deployment Manager now, to install a cluster in your environment. There are several ways to start this installation. With NetWare 6.5 and OES, you will have access to iManager which contains the Install/Upgrade options. You can also start NWDEPLOY.EXE to install a cluster.

    In Deployment Manager, select **Install/upgrade Cluster** and click the link to run the **Novell Cluster Utility**.

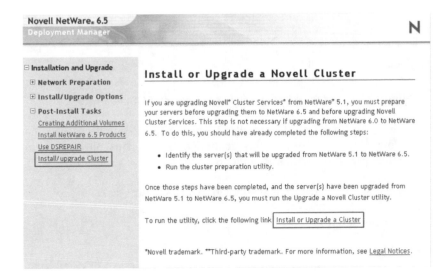

Figure 28.1: Start the installation from deployment manager.

2. In the welcome screen, click **Next**.

3. In the action selection window, select Create a new cluster. Leave the checkbox **Skip the file copy** enabled. The Cluster software files are already installed on your server during server installation.

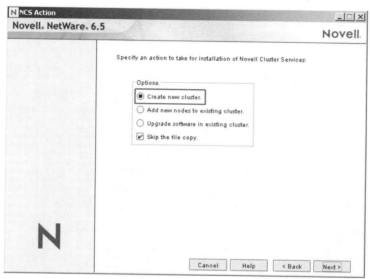

Figure 28.2: Create a new cluster.

4. Enter a name for the cluster object, the name of your tree, and the context where the cluster object must be created.

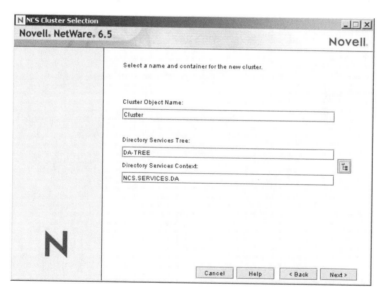

Figure 28.3: Specify a name and the eDirectory tree details.

5. In the cluster node selection screen, click the Browse button and select the two servers that you want to add to your cluster.

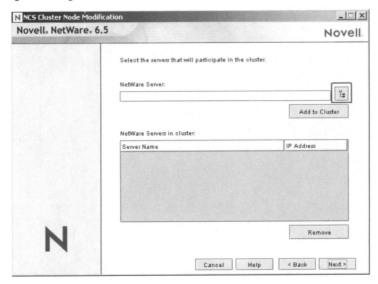

Figure 28.4: Browse for the servers to add to the cluster.

6. Select the servers in the Browse window and click **Add**.

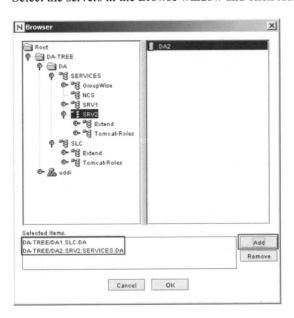

Figure 28.5: Select the servers to add to the cluster.

7. At this time, the cluster installation NLMs will be loaded on both servers. This process will also search for a common shared disk between the two servers. If both servers were contacted successfully, the summary will show you the following overview:

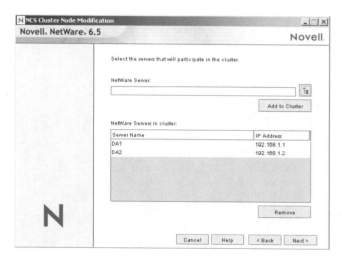

Figure 28.6: Overview of servers to add to the cluster.

8. Click **Next** to go to the **Cluster IP Address Selection** window. Enter a common IP address here which will be used as the Master IP address. You can use this address to access the cluster. The Master Node will always be available if the cluster is active.

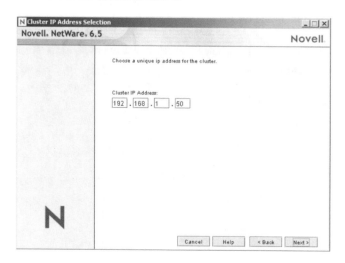

Figure 28.7: Specify the cluster Master IP address.

9. In the **NCS Shared Media Selection** window, the **Yes** button should be enabled for the question, if the cluster has shared media. The drop down list should list your shared disk. The first image here is of a shared virtual SCSI disk, the second image is of an iSCSI target disk.

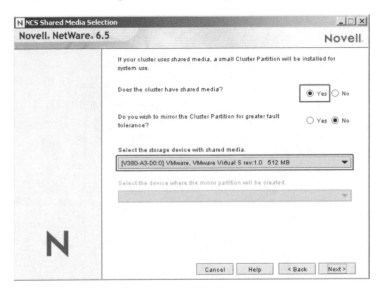

Figure 28.8: Select the disk where to install the SBD partition.

If your shared disk is not listed and the **No** button is selected, then you will have to troubleshoot this first, before continuing on further. The NetWare Cluster Troubleshooting paragraph at the end of this chapter contains some tips on what to do if your shared disk is not recognized.

10. In the Start Clustering window, select whether you want to start clustering automatically after installation.

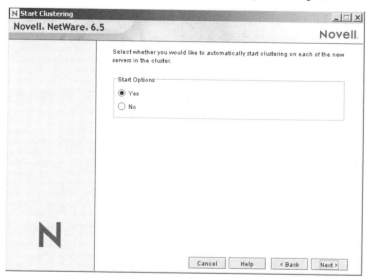

Figure 28.9: Start the cluster after installation.

11. After the installation is complete, you will see a window asking you if you want to read the Readme file. The Novell Cluster Services software is started on both servers.

12. At this time, you have an up and running cluster on your servers. The Cluster Membership Monitor (CMON.NLM) will display the two servers in the cluster with the Up status.

    You can use iManager (if you have SP1a), Remote Manager or ConsoleOne to manage the cluster.

Have fun with your newly built cluster!

28.1 Be Careful to Suspend the Cluster Nodes

The cluster nodes will continuously keep each other informed about their status. If a node is not available, it will be marked as off-line. If you suspend a cluster node, it will no longer be available to the other node(s) in the cluster.

You may think that suspending both cluster nodes at the same time is the solution. This could work if you are fast enough, but if you bring the server back on-line from the suspend mode, the resume operation could take some time. This is especially the case if you resume two servers at the same time. There is a fair chance that they will not be resumed exactly at the same time (depending on your hardware), or that your host is so busy with this operation that the guests are slow and the heartbeat between the cluster nodes gets lost.

The best thing to do is to either take all (or all but one) of the servers in the cluster off-line, and then suspend all of them; or, just shut down the operating system and power off the virtual machines.

28.2 No Shared Media is Available

If during the cluster installation the software reports that no shared media is available, there are three known common problems:

1. The servers do not have access to the shared disk. Check with `list devices` to find out whether both servers can see the shared disk.

2. One of the servers does not have the `disk.locking = "false"` line in the `.VMX` file. In this scenario, one of the servers does not lock the disk and the second one does, which prevents the other server to write to the disk.

3. There is data on the disk that prevents the Cluster Services installation from creating the Split Brain Detector (SBD) partition. In this case, replace the disk with a new one or use the NSS Management Utility (`NSSMU.NLM`) to initialize the disk. This is shown in Figure 28.10.

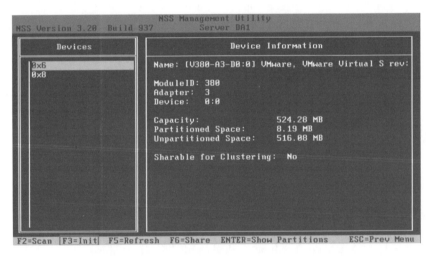

Figure 28.10: The shared disk can be initialized with the NSS Management Utility

28.3 Disk with SBD Partition Deleted or Corrupt

If your disk that contains the SBD partition is corrupt or for any other reason missing, then you can very easily re-create the SBD partition.

1. You start out by adding a new shared disk to your servers via either a shared SCSI channel or an iSCSI channel.

2. Set up this disk to be sharable from the Devices menu in the NSS Management Utility (NSSMU.NLM) on **BOTH** servers. Remember the Device ID for this disk (if you have multiple disks), because the SBD install utility will show your disks based on their IDs.

3. Make sure that the cluster services software is loaded (LDNCS.NCF).

4. Type SBD INSTALL at the console prompt to recreate the SBD partition.

```
CLUSTER-<INFO>-<6135>: Searching for SBD partition ...
CLUSTER-<INFO>-<6135>: Searching for SBD partition ...
CLUSTER-<INFO>-<6135>: Searching for SBD partition ...          OK
CLUSTER-<INFO>-<6135>: Searching for SBD partition ...

Do you want to create Mirrored SBD Partition(y/n): n

6 -> Device Number for: [V380-A3-D0:0] VMware, VMware Virtual S rev:1.0
7 -> Device Number for: [V380-A3-D1:0] VMware, VMware Virtual S rev:1.0

Select device to install Persistent Cluster Map (SBD), Device Number = 7
CLUSTER-<NORMAL>-<6035>: SBD partition was created
```

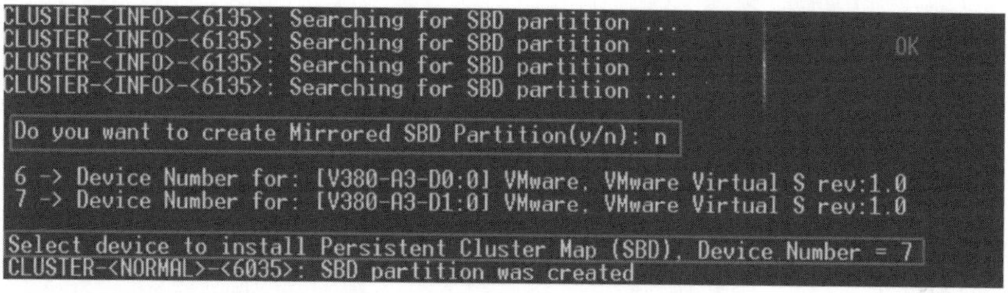

Figure 28.11: Re-create the Split Brain Detector partition.

If you do not have two disks to use for the SBD partition (and no space is available to create a mirrored SBD partition), then select **No** to create a single SBD partition. Select the device number where you would like to create your SBD partition.

5. At this point if your SBD partition has been re-created, type cluster join to start the cluster. If it still reports an SBD failure, unload the clustering software (ULDNCS.NCF) and reload it (LDNCS.NCF).

29 Configuring Microsoft Cluster Services Software

This chapter covers the configuration of Microsoft Cluster Services Software on your Windows Server 2003 Enterprise Edition servers. You must have taken the prerequisite steps in chapter 23: "Preparing for a Windows Server 2003 cluster" and you should have read one of the shared disk configuration chapters for VMware Workstation, GSX Server or ESX Server.

During the installation of your cluster, it is critical that some nodes are powered on while other nodes are powered off at some points. So, make sure that you follow the steps that instruct you to power a node off or on. Table 29.1, from Microsoft Clustering manual, provides an overview of the installation steps as well as the status which every node must be in.

Table 29.1: Overview of Cluster Installation Steps and Node States.

Step	Node one	Node two	Storage	Comments
Setting up networks	On	On	Off	Verify that all storage devices on the shared bus are turned off. Turn on all nodes.
Setting up shared disks	On	Off	On	Shutdown all nodes. Turn on the shared storage, then turn on the first node.
Verifying disk configuration	Off	On	On	Turn on the first node, turn on second node. Repeat for nodes three and four if necessary.
Configuring the first node	On	Off	On	Turn off all nodes; turn on the first node.
Configuring the second node	On	On	On	Turn on the second node after the first node is successfully configured. Repeat for nodes three and four as necessary.
Post-installation	On	On	On	All nodes should be on.

1. Start out with node one powered on and node two powered off.

2. In node one, open the Computer Management via the Administrative tasks menu item and select Disk Management.

⚠ **Note:** If the **Write Signature and Upgrade Disk Wizard** runs, then do not convert your new disk to a dynamic disk. If it is converted to a dynamic disk, then right-click the disk in Disk Management and select **Revert to Basic Disk**.

3. Right-click the **Unallocated** disk space on your new disk and create a new primary partition. The minimum size for your quorum disk must be 50 Mb. If you have created a 100 Mb or a 500 Mb disk, you should use the entire disk at this point. Format it as NTFS and assign it a drive letter. Q: is a commonly used letter for the Quorum disk.

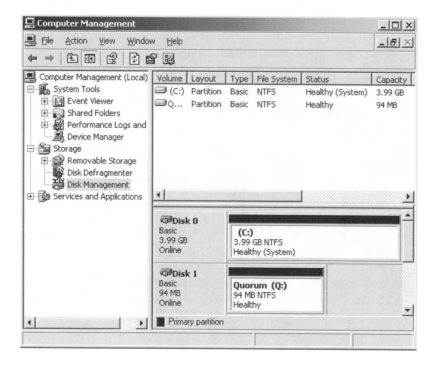

Figure 29.1: The Quorum disk is configured in the first node as drive Q:.

4. At this point, it is important to verify that you can access the disk. Add a text file to the newly created Quorum disk and enter some information in the file.

⚝ **Tip:** Also, check that you still have your **Private and Public network adapters** because if they have moved to another slot, they could be replaced by a new adapter called **Local Area Connection**. If needed, re-configure the adapter to be the Private or Public network adapter with the correct IP address. Repeat this step on node two in the next step.

5. Now power off the first node and power on the second node. The disk should now be available in node two. Go to **Disk Management** and assign the drive letter Q: to this disk. In Windows Explorer, you should now see the file that you have created from the first node. You can open this file and view the contents that you have added to the file from the first node. Also, check the network adapter configuration as described in the previous step.

   If everything works, then power off node two again and power on node one.

6. On node one, start the Cluster Administrator (Go to **Start → All Programs → Administrative tools**).

7. Select **Create new cluster** from the dialog box.

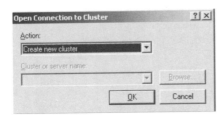

Figure 29.2: Create a new cluster.

8. The **New Server Cluster Wizard** has started. Click **Next** on the introduction screen.

9. In the Cluster Name and Domain Name selection screen, select your domain and enter a name for your cluster. This must be a unique and valid NETBIOS name.

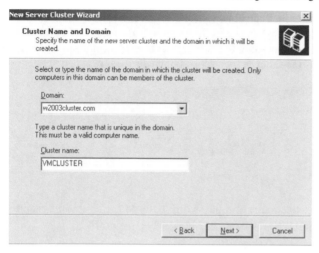

Figure 29.3: Specify a name and domain for the cluster.

10. You will be prompted for the first node in the cluster. This will typically be the node where you are configuring these first steps of your two node VMware cluster.

11. Your configuration will be analyzed, and an overview of any problems will be displayed. Fix any problems that are critical before continuing with the next step.

12. Provide a unique IP address that will be used for the cluster.

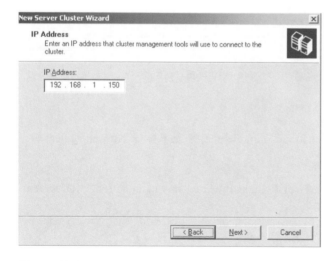

Figure 29.4: Specify the cluster IP address.

If you get the error message in Figure 29.5, it means that either you have selected an IP address that is not in the range of any locally bound addresses, or you have changed the address while the Cluster Configuration Wizard was already running. If the latter is true, close the wizard and restart it.

Figure 29.5: IP selection error message.

13. Provide the cluster username and password that you configured in chapter 23: "Preparing for a Windows Server 2003 cluster" on page 216.

14. Click **Next** and let the **New Server Cluster Wizard** re-analyze the cluster environment. If everything is OK, then the cluster is created. Close the wizard.

15. In the Cluster Administrator verify that all resources are online. Your configuration should look similar to the one in Figure 29.6.

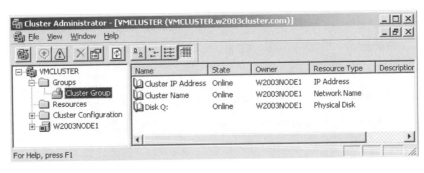

Figure 29.6: The cluster software is running on node one.

16. Now power node two on.

17. In Cluster Administrator on node one, click **File → New** and select to add a node.

18. The **Add Nodes Wizard** will start. Click **Next** in the introduction screen.

19. Enter the name of your second node and click **Add**. Then click **Next**.

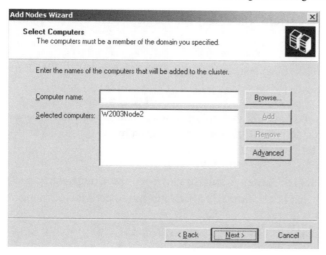

Figure 29.7: Enter a name for the second node.

20. The cluster configuration will be analyzed. If the communication with the second node fails, for example if the message: "Connection failed because the RPC is not available" appears, then check the log file for the IP address that is being used to access the second node. Check the IP connectivity between your nodes for Private and Public network connections.

21. Enter the password for the Cluster Service user.

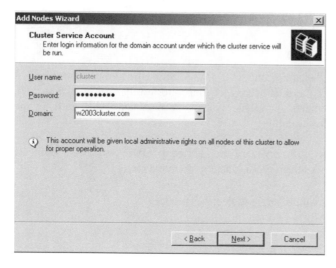

Figure 29.8: Enter a password for the cluster user.

22. On the summary screen, click **Next** and let the Wizard configure the cluster for node two.

23. When all the tasks have been completed, click **Next** and click **Finish** to close the Wizard.

    At this point, you have configured a two node Windows 2003 Server cluster. The next step is to test the cluster and to configure the Cluster Heartbeat and a shared disk for your data.

24. In the left panel of Cluster Administrator, open the Groups entry and select Cluster Group. Right-click the Cluster Group and select Move Group.

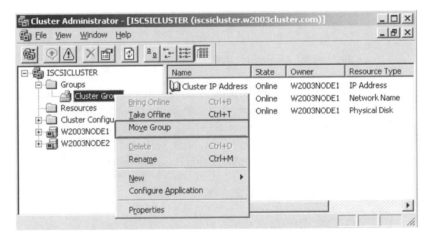

Figure 29.9: Test the cluster by moving a group to another second node.

The resources in the group will now be moved to your second node in the cluster. Check the disk access to your Quorum disk and make sure that the changes you make in the file system are persistent when moving the disk from one node to another.

The next steps will configure the heartbeat network so that it only uses the Private network adapters for cluster communications.

25. In the Cluster Administrator select **Networks**.

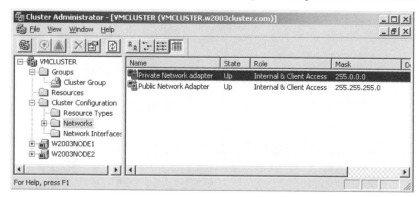

Figure 24.10: Select the private network to configure the heartbeat.

26. Right click on Private network adapter (you can distinguish the adapter based on the name or the subnet mask). Select Properties to configure this connection.

27. Set this private adapter to be used for **Internal cluster communications only**.

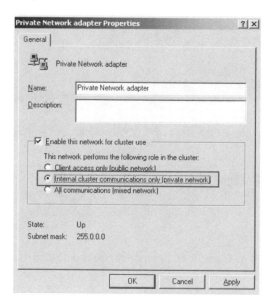

Figure 24.11: Configure the private adapter.

28. We will now add a data disk to our cluster to test the failover.

---

29. Power off the two nodes and add a Fixed Sized SCSI disk to both node one and node two. Do not forget to click **Allocate disk space now**. Make sure it is configured on SCSI bus 1 just as it is on your quorum disk. For example, if your quorum disk is SCSI 1:0, configure your new disk as SCSI 1:1.

After adding your disk, your configuration should look like the one in Figure 24.12.

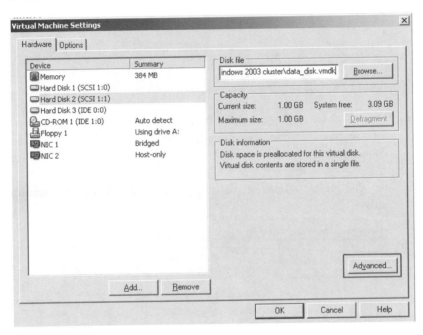

Figure 24.12: Add a second SCSI disk to the Windows cluster for shared data.

Tip: If you forget to specify the disk for channel 1, you can always click the **Advanced** button (see Figure 24.12) to change the disk to SCSI 1:1.

30. First power on node one.

31. Open **Disk Management** in **Computer Management** and format the disk and assign a drive letter.

32. Next, we are going to create a new group in Cluster Administrator. Click **Groups** in the left panel and select **New → Group**.

Clustering Virtual Machines

33. Enter a name for the group (for example **Shared Disk**) and click **Next** to create the group. In the **Preferred Owners** window, select the nodes where the new Group will be available.

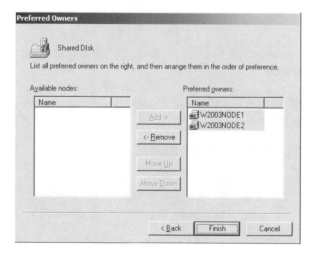

Figure 24.13: Assign nodes to the shared disk group.

34. Right-click the newly created group and select **New → Resource**.

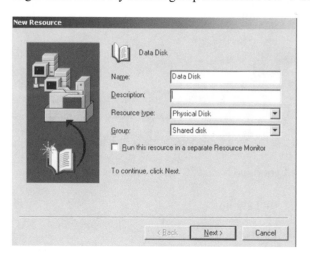

Figure 24.14: Data Disk configuration.

Enter a name such as Data Disk for the resource , and select **Physical disk** as the Resource Type.

35. In the next window, select the cluster nodes for which the disk will be available.

36. In the next window, select the newly added disk and click **Finish** to create the resource.

37. At this point the resource will become available online and it is accessible from Windows Explorer.

38. Start node two and when it is online use Cluster Administrator to move the group to node two. The disk is now accessible via node two.

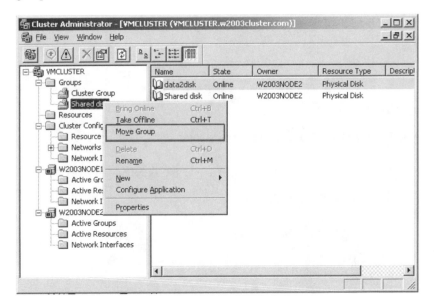

Figure 24.15: Test the cluster by moving the data disk to another node.

You have now configured your two node clusters in Windows Server 2003.

Have fun with your newly built cluster!

Be careful to suspend the cluster nodes

The cluster nodes will continuously keep each other informed about their status. If a node is not available, it will be marked as off-line. If you suspend a cluster node, it will no longer be available to the other node(s) in the cluster.

You may think that suspending both cluster nodes at the same time is the solution. This can work, if you are fast enough, but if you bring the server back on-line from the suspend mode, resuming operation could take some time. This is especially the case if you resume two servers at the same time. There is a fair chance that they will not resume exactly at the same time (depending on your hardware), or that your host is so busy with this operation that the guests are slow, and the heartbeat between the cluster nodes gets lost.

The best thing to do is to either take all the servers in the cluster (or all but one) off-line, and then suspend all of them. Otherwise, just shutdown the operating system and power off the virtual machines.

Part 5

Introduction to VMware GSX Server

30 Introduction to VMware GSX Server

Now that you have made it to this chapter of the book, you should already know what VMware Workstation is. Also, you should be familiar with creating and running virtual machines and you should know how the virtualization technology can be used. But you may wonder why you would use a VMware server version instead of the Workstation software. In this chapter, I will explain in which scenarios it is better to use a server product instead of the Workstation version. Next, I will explain how to install VMware GSX Server on Windows and Linux. The next chapters in this part of the book contain information about management and configuration.

30.1 When to Use a VMware Server Version

Running multiple virtual machines on one hardware box is the basic functionality of any VMware product. You can use an existing machine in your organization, install VMware Workstation, and run several servers from your production environment, by using virtual machines. So, why bother using a server version?

There are several reasons, and some of them are technical, which I will discuss later. Let's start with the manageability of your environment. With individual virtual machines in VMware Workstation, you can only manage them from the actual PC or server, where they are running. Powering on and off and changing the configuration requires access to the VMware application on the host computer. You may have to go to the machine physically. Or, you may be able to access the display with VNC. But you can still only do that with one administrator at a time. So as soon as more than one administrator needs to manage the virtual machines, you will need more advanced management capability.

 Note: not only are there technical and usability issues with using VMware Workstation in this way. You also do not comply with the End User License Agreement for VMware Workstation that is very specific that the product is intended for one specific individual user only.

VMware GSX Server and ESX Server provide the management capability that you need for working with virtual machines from different locations. First of all, you can power your virtual machines on and off from a browser based management interface. The management interface also allows you to monitor the usage and performance of virtual machines. In addition, you can use the Remote Control utility to access the virtual machine at the hardware level. This allows you to work with the machine just as if it was a regular virtual machine running on your own PC, even when the operating system inside the VM has crashed. And last but not least, more than one administrator can work with a machine simultaneously. So, a server version takes away all of the manageability issues that you may encounter with VMware Workstation.

From a technical perspective, there are not that many VMware GSX server features compared to Workstation version 5. Workstation version 5 even has a few advantages over VMware GSX Server 3.2 in terms of memory management and performance improvements in suspend/resume and snapshot technology. At the time of writing this book, it is not clear when these new technologies may be implemented in VMware GSX Server. However, VMware traditionally introduces new functionality in Workstation first (where it can be exposed to the largest number of customers), and then rolls it out over time in to the other products.

The greatest technical advantages over using VMware Workstation can be found in VMware ESX Server. Chapter 1 contains an introduction to this product. The benefits include huge improvements in hard disk performance, memory management, and stability. For running multiple production servers, VMware ESX Server is certainly the platform of choice.

One final difference between purchasing a server version over VMware Workstation is that the server version always comes with a support contract. If you are seriously thinking about running virtual machines in a production environment, you must definitely consider buying a server version with support.

30.2 Choosing Between GSX Server and ESX Server

When you decide to virtualize the servers in your environment with a VMware server version, you need to decide whether you want to do that with VMware GSX Server or VMware ESX Server. Many consultants and resellers will always recommend the ESX Server and tell you that it is the only mature server virtualization product. However, it is my belief that there are still many usage scenarios where GSX Server is an excellent choice.

First, let's take a look at some of the differences between the two products. An extensive comparison can be found in chapter 1, the introduction to VMware ESX Server. The main advantages of VMware ESX Server over VMware GSX Server are:

- Immunity to host operating system stability risks
- Better hard disk performance
- Better memory management

When looking at the above advantages, it is clear that for an environment where availability and performance are important, VMware ESX Server is the platform to choose. No doubt that when you want to consolidate multiple servers on one hardware platform and you want to keep the performance you have on your physical hardware that you will have to choose the VMware ESX Server. Also, when you want to make use of the vMotion technology to increase the availability

---

and flexibility of your virtualization platform, you have to choose VMware ESX Server because it is the only platform for which the product is available.

So, what are some of the usage scenarios, when it makes sense to choose the VMware GSX Server? In general, I would say that you can choose this product, if the servers you are consolidating are not too dependent on the best performance you can get. For example, this can be the case for servers that do not have a very high disk activity. For example, high end database servers will not be the ones that you want to consolidate on VMware GSX Server. Departmental e-mail servers, Intranet servers, and other not-too-busy servers are good examples of servers that you could still very well virtualize with VMware GSX Server.

Another valid scenario for running a GSX Server is when the number of servers that you want to consolidate is small. If only two or three servers need to be running on one single hardware box, then you can still get very good performance compared to running physical machines and still benefit from all the advantages of virtualization. An example of this is where a company has several small branch offices. You can set up these offices with multiple physical servers, but if you do the math then it could be less expensive to buy just one hardware box and VMware GSX Server. A machine with a single CPU with 2 GB of RAM and VMware GSX Server costs about USD 2500, and three physical machines with one CPU and 1 GB of RAM each cost USD 6000. And that is only when you buy the hardware initially. What if some reseller or manager asks you to add a server to every branch office for product XYZ? You do not need to buy a new hardware box; instead, you just configure a new virtual machine and you are ready. This is assuming that the hardware is still sufficient for the needed performance. Nevertheless, a memory and disk upgrade will be less expensive than a complete new server.

31 Hardware & Software Requirements and Design

This chapter will help you decide what hardware and software you need to set up your VMware GSX Server environment. This includes the selection of your host operating system and the hardware requirements for your host.

31.1 Choosing your Host Operating System

When you start a discussion on this topic, there is no end to it. It is like being at a birthday party where your two brothers-in law try to convince each other about a Mercedes being a better car than a BMW and vice versa.

Choosing between Windows and Linux, fits into the same category. Neither of these choices is better than the other one by definition. In reality, both are composed of software created by humans so they both will contain bugs and features that may be implemented the wrong way. But we will have to work with what is available, which means that we have to make a choice. It is best to make your selection before you buy the product, because once you buy a license for GSX Server on Windows you can only run it on that platform. For a Linux, host you are required to obtain another license.

If you browse the net, you will find some documents that describe the benefits of running Linux over Windows and vice versa. I have never found any reliable and thoroughly detailed documents that could convince me to use one over the other. You could argue about the stability and performance. That is what I very often hear when it comes to choosing Linux over Windows. But with Windows Server 2003, the stability has improved enormously over previous versions so it is my belief that this is not a real criterion.

My recommendation is that the first selection criteria should be: what platforms does the organization already use and what is the experience of the administrators with Windows and Linux? If you consider yourself a true Windows organization, then stick to Windows. You would really have to learn Linux, before you can start using it. If, on the other hand, you have a mixed environment with Linux servers in place and your administrators have the knowledge to manage the Linux environment then Linux is a very good choice.

31.2 Operating System (OS) Requirements

For Windows, you need a server version of the operating system to run VMware GSX Server. This can be either Windows 2000 server or Windows Server 2003. For a list of all current supported versions and supported service pack levels check VMware's on-line documentation at the following URL:
www.vmware.com/support/pubs.

When installing your Windows server for use with VMware GSX Server do not forget to also install IIS if you want to use the Management Interface for web based management.

For Linux, the list of supported distributions is also available on the previously mentioned URL. That list is quite long, because there are many distributions out there. In general, most GSX Server implementations are done on an Enterprise Server (ES) or Advanced Server (AS) version of Red Hat (version 3 or 4) or SuSE Linux Enterprise Server version 8 or 9.

31.3 Hardware Requirements

VMware GSX Server runs on the Intel x86 platform including machines which have an AMD processor. For the most current and detailed listings of supported CPUs, check out the on-line documentation at the following URL: www.vmware.com/support/pubs.

Processor

GSX Server supports systems with multiple processors up to a maximum of 32. There are two versions of the software available: one that supports two processors in your host system and one that supports an unlimited number of processors (or actually 32 that is, in real life). It makes sense to have multiple CPUs in your host system. As a general guideline, VMware suggests running no more than four virtual machines for every processor. However, what you will choose as a hardware platform depends on many criteria. In the next paragraph, you will read more about these criteria. In any case, keep in mind that the maximum number of virtual machines you can run on a GSX Server is 64.

A very important thing to keep in mind is that GSX Server will not give you the same performance with multiple CPUs that a VMware ESX Server will give you. When looking at the price list, you may be tempted to choose an 8-way CPU machine with a GSX Server unlimited CPU license for only a fraction of the cost of an ESX Server 8 CPU license (about five times as expensive). However, be aware that the way that ESX Server divides the load over multiple CPUs is much more efficient. This is especially true when using the additional virtual SMP product, which is only available for the ESX Server. This product allows you to assign multiple processors to your virtual machines to be used with your Guest Operating system. With the VMware GSX Server, your virtual machines will always have only one CPU, no matter how many processors you have in your host system.

One last thing that should be mentioned about processors is that dual core processors are also supported with VMware GSX Server version 3.2. At the time of writing this book, AMD has a dual core Opteron processor available and Intel is about to release the first Itanium dual core CPU and XEON based dual core CPU by the end of 2005. Simply put, a dual core CPU is a physical processor with two complete execution cores. This allows the processor to run two software threads simultaneously in parallel. With the already existing Hyper Threading technology, two software threads also work simultaneously, but not in parallel. Even more performance gain will result from dual core processors which also support Hyper Threading technology.

32 bit versus 64 bit
Of course another choice you have to make is between a 32 bit or 64 bit processor. VMware GSX Server version 3.2 runs on the 64 bit Intel XEON and AMD Opteron and Athlon processors. It is not as simple as saying that performance will be better on the newer 64 bit platform (if you also run a 64 bit OS), since VMware itself is a 32 bit application. There are some other important benefits with the 64 bit platform that will be discussed later on regarding memory optimization on page 273.

Memory
You can not have enough of it! That is a general rule with virtualization and memory. The minimum requirement for GSX Server is 512 MB but that really does not leave any room for virtual machines. The next paragraph describes some optimization criteria. The maximum amount of RAM on both Windows and Linux is 4 GB for Non-PAE enabled systems and 64 GB for PAE enabled systems. On Linux, an extra limitation to keep in mind is that servers based on the 2.2 kernel only support a maximum of 2 GB of RAM.

Miscellaneous
Your system needs a CPU and memory, but there are more components that are also needed. I am not going to duplicate the list here which you can find on the VMware website. This list will tell you what type of display adapter, hard drive or network card you need. After you have read the next paragraph about optimization, you will be able to decide for yourself what hardware you really need.

31.4 Hardware Optimization and Design Guidelines

The previous paragraph described the minimum hardware requirements that you must meet to run your GSX Server. Just like with every system, you will need more than that. You will need more processors, more memory, and more disks; but how much more? There is no simple formula that tells you how many CPUs and how much RAM you need for a given number of virtual machines. There are too many parameters that will influence your decisions. In this section, I want to give you some information that will help you choose the right hardware platform for your virtual infrastructure environment.

Processor
VMware GSX Server supports a minimum of two CPUs. There is also a version that supports an unlimited number of CPUs. In real life that will be 32 processors in one system. So, it is extremely important to decide if you need support for more than two CPUs in your GSX Server before purchasing the product.

A general guideline from VMware is that you run four virtual machines on every physical CPU. When deciding how many CPUs you need, you should also take into consideration if you will be running CPU intensive applications inside your guest operating systems. Running a file and print server for 50 users relies more heavily on disk and network access instead of CPU usage, compared to a server running a high end Java2 Enterprise Edition application that is continuously accessed by several hundred users.

Choosing the number of CPUs for the virtual machines that you plan to run can not be done without looking into other factors, such as hard disk and network activity which will impact your server's performance. As an example, let's assume that you have a four processor machine and you are planning on running the suggested sixteen virtual machines. This may sound good on the processor side, but if that server has only one hard disk that all virtual machines need to read from and write to, you will end up with poor performance, even with non-disk intensive applications.

Memory
The second component of your server that will heavily influence the performance of your virtual machines is the available memory. A general rule with most servers and operating systems is: the more the better. But there are a few things to keep in mind before ordering all your servers with 64 GB by default.
First of all, you need to determine how much memory you really need for your virtual machines and how much memory you need for future installations. The great advantage of VMware's current generation of products is that it does not pre-allocate the memory that you assign to a virtual machine. In other words, if you start four machines with 512 MB each, your GSX Server software does not consume 2 GB of memory from the start. If those guest operating systems are only using 256 MB each, the total memory usage will be around 1 GB or even less.

When you encounter such a situation, you can optimize the memory settings of your GSX Server and virtual machines. Therefore, when calculating the amount of RAM that you really need for your server, you do not have to add up the amount of RAM that you would typically buy for your independent physical servers. Of course, you also benefit from using VMware technology with the capability of removing and adding memory to virtual machines very easily, especially compared to swapping physical memory modules.

 Note: It is important to remember to reserve enough memory for your host operating system. When your host OS starts using virtual memory (for swapping, paging, etc.), the performance of your virtual machines will degrade noticeably.

For configurations of up to 4 GB, there are not too many special configurations that you have to consider. As long as you remember that besides the amount of RAM required to run a given number of virtual machines, you also need to have sufficient processing power and hard disk availability.

When you plan to exceed 4 GB with the VMware GSX Server, you need to look into some special configurations. Whether more than 4 GB can be used will depend on your hardware platform and your operating system. First, let's take a look at the 32 bit architecture. The memory limit for an Intel 32 bit systems is 4 GB. With the support for Physical Addressing Extension (PAE), this memory limit can be extended. The amount of memory you can use depends on your operating system. With Windows 2000 Advanced Server, the limit can be extended to 8 GB and for Windows 2000 Datacenter Server the limit is 32 GB. For Windows Server 2003, the limit of the Standard Edition is always 4 GB because it does not support PAE. With Windows Server 2003 Enterprise Edition the limit is automatically extended to 64 GB.

To enable PAE on a Windows host, you need to edit the boot.ini file and add the /PAE switch to the end of the line, where you load the operating system. The following is an example of a Boot.ini file, where the PAE switch has been added:

```
[boot loader]
timeout=30
default=multi(0)disk(0)rdisk(0)partition(2)\WINDOWS
[operating systems]
multi(0)disk(0)rdisk(0)partition(2)\WINDOWS="Windows
Server 2003, Enterprise" /fastdetect /PAE
```
Whether Linux supports PAE depends on your distribution. You will have to check with your vendor if you want to use more than 4 GB of RAM on your Linux host. However, most of the recent professional distributions from SuSE and RedHat support PAE.

64 bit platform
On the 64 bit platform with Windows Server 2003 for 64 bit Extended Systems, the operating system can handle 64 GB by default. The 32 Bit applications, such as VMware GSX Server, run in a subsystem that accommodates loading, execution, and management of 32-bit applications. This subsystem is called WOW64, or Windows-32-on-Windows-64. This subsystem only assigns 4 GB to a 32 bit application. There is one slight advantage over the typical 4 GB, which you get on a normal non-PAE enabled system. In this case, the memory is also used by the operating system and other applications. Whereas on the 64 bit platform, the application is assigned a total of 4 GB for dedicated use (as long as the server has more than 4 GB total, so the OS itself and other applications are loaded in the remaining available memory).

Therefore, the bottom line is that you will get some benefits from buying a 64 bit platform to run VMware GSX Server but you might want to spend your money on an additional optimized 32 bit server to balance the load of your virtual machines.

⚠ **Note:** All this information about the 64 bit platform does not cover running 64 bit guest operating systems. If you need to do that, you need to buy a 64 bit platform first and it is important to know that VMware GSX Server runs on that hardware.

Note: Support for the 64 bit platform is something that most likely will become available with version 3 of VMware ESX Server. There is no information available at the time of writing this book to suggest that a 64 bit version of VMware GSX Server or VMware Workstation will become available soon.

32 Upgrading GSX Server Software

For both Windows and Linux, it is important to take the following actions if you are going to install a newer version of VMware GSX Server. This is especially important if you are planning to install from an older generation of GSX Server. As an example, if you are running GSX Server version 2.x and are now upgrading to version 3.2:

4. Make sure that all virtual machines are in the Power Off state. If your machines are suspended, resume them first, shut down the guest operating system and then power them off. After installing the new GSX Server software, you will need to upgrade the virtual hardware. See the GSX Server Administration Guide if this applies to you. Also check out the information about VMware generations on page 98.

5. Save all undoable disk mode information into the virtual disks. When you have disks that are in the legacy undoable mode, make sure that you save all the changes into virtual disks or discard the changes before powering off.

Also, make sure that you create a backup of your virtual machines and your GSX Server Host machine. And last but not least, test the newer version of VMware GSX Server before you install it into your production environment.

Before you can install a newer version of VMware GSX Server on Windows, you must uninstall your current version. For Linux, it depends on the previous installation method. If you have used the tar installer, you do not have to uninstall the previous version. You only need to ensure that no old extracted files from a tar installation exist in the directory where you extract your download. When you use the RPM installer, you must first uninstall the current version before you can install a new one. To find out whether you have installed with the RPM package, use the following command to query the RPM database:

```
rpm -qa | grep VMware
```

If no entry from the database is shown, then you can assume that the installation was done with the installer from the tar archive. If you need to uninstall the application, which was installed with the RPM package, use the following command:

```
rpm -e VMware-gsx
```

The RPM database listing that you performed with the query command shows all the installed software. The keyword VMware-gsx is used to uninstall the GSX Server, but the VMware console could also be shown in this listing.

33 Installation and Configuration on Windows

The first step in setting up your Windows GSX server is to get your hardware up and running. I am assuming that you have read the previous sections about the hardware system requirements, design, and optimization and that you have set up the hardware at this point.

Meeting software system requirements
Next, you need to install your host operating system. Before you install the OS, you need to decide if you want to run the VMware Management Interface on you server. With this component, you can manage your GSX Server from a web browser and use it to start and stop virtual machines, create or delete them, and configure existing ones. To use this feature, your Windows server must have a version of IIS installed.

You can use either version 5 on the Windows 2000 Server or version 6 on Windows Server 2003. Make sure to install IIS if you have not already done so during the Windows Server installation. If you have not installed IIS, you can not continue with the installation of the Management Interface during your GSX Server installation.

Get the software
The next step in setting up your Windows GSX server is to obtain the software. It is possible to buy a media kit from VMware which contains a CD-ROM with the software. But your best choice, assuming that it is no problem to download just a little more that 100 MB, is to download the latest version from www.vmware.com/download.

To download the software, you must be registered as a customer or you need to be enrolled in the evaluation program. You can enrol to evaluate the program, by selecting the **evaluate** link on the download webpage.

Get a discount
If you have not already bought the software, it is good to know that you can receive a discount when you buy your license at the VMware online store. You are eligible for a 5% discount if you enter the following discount code when buying your product online at the VMware Store: VMRC-ROBBAS389.

This code is valid for VMware Workstation and VMware GSX Server purchases.

Software installation

The most recent version at the time of writing this book is v3.2, build 14497, dated July 1, 2005. To start installing your software on your Windows server, run the downloaded executable, in this case VMware-gsx-server-installer-3.2.0-14497.exe. The installation process is very straightforward. If you select the typical installation method, all you have to do is click **Next** a couple of times and click **Finish** once you are ready to install. When choosing the custom installation, there is an extra step where you can choose what features you want to install.

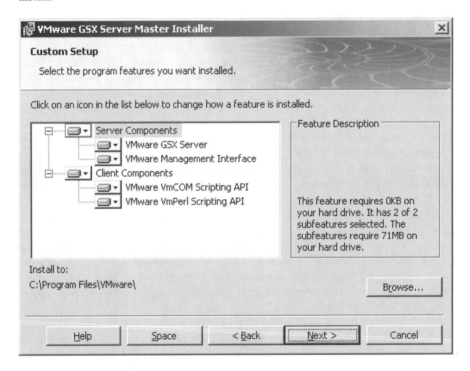

Figure 33.1: Features can be selected when selecting the custom installation.

From the list of available features, **GSX Server** is the minimum selection you want to make. The VMware Management Interface can be used to manage your GSX Server remotely from a web browser. The two available scripting APIs can be used to run your own customized scripts to manage virtual machines. An example of this is to start or stop them from your own application.

Note: The scripting APIs can still be used today, but there is also a Virtual Infrastructure Software Developer's kit available. With this set of web services, you can do the same and much more.

During installation, you will be prompted with the following question regarding Windows Autorun:

```
Your machine currently has CD-ROM autorun enabled.
Autorun can have unexpected interactions with virtual
machines. Do you want to disable autorun now?
```

I suggest that you always turn off the autorun for CD-ROMs so that you do not get any unwanted actions. If a CD-ROM is loaded into your server's CD-ROM drive and is also attached to your virtual machines and both the physical server and virtual machines start accessing the disc at the same time, it will cause performance degradation for your virtual machines.

After the installation is complete, you will have a VMware GSX Server console and a VMware virtual machine console on your Windows Server, which you can use to manage your GSX Server and your virtual machines.

34 Installation and Configuration on Linux

The first step in setting up your Linux GSX server is to get your hardware up and running. I am assuming that you have read the previous sections about the hardware system requirements, design, and optimization and that you have set up the hardware at this point.

Meeting software system requirements
Next, you need to install your host operating system. There are a lot of Linux distributions out there and they all have their small specific issues. Check the online VMware documentation for any issues you may encounter with your Linux distribution and version.

Get the Software
The next step in setting up your Linux GSX server is to obtain the software. It is possible to buy a media kit from VMware which contains a CD-ROM with the software. But your best choice, assuming that it is no problem to download just a little more that 100 MB, is to download the latest version from www.vmware.com/download. To download the software, you must be registered as a customer or you need to be enrolled in the evaluation program. You can enrol to evaluate the program, by selecting the **evaluate** link on the download webpage.

Get a discount
In case you have not already bought the software, it is good to know that you can receive a discount when you buy your license at the VMware online store. You are eligible for a 5% discount if you enter the following discount code when buying your product online at the VMware Store: VMRC-ROBBAS389. This code is valid for VMware Workstation and VMware GSX Server purchases.

Software installation
At this point, I am assuming that you have downloaded the installation files, copied them to your server, or you have mounted the CD-ROM which contains the installation files. It is also very convenient to have the Management Interface files in place to install that part right after your server installation. Copy the VMware-mui-3.2.0-14497.tar.gz file to the /tmp or another directory where the GSX Server install package is located.

Follow the following steps to install the software:

1. Log on to your Linux host and open a terminal window.

2. You need to install the software as a root user so use the su - command to become root. Move to the /tmp directory or another directory where you want to extract the files.

Introduction to VMware GSX Server

3. For the RPM version, execute the following command to install the software:

```
rpm -Uhv VMware-gsx-3.2.0-14497.i386.rpm
```

4. For the tar archive version, execute the following command to install the software:

```
tar -zxf <path>/VMware-gsx-3.2.0-14497.tar.gz
```

5. Change the present working directory to the location of the installation files:

```
cd vmware-gsx-distrib
```

6. Start the installation script:

```
./vmware-install.pl
```

7. The installation script will prompt you for the directories where the software and documentation will be installed. Here is a list of the default directories that are suggested during installation:

binary files	`/usr/bin`
init directories	`/etc/init.d`
init scripts	`/etc/init.d`
daemon files	`/usr/sbin`
library files	`/usr/lib/vmware`
manual files	`/usr/share/man`
documentation files	`/usr/share/doc/vmware`

8. When the installation is complete, you will be prompted to run the configuration script. You can accept the default answer (yes), or run the script later by executing the following command:

```
vmware-config.pl
```

9. At this point, read and accept the licensing agreement. Press q when finished reading and type yes to agree.

10. Whether the VMware modules will load or not at this point, depends on your distribution. For most recent professional server distributions, the modules will load perfectly.

11. Next, you will be prompted with several networking questions. Answer these questions according to your needs.

Do you want networking for your virtual machines?
(default: yes)

Do you want to be able to use NAT networking in your virtual machines?
(default: yes)

> If you select to install NAT:
> Do you want this program to probe for an unused private subnet?
> (default: yes)

Do you want to be able to use host-only networking in your virtual machines?
(default: no)

> If you select to install host-only networking:
> Do you want this program to probe for an unused private subnet?
> (default: yes)

12. Next, you will be prompted for the location of you virtual machine files. The default directory for this is `/var/lib/vmware/virtual machines`.

13. The final step is to enter the 20 character serial number for your GSX Server installation.

Now that you are still a root user and you are installing software, you might find it convenient to start the installation of the Management Interface right away. Follow these steps to perform this installation:

1. Go to the directory where the tar archive is located and extract the files:

```
tar zxf VMware-mui-3.2.0-14497.tar.gz
```

2. Change the present working directory to the location of the installation files:

```
cd vmware-mui-distrib
```

3. Start the installation script:

```
./vmware-install.pl
```

4. Read and accept the license agreement.

5. The installation script will prompt you for the directories where the software and documentation will be installed. Here is a list of the default directories that are suggested during installation:

binary files	`/usr/bin`
init directories (rc0.d/ to rc6.d/)	`/etc/init.d`
init scripts	`/etc/init.d`
VMware Management Interface files	`/usr/lib/vmware-mui`
documentation files	`/usr/lib/vmware-mui/doc`

6. When the installation is complete, you will be prompted to run the configuration script. You can accept the default answer (yes) or run the script later by executing the following command:

    `/usr/bin/vmware-config-mui.pl`

7. The final question is to specify the number of minutes before an http session will time out. The default value is 60 minutes. You can set it to 0 to disable access to the Management Interface or to -1 to configure sessions to never time out.

Now that the installation is complete, you can move to the next chapter where you can read about how the VMware GSX Server can be managed.

35 Managing GSX Server and Virtual Machines

The main advantage of VMware GSX Server compared to the Workstation product is that you can manage your server and the virtual machines from remote connections. You do not have to be present at the GSX Server console and there is no need to connect to the host with a remote control utility such as VNC. With VMware GSX Server, management can be performed with Windows and Linux client applications and the Management Interface.

35.1 Using the Management Interface

With VMware GSX Server's Management Interface, you can manage the host itself as well as the virtual machine environment. The web based console allows you to create and delete virtual machines, change the properties of existing machines, and power the machines on and off. The console also allows you to check the status and performance statistics of your GSX Server.

Tip: If you have more than one GSX Server, you need to login to each individual Management Interface to manage them. To simplify the management task and to gain even more control over your virtual machine environment, I recommend that you use the VMware VirtualCenter application. It allows you to manage all your GSX and ESX Servers from one console. You can read more about this application in chapter 1: "Introduction to VMware ESX Server".

At this point, I am assuming that you have the Management Interface up and running on your server. Instructions on how to install this feature can be found in the previous sections regarding the VMware GSX Server installation.

To login to the Management Interface, start your browser and enter the following URL:

```
https://hostname-or-ip-address:8333
```

An example of the URL and login page is shown in figure 35.1.

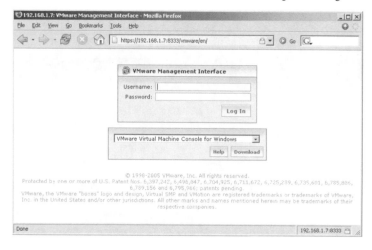

Figure 35.1: The login page for the VMware Management Interface.

By default, the Management Interface is configured to use SSL. This is why you need to connect to the server with the HTTPS protocol. If SSL is not available on your server, you can access the service on port number 8222 with the regular HTTP protocol. This is not secure, of course. Your username and password will be transported across the network in clear text. Therefore, if you contact the service through HTTP on port 8222, and if SSL is available, you will automatically be redirected to HTTPS port 8333.

The login page allows you to download the console applications for both Windows and Linux. You can also download these when you are already logged in to the Management Interface.

You can now log in to the Management Interface with a user name and password. This could be **Administrator** for Windows or **root** for Linux; however, I suggest that you always use another user name than the default administrative account. This is common practice anyway. The user account that you use to login to the Management Interface will define what rights you have. How to set up the users' rights is explained later on in this chapter.

Using different levels of access for users enables you to create roles in your organization for different types of administrators. For example, you can have a group of administrators that is only allowed to manage the existing Windows servers in your environment and is not allowed to create any new machines. In that case, you can give them the rights that they need on the Windows server virtual machines and the minimal right to see the other servers that are running.

Once you are logged in, you will see a list of virtual machines, their status, and the status information of your VMware GSX Server. An example of a Management Interface browser window is displayed in Figure 35.2.

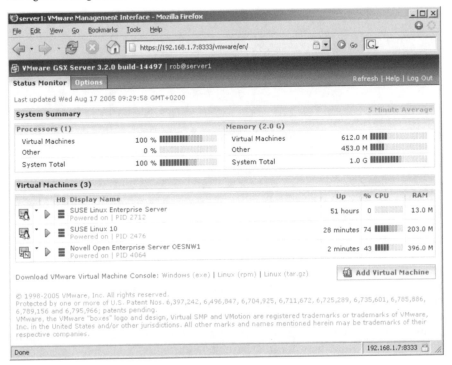

Figure 35.2: VMware GSX Server and its virtual machines can be managed from the web based Management Interface.

Most features available in the Management Interface are simple and self explanatory. If you need any information about how to create a new virtual machine, change the properties of a machine and so on, I suggest that you check out the VMware GSX Server documentation.

Figure 35.3 displays the controls of the Management Interface that are available for each virtual machine.

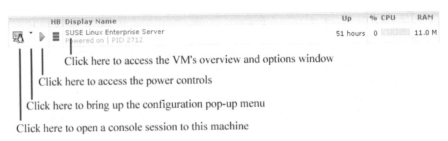

Figure 35.3: Every virtual machine can be managed with these controls.

Tip: If you have any problems with your virtual machines' controls or with accessing the properties windows for your machines, check the pop-up settings for your browser. It might prevent your browser from showing the configuration windows that you are trying to access.

There are a few specific items that I would like to explain about working with the Management Interface.

Heartbeat

One of the items that I would like to explain regarding the Management Interface is the meaning of the heartbeat which is displayed next to the power control button of the virtual machines. When the VMware tools have been loaded inside your virtual machine, it will continuously send heartbeats to the GSX Server. When all heartbeats have been received within the minute before the screen was refreshed, the percentage of received heartbeats is 100% and the indicator will be green. When all the heartbeats have not been received, the percentage drops and the indicator will be orange. When you have not loaded the tools, the indicator will be greyed out because in that case the heartbeat is not available at all.

 Tip: If you notice strange heartbeat behavior, such as when the percentage is low but the virtual machine is performing very well by itself, check if you have the correct version of the VMware tools loaded inside the guest operating system.

Start up and shutdown options

The Management Interface also allows you to configure the startup and shutdown options for your virtual machines. It allows you to configure specific actions for your machines when the GSX Server is started on your Windows or Linux host. There might be virtual machines that always need to be available, whereas others should only be started when you need them, such as servers that you use for testing purposes.

By default, the settings are not to start the virtual machine when the host starts and to power off the virtual machine when the host shuts down. You can change these settings from Management Interface. Click on the name (hyperlink) of the virtual machine that you want to manage, or select **configure options** from the pop-up menu by clicking the arrow next to the virtual machine icon. In the Options tab, you will find the configuration options, as displayed in Figure 35.4.

 Note: On a Windows host, the startup option can only be set to automatically start the virtual machine if the machine is configured to run as the local system account or as a specified user.

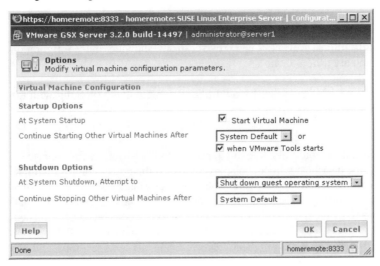

Figure 35.4: Startup and shutdown options can be configured on a per virtual machine basis from the Management Interface.

Note: Selecting the shutdown option, and shutdown guest operating system, requires that the VMware tools are running inside the guest operating system. Be aware that only Windows and Linux guests support the shutdown option through the tools.

Tip: VMware GSX Server does not support suspending virtual machines when your host is being shut down. Using suspend and resume saves a lot of time compared to stopping the guest operating system and restarting it again when the GSX Server is started. The GSX Server scripting facility allows you to suspend your machines from a script. Therefore, if you configure a script that is used for a server shutdown, it can suspend your machines. You can even specify the order in which to shutdown the machines. See the scripting section that starts on page 307 for an example of such a script.

Virtual Machine Configuration
We have looked at the virtual machine configuration options from within the Management Interface. Based on my personal experience, I can say that it is easier to configure those options, which are available both from the virtual machine console or VirtualCenter, from these respective applications. The reason is that the graphical interface on Windows (for both) and Linux (for the Remote Console) allows you to work much easier with the configuration options. One example is attaching an ISO file to a virtual machine. With Management Interface, you have to type the path and filename for the ISO image, whereas in the graphical utilities you can browse to the file.

Introduction to VMware GSX Server

35.2 Using the VMware Virtual Machine Console

After the installation of GSX Server on a Windows host, you will automatically have two console options available. A shortcut will be made on the desktop. These two options are the VMware GSX Server console and the VMware virtual machine console. The latter is the same application which you can install on your clients. The specific VMware GSX Server console automatically connects to the local server. The client version asks you what host you would like to connect to.

On a Linux host, the VMware virtual machine console is the only one that is installed and it always works in the same way as it would on the client. It prompts you to login to the local server or a remote GSX Server. An example of a login prompt is displayed in Figure 35.5. The Windows client window has the same layout as this Linux window.

Figure 35.5: An example of connecting to a GSX Server
host, where the port number has been changed
to something other than the default value of 902.

In order to work with your virtual machines from a client computer, you need to install the VMware virtual machine console application on your Windows or Linux computer. The easiest way to obtain the software is to login to the Management Interface from a browser. On the login page and on the main page after the login, a link is available to download the client application for both Windows and Linux. Another way to obtain the software is to download it from the VMware website.

Windows installation

To install the client application on a Windows computer, you simply need to run the executable that you download. At the time of writing this book, the file name is VMware-console-3.2.0-14497.exe. After the installation, you can simply start the application by selecting the **VMware virtual machine Console** shortcut from **Start → Programs → VMware**.

Linux installation

The easiest way to install the client application on a Linux computer is to download the RPM package (VMware-console-3.2.0-14497.rpm) and let it install automatically with a package manager. Many recent Linux distributions come with the RedCarpet client. When you select to download the RPM from a browser, one of your options is to open the file with RedCarpet. If you choose this option, the only extra step is to click **Continue** in the summary windows as is displayed in Figure 35.6.

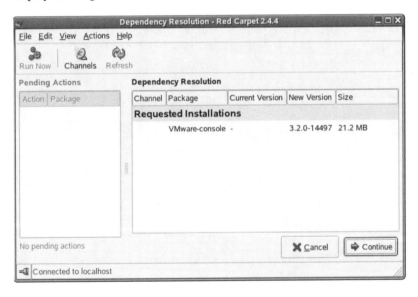

Figure 35.6: Using RedCarpet is the easiest way to install the Linux version.

You can also manually install the RPM version by using the following command:

```
rpm -Uhv VMware-console-3.2.0-14497.rpm
```

Of course, the version number in this example can be different if you are using a newer version of the software.

If you do not have RedCarpet, or for any other reason, you do not want to install the application from the RPM, you can download the tar version (VMware-console-3.2.0-14497.tar.gz) instead.

If you have downloaded the file as a ZIP file from the VMware download site, you will first have to unzip it. In this example, I extract the files to the tmp directory:

```
unzip VMware-gsx-server-linux-client-14497.zip -d /tmp
```

If you have the tar archive on your system, you have to decompress and extract it. You can do that simultaneously by using the z and x parameters:

```
tar -zxf VMware-console-3.2.0-14497.tar.gz
```

The archive will be extracted into a subdirectory called vmware-console-distrib. Use the cd command to enter that directory and start the installation from there:

```
vmware-console-distrib

./vmware-install.pl
```

This will start the VMware virtual machine console installation script. I have listed the questions and the default answers here for your reference. In most cases, you can leave the defaults in place. First, you need to read and accept the end user license agreement.

1. In which directory do you want to install the binary files?
   /usr/bin

2. In which directory do you want to install the library files?
   /usr/lib/vmware-console

3. In which directory do you want to install the manual files?
   /usr/share/man

4. In which directory do you want to install the documentation files?
   /usr/share/doc/vmware-console

After the installation has been completed, you will be prompted to run the configuration script. You can answer yes; or you can run the script later with this command:

```
/usr/bin/vmware-config-console.pl
```

The only configuration script question that you will be asked is: What port do you want the remote console to use to connect to the server? The default answer is 902.

35.3 Restricting Virtual Machine Management

In a small organization, things can sometimes be pleasantly simple. There is only one administrator and he or she does all the work. There is no need to tell the other administrators what to do and no need to restrict anything for all users other than: no access at all. But even with small organizations, it is never as simple as that. There will always be an intern that needs to be able to do something on your system or a user that needs to look after things when you are on vacation. And you do not want to just give them the administrator or root password.

Therefore, it is good to know that you can configure access rights to virtual machines and to define what your users can do with them.

 Tip: If you have many users, and especially if you have more than one GSX Server or ESX Server, my advice is to use VMware VirtualCenter to configure delegated administration. It allows you to configure users from one central location with their specific rights. This saves time compared to setting up users and file permissions on your individual VMware GSX Servers.

Access rights to virtual machines are managed by defining file permissions on the virtual machine configuration file (.vmx). The levels of access that you can define are listed in Table 35.1, along with the file rights that you need for that level.

Table 35.1: Overview of permissions and rights for VMware GSX Server.

Access level	Allowed operations	Rights needed
Browsing virtual machines	This allows you to see the virtual machine in the Management Interface and attach to it with a console. You can not change the power state or modify the configuration.	Read right on the vmx-file
Interacting with virtual machines	This allows you to work with the console, change the power state, and connect and disconnect removable devices (such as a CD-ROM). You can not modify the configuration.	Read and Execute rights on the vmx-file
Configuring virtual machines	This allows you to modify the configuration, such as adding or removing hardware.	Read and Write rights on the vmx-file (you also need rights to other resources, such as folders where you store virtual disks)

Administering virtual machines	This gives you complete access to the virtual machines.	Read, Write and Execute for a specific virtual machine.
Administering the host	Allows you to modify the GSX Server settings.	Be a member of the Administrators group (Windows) or have root access to the VM's directory (Linux).

When creating a virtual machine, the default setting is to make it a private virtual machine. This means that the virtual machine is only stored on the inventory list of that user and that only that user can work with the machine. Other users have no permissions and can not work with the virtual machine at all. Figure 35.7 shows the window that prompts you to choose a private configuration, when creating a new virtual machine.

Figure 35.7: By default, all virtual machines are created as private virtual machines.

It is also possible to configure a virtual machine to become private after it has been created. From the **VM** menu in the VMware virtual machine console, select **Settings** and in the **Options** tab, click **Permissions** to change the virtual machine into a private one or to remove this setting. When you make a machine private, it will be removed from the inventory of other users who were using the machine.

35.4 User Accounts Used to Run Virtual Machines

On a Windows host, a virtual machine can run under different user accounts, depending on how the machine is configured. Figure 35.8 shows the three possible options that can be configured in the Virtual Machine Settings dialogue box.

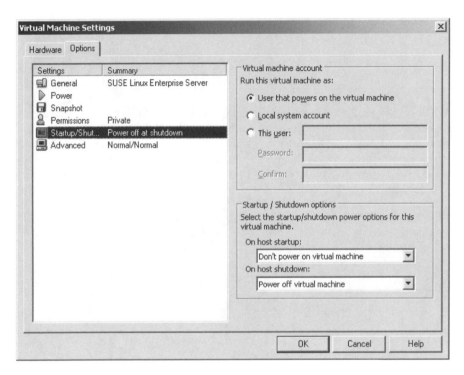

Figure 35.8: A virtual machine can be configured to run in a specific user account.

The default setting when creating a virtual machine is that it runs as the user who powers the virtual machine on. This implies that the user must have rights to the virtual machine's files, such as the configuration file and disk files. These rights can easily be configured by assigning them to the directory, where the virtual machine files are stored. The rights are then transferred to the individual files. Using a specific user to run the machine requires the same rights to the virtual machine files for that user. When the virtual machine has to work with physical devices that are attached to the host, such as an SCSI device, a physical disk, or a USB device, then the user who is running the machine must be a member of the Administrators group.

Using the local system account is the easiest configuration, because that account always has complete access to all the files and has administrative rights to the host.

Something else to keep in mind when running a virtual machine, as a user that is logged in to Windows, is that the virtual machine will be powered off when you close the session. You will receive a warning message like the one displayed in Figure 35.9.

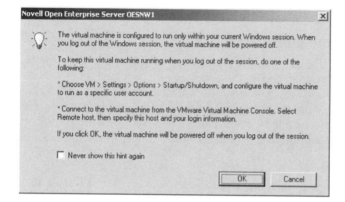

Figure 35.9:   Starting a virtual machine as the current
user will power off the machine when you log off.

For virtual machines that always need to be available, you need to configure them to run under the local system account. Figure 35.10 shows an example of three virtual machines that run under the system account. You can check this yourself for running virtual machines with the Task Manager on your environment.

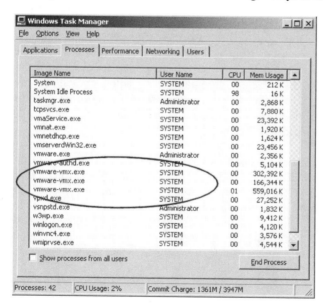

Figure 35.10: Virtual machines running under the system account.

Linux
On a Linux host it works differently than described earlier for Windows. Also, you can not configure the user account which is used to run the virtual machine as you can do from the virtual machine settings for a Windows host. On Linux, the virtual machine runs as the user who is the owner of the virtual machine's configuration file.

35.5 GSX Server Backup

Creating backups of a VMware GSX Server is different from backing up other server systems. This is because you now have to deal with both the host system and the running virtual machines. It is not as simple as installing a backup solution on your Windows or Linux host and then performing a daily backup. Your running virtual machines are accessing the virtual disk files, which prevents them from being copied by the backup software. These applications require exclusive access to those files.

There are a lot of backup solutions available on the market, all with their advantages and disadvantages and of course with a different price tag. I can not list these solutions here; instead I will simply direct you to the correct solution for your environment. I can only provide you an overview here, and it is up to you to select the backup solution that best fits your needs.

Running backup agents in your guest operating systems
This is a backup solution that is not different from creating backups in a normal server environment. One of the servers in your environment has a backup device attached and runs the backup software. The server contacts the agent in every virtual machine to create a backup of the operating system and data. Do not forget to also create a backup of the host itself in case the entire GSX Server fails. An advantage of this is that it is easy to set up and maintain. It is also the best solution, if you want to be able to restore single files from a backup. The disadvantage is that it may take too long to create the backup, depending on the amount of data and the available backup window. Something else to keep in mind is that restoring an entire server will require setting up the virtual machine and performing the restore just as you need to do when a physical server fails.

Creating backups of the entire host and its virtual machines
With this approach, you will have a backup of all the virtual machines with all their configuration and disk files. The advantage is that it is very simple to restore an entire machine. Just restore all the files for the virtual machine and you are done. The disadvantage is that the virtual machines need to be shut down, or suspended, to be able to create the backup. Therefore, for servers with a short backup window that is not an option. Also, it requires you to create a script that stops or suspends the virtual machines and starts them again after the backup. How to create such a script is explained in section 37.5. The disadvantage of backing up entire virtual machines is that you can not restore individual files from your guests.

Snapshots and other technologies

There are a few solutions left that can be used to back up your virtual machine environment, but they are not specific for such an environment. An example of this is the feature to create snapshots that some SANs will support. This allows you to create a full backup of the 'frozen' environment without any problems with open files. The disadvantage of this is that you can not restore individual files from your guests. Also, depending on your backup solution, you might even have to restore an entire server instead of being able to restore individual virtual machine files.

36 Creating and Configuring Virtual Machines on GSX Server

Your knowledge of virtual machine technology, which you may have gained from working with VMware Workstation, also applies to VMware GSX Server. If you have never worked with a VMware product in the past, I encourage you to first read the chapters in this book about the Workstation product.

The virtual hardware inside the virtual machine is the same as that in the Workstation version. It also does not matter whether you have installed your virtual machine on a Windows or a Linux host and later transferred it between these two supported host operating systems. The hardware inside the virtual machine stays the same. The only component that will be different is the processor, since the virtual machine will work with the underlying processor from the host machine.

Every virtual machine has these hardware specifications:

- Same processor as on the host computer
- Intel 440BX-based motherboard with NS338 SIO chip and 82093AA IOAPIC
- PhoenixBIOS™ 4.0 Release 6 with VESA BIOS (DMI/SMBIOS-compliant for system management agent support)
- A maximum of 3.6 GB of RAM for each individual virtual machine
- VGA adapter that supports SVGA
- A maximum of 60 SCSI devices on a maximum of four controllers (the SCSI controller can be either a Mylex® (BusLogic) BT-958 compatible host bus adapter, or an LSI Logic Ultra160 LSI53C10xx SCSI controller)
- Virtual SCSI disks with a maximum size of 256 GB
- A primary and secondary IDE channel for up to four devices
- Virtual IDE disks with a maximum size of 128 GB
- A maximum of four AMD PCnet-PCI II compatible Ethernet adapters
- Creative Labs Sound Blaster® AudioPCI emulation
- Virtual floppy drives (maximum of two), parallel and serial ports, and two USB ports

Creating a virtual machine can be done from the Management Interface, from VMware virtual machine console, or from VirtualCenter if you have that software installed in your environment. I will not go into the details of how to create a virtual machine here. First, all the necessary information about selecting the correct operating system, disk types, etc. are already covered in the VMware Workstation section of this book. Secondly, I am assuming that since you started working with VMware GSX Server, you are an experienced administrator. What I will do in this chapter is to pick out the specific topics for VMware GSX Server which you need to know before you get started in working with virtual machines in your environment.

Pre-allocate virtual disk space
By default, when you create virtual machines in VMware, you will be prompted for the hard disk capacity of the new virtual hard disks. This is shown in Figure 36.1. In this window, you must also choose if you want to pre-allocate the disk space for your virtual disk. By default, the checkbox for this setting is enabled.

Figure 36.1: By default, disk space will be pre-allocated for your virtual disks.

To achieve the best performance for your virtual machine, leave this checkbox enabled. The vmdk file(s) will be created when you click **Finish**. This will take a while, depending on the size of your virtual disk and your hardware specifications.

The reason for the performance improvement is that the virtual machine does not have to perform any tasks to increase the size of the virtual disk file. Also, the file will not become fragmented as it normally would, when small amounts of file system blocks are continuously added to the file. That is, if you make sure that your disk is defragmented when your disks are created.

Another advantage of pre-allocating the disk size is that the virtual machine is guaranteed to have the disk space it needs. Therefore, there will be no surprises. On the other hand, there can be some scenarios when you want to work as efficiently as possible with your host's available disk space. By allowing your virtual disks to grow dynamically, you can overbook your disk capacity. Depending on your virtual machine's specifications and guest operating system's configuration, you can add additional disks to your machine or you can increase the size of your virtual disk files.

Split files into 2 GB chunks

The default setting, shown in Figure 36.1, is to create one big virtual disk file. This will give you the best performance; but, whether there are any benefits to splitting the virtual disk file into 2 GB chunks depends on the use of your virtual machines.

There can be technical reasons for splitting the disks into smaller pieces. For example, the FAT32 file system only supports files with a maximum size of 4 GB minus 1 byte (2^{32} bytes minus 1 byte). You may have NTFS on your system, but let's assume that you would like to move the virtual machines to another server that uses FAT32. By starting off with virtual disks that are already split, that operation becomes a no-brainer.

Also, I personally find it useful to split files into smaller pieces for occasions when you need to copy or move virtual machine files to another location. Copying a 100 GB file where the transaction in Windows Explorer is stopped after 99 GB requires you to start all over again, unless you had already copied or moved all partial files except for one.

A final reason to split your files into smaller pieces is that you may want to burn a virtual machine to a DVD. Of course, you can archive the files into multiple files, but if they already are split into smaller pieces that fit with two on a DVD then it saves some extra steps.

Use multiple virtual disks

It is very simple to create a new virtual machine with one 30 GB virtual disk and to install the operating system on it. You need to create one or two partitions and then store the OS and its data into the single virtual disk. But that also means that in case of a failure, you will have to restore the entire virtual disk. Using multiple virtual disks gives you more flexibility and makes it easier to swap pieces of a virtual machine.

Let us take a look at the following scenario. In Figure 36.2, you see the disk configuration for a Linux host with some system partitions; a partition called home for user data and another partition called data used for corporate data.

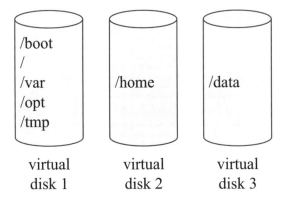

Figure 36.2: An example of dividing partitions over virtual disks.

By dividing the partitions over three virtual disk files, you can restore any of them when required. That could be done for disaster recovery. But also, let's consider test environments where you need to run several different tests with different data. You could easily copy the entire virtual machine initially to a test environment and later only copy the newer data into the test environment, without having to touch the rest of the virtual machine. And it also works the other way around. You can test an update on the guest operating system in a test environment and if it fails, you will only have to copy the virtual disks' operating system again to re-run the test.

37 GSX Server Advanced Configurations

This chapter contains several tips and configuration information for your VMware GSX Server environment, which you can use when you need to make modifications, such as changing ports and startup/shutdown options.

37.1 Assigning virtual Machines to a Specific Processor

If your host has multiple CPUs, you can define the processors that you want your virtual machines to run on. Actually, you can only define the CPUs that you do not want them to run on. You can specify this with the following parameter which you add to the machine's configuration (.vmx) file:

```
processor<n>.use = false
```

The processor number specified with <n> is the processor that your virtual machine should not use. On most operating systems, the processor numbering starts with 0. For example, if you have specified to not use processor 0, the machine's log file located in the same directory as the configuration file, will show the following message:

```
Not using processor 0
```

For Windows, you can find specifications for the available processors in the registry. Check the following key which lists the available CPUs:

```
HKLM\HARDWARE\DESCRIPTION\System\CentralProcessor
```

For Linux hosts, information about the available processors in the system can be found in the file /proc/cpuinfo.

 Note: For Windows, this feature is available on VMware Workstation and VMware GSX Server version 3.2. On Linux, it only works with VMware GSX Server, but only when you have kernel version 2.6 or higher.

Now that we have looked into the configuration of this feature, let us take a look at how we can effectively use it. If you have a two CPU machine, or a server with a CPU which supports hyper threading, it does not make much sense to configure the CPU load balancing. With four processors or more, there are several scenarios where it makes perfect sense.

An example of this is when you have one or two important virtual machines that you want to run with the best performance and another four machines that are less important. In that case, you could configure the first two to run on processors 0 and 1 and the other ones on processors 2 and 3. If you are planning such a scheme, always create a table where you define the machines and the processors that they are not allowed to use. Table 36.1 shows an example of such a table.

Table 36.1: Planning for CPU load balancing.

Virtual machine	CPU0	CPU1	CPU2	CPU3
Main file and print server	true	true	false	false
E-mail server	true	true	false	false
Intranet server	false	false	true	true
Accounting server	false	false	true	true
IT test server	false	false	true	true

 Note: When you need to transfer any of these virtual machines to another server that has more or less processors, make sure that you reconfigure the CPU scheduling for the new server.

37.2 Changing Port Numbers for VMware Virtual Machine Console

By default, your GSX Server listens on port 902 for connections from the client console application. If for any reason you need to change this to another port, you can do that by changing the parameters in the configuration files. After changing the port number, you can access the GSX Server by adding the new port number to the host name or IP address with a colon. For example: 192.168.1.10:9020.

Windows
On the VMware GSX Server, add this line to your configuration file or modify it when it already exists:

```
authd.port = <portNumber>
```

This configuration file is called config.ini and it is located at the following location: C:\Documents and Settings\All Users\Application Data\VMware\VMware GSX Server. After modifying this setting, you need to restart the **VMware Authorization Service**. You can do that from the Services Control Center, in Administrative Tools. Running virtual machines are not affected.

Linux
On a Linux host, the files you need to modify will depend on whether you are using xinetd or inetd. If you are using inetd, the port number will be specified in file /etc/inetd.conf. If you are using xinted, modify the already existing port number parameter in the file in /etc/xinetd.d/vmware-authd:

```
port = 902
```

Also modify your services file (/etc/services). Find the vmware-authd entry and change the port number that you want to use.

```
vmware-authd 902/tcp
```

Next, you need to restart the xinetd daemon:

```
/etc/init.d/xinetd restart
```

37.3 Setting the Session Length for the VMware Management Interface and Disabling Login

The default timeout setting for sessions with the Management interface is 60 minutes. This timeout value can be changed by modifying the Management Interface configuration file.

Windows

Change the setting of vmware_SESSION_LENGTH in the file C:\Program Files\VMware\VMware Management Interface\htdocs\init.pl

```
$ENV{vmware_SESSION_LENGTH} = 60;
```

Linux

For Linux, you need to run the configuration script for the Management Utility. This will prompt you for the number of minutes that you want.

```
/usr/bin/vmware-config-mui.pl
```

For both Windows and Linux, you can also disable the access to the Management Interface by specifying 0 as the timeout value. The login screen will display a message to warn users that login is prohibited: The VMware Management Interface is closed and no logins are permitted.

When you specify -1 in the configuration file, the sessions will never time out.

37.4 Accessing VMware GSX Server Log Files

If you experience any problems with your VMware GSX Server environment, the log files are a good place to start your investigation. This paragraph simply points you to the correct log file locations.

Virtual machine log file

Every virtual machine keeps its own log of what's happening. It is created in the virtual machine's configuration directory, which is where the .vmx file is located.

Virtual machine event log file
For every running virtual machine on your GSX Server host, a log file is used to store information about the events and problems with that machine. The most basic information is that it has been powered on or off. This information is also displayed in the Management Interface in the **Users and Events** tab of the VM's properties. The log files for the machines are stored at the following path:

For Windows:

```
C:\Program Files\VMware\
                VMware GSX Server\vmserverdRoot\eventlog
```

For Linux:

```
/var/log/vmware
```

VMware virtual machine Console log file
The client application used to access the virtual machine consoles also stores a log file. It is stored in the user's TEMP directory. You can find out about the active log file and location. The easiest way to do this is to check this information in the **About** information from the VMware virtual machine Console **Help** menu.

VMware Management Interface log file
The web server for managing your VMware GSX Server also keeps a log file. On a Windows host, it is called mui.log and it is stored in C:\Program Files\VMware\VMware Management Interface. On Linux, the log file is called error_log and it is stored in /var/log/vmware-mui.

VMware Authorization Service Log File
Logging for the Authorization Service is not enabled by default. You will have to add the following lines to your configuration file to enable the logging:

```
vmauthd.logEnabled = true
log.vmauthdFileName = "vmauthd.log"
```

For Windows, the configuration file is called config.ini and it is located at the following location: C:\Documents and Settings\All Users\Application Data\VMware\VMware GSX Server. On a Linux host, the file is called config and it is stored in the /etc/vmware directory.

After modifying this setting, you need to restart the **VMware Authorization Service**. For Windows, you can do that from the Services Control Center in Administrative Tools. For Linux, restart the xinetd daemon:

```
/etc/init.d/xinetd restart.
```

VMware Registration Service log file

All general VMware GSX Server activity is logged in a file called `vmware-serverd.log`. It is stored in the following directories:

For Windows:

`C:\Windows\Temp`

For Linux:

`/var/log/vmware`

Installation log files

During the installation of VMware software, an installation log is created. For Windows, the file is called `VMInst.log`. It is saved in the TEMP directory for the user who performed the installation. An example is `C:\Documents and Settings\Administrator\Local Settings\Temp`. On a Linux host, the log file is called `locations` and it is stored in `/etc/vmware`.

37.5 Using VMware GSX Server Scripting Commands

Vmware has created a very comprehensive scripting API that can be used for VMware GSX Server and ESX Server. The APIs can be used from within COM-based languages, such as Visual Basic or with the Perl scripting language.

For those administrators who are into programming and for third party developers who want to create software to manage a VMware environment, the scripting APIs are very valuable. But for the average administrator, simple tasks to run from a batch file or shell script will most likely be sufficient. For those purposes, VMware has included the vmware-cmd utility which can be used on both Windows and Linux to automate tasks.

 Note: The scripting APIs can still be used today, but there is also a Virtual Infrastructure Software Developer's Kit available. With this set of web services, you can do the same and much more.

Actions that can be performed range from starting and stopping virtual machines to changing the configuration parameters and connecting removable devices.

Suspending virtual machines
A practical scenario where a script can be used is when you want to suspend your virtual machines while shutting down a host instead of having them shut down; with the need to start up the entire guest OS again after the host has rebooted. Here is a simple script that suspends the virtual machines and then reboots the machine:

```
#script to reboot the server
#first suspends the virtual machines and then reboots
vmware-cmd /data1/vmware/nw65/nw65.vmx suspend
vmware-cmd /data1/vmware/suse10/suse10.vmx suspend
vmware-cmd /data1/vmware/sles9/sles9.vmx suspend
#maybe do some other stuff;-)
reboot
```

This sample script demonstrates the syntax of the utility. The vmware-cmd command is followed by the path and name of the configuration file and it is concluded with the action to be taken.

Preparing for a backup
In section 35.5, I explained that creating a backup of a VMware GSX Server host that has running virtual machines is a bad idea. Also, I suggested to stop the virtual machines, and to start them again after the backup. The following scripts extend the script that I created to reboot the host. In this script, I do not list the virtual

machines manually, but instead I list all the listed virtual machines with the
vmware-cmd -l command:

```
for vm in $(vmware-cmd -l); do
    vmware-cmd $vm suspend
done
```

If you run this script and the virtual machine is already suspended or it is in a
power off state the utility will generate an error message, explaining that the
machine is in the wrong state. So, if you have some time on your hands and you
have scripting skills, you could extend this with a check on the virtual machines'
state with the vmware-cmd getstate command.

Command reference
At the end of this section, I would like to provide you a full set of options that are
available for the vmware-cmd utility. To work with virtual machine actions, use the
following sytax:

```
vmware-cmd <options> <vm-cfg-path> <vm-action> <arguments>
```

To work with server based actions, add the -s parameter to the command.

```
vmware-cmd -s <options> <server-action> <arguments>
```

Table 37.1: Options for the vmware-cmd command.

Option	Description
-H <host>	Specifies an alternative host (if set, -U and -P must also be set)
-O <port>	Specifies an alternative port
-U <username>	Specifies a user
-P <password>	Specifies a password
-h	More detailed help
-q	Quiet - Minimal output
-v	Verbose

Table 36.2: Server actions for the vmware-cmd utility.

Option	Description
-l	Lists the registered VMs
-s register <config_file_path>	Registers a VM
-s unregister <config_file_path>	Un-registers a VM
-s getresource <variable>	Retrieves a server resource
-s setresource <variable> <value>	Sets a server resource

Table 36.3: Workstation actions for the vmware-cmd utility.

Option*	Description
Getconnectedusers	List users connected to the VM and their IP address
getstate	Gets the execution state of the VM
start <powerop_mode>	Powers on or resumes a VM
stop <powerop_mode>	Stops a VM
reset <powerop_mode>	Resets a VM
suspend <powerop_mode>	Suspends a VM
setconfig <variable> <value>	Sets a configuration variable
getconfig <variable>	Retrieves the value for a configuration variable
setguestinfo <variable> <value>	Sets a guest info variable
getguestinfo <variable>	Retrieves the value for a guest info variable
getid	Retrieves the VM ID
getpid	Retrieves the process ID of the running VM
getproductinfo <prodinfo>	Gets various product information
connectdevice <device_name>	Connects a virtual device to a VM
disconnectdevice <device_name>	Disconnects a virtual device from a VM
getconfigfile	Retrieves the path to the configuration file
getheartbeat	Retrieves the heartbeat value of the guest OS
getuptime	Retrieves the uptime of the guest OS
getremoteconnections	Retrieves the number of remote connections to a VM
gettoolslastactive	Retrieves the number of seconds since last notification from the tools
getresource <variable>	Retrieves a VM resource
setresource <variable> <value>	Sets a VM resource
setrunasuser <username> <password>	Sets the user that the VM runs as
getrunasuser	Retrieves the user that the VM runs as
getcapabilities	Retrieves the access permissions of the current user on a VM
addredo <disk_device_name>	Adds a redo log to a virtual disk
commit <disk_device_name> <level> <freeze> <wait>	Commits the redo log of a virtual disk
answer	Answers a question for a VM requesting input

*Workstation options must always include the full path to the virtual machine's configuration file.

Part 6

Introduction to VMware
ESX Server and VirtualCenter

38 VMware ESX Server Introduction

If you have worked with VMware Workstation or with VMware GSX Server, then you understand the concept of virtual machines. You know that multiple virtual machines can run on top of one hardware box and share resources such as memory, CPU, and hard disk. This is also true for VMware ESX Server, but it is also where the comparison stops: it is a hardware box that runs virtual machines. The way that you create them seems to be the same but there are important differences. Also, the VMware ESX Server configuration and management are completely different from VMware Workstation and they are more advanced than for VMware GSX Server.

This chapter serves as an introduction to VMware ESX Server. If you have worked with this product already, you should not find anything new here. I expect that you are familiar with VMware's hosted products such as Workstation or GSX Server, so I will start with an overview of the similarities and differences between these products and the VMware ESX Server. Afterwards, I will go into detail on what hardware and software you need to run a server and how to perform a simple installation.

Hosted versus native operating system

The biggest difference is that VMware ESX Server is not a so called "hosted product". You do not install Windows or Linux on the hardware box which you use for your server. Instead, the installation procedure installs a version of Linux that has been modified by VMware to be used solely for running virtual machines. You can login to the Linux environment to perform maintenance or configuration tasks, but it is not the intention of VMware to let you install your own additional Linux software onto the ESX Server. Running a dedicated Linux version may seem to bring limitations to your environment because you can not install the drivers or software which you might find useful. But on the positive side, this is exactly why VMware ESX Server is so powerful. All the drivers for the supported hardware are included and with the VMware approved drivers and software, you get an ultra stable operating environment for your virtual machines.

Fixed sized virtual disks

Creating virtual machines may look the same as in VMware Workstation of VMware GSX Server if you see it for the first time, but there are a few significant differences. First, you will have to allocate all the needed disk space for the virtual machine at the time of creation. There is no such thing as dynamically growing virtual disks. These virtual disk files are stored on the special VMFS file system, which is optimized for these large files. Also, the virtual disks in your virtual machines will always use an SCSI disk and will need to be stored on a physical SCSI disk as well. This is because it is the only disk type that is supported for the VMFS file system.

Only remote management

For the management of your virtual machines, you rely solely on remote management with a web-based management interface, the remote console client application, or the additional VMware product VirtualCenter. You can change the status of a virtual machine from the command line in the Linux environment, but there is no graphical environment to work with the virtual machine locally on the ESX Server.

Advanced memory management

Some of the memory management technologies from ESX server have been implemented in the recent version of VMware Workstation. When VMware follows its own regular product feature roadmap, some of it will also be implemented into GSX Server in the future. But even then, it will never be able to come close to what ESX Server can do to get the most out of your hardware.

High availability and scalability

A single VMware ESX Server will already give you a higher availability than what you can normally get with individual servers. The selection of supported hardware, together with a dedicated operating system and drivers make it a very stable platform. Of course, you can still encounter a hardware problem or some peak usage of your virtual machines, which may impact the performance in a negative way. When running two or more VMware ESX Servers that are connected to a Storage Area Network (SAN), you can achieve a higher availability level and it becomes possible to manually balance the load of the virtual machines between your servers. The magic words here are VirtualCenter and vMotion. With this software which you can purchase from VMware, it is possible to migrate a running virtual machine from one ESX Server hardware box to another. To be able to do this it is required that the virtual machine's hard disk file is on the SAN and it can be accessed by both servers. The magic trick to moving the machine is to copy the memory pages from server to server and when the machine is completely copied, to activate it on the other server. The time needed to switch the machines is so short that your client workstations will never be impacted by it.

39 Getting Started with VMware ESX Server

Now that we have looked into what VMware ESX Server is, compared to the hosted products, it is time to take a look at what you need to get started. First of all, you need the software. You can not simply download an evaluation copy from the VMware website. However, you can request an evaluation version, by contacting VMware sales directly or by contacting your local VMware reseller. They will then set you up for an evaluation account which allows you to download the software and use it for 30 days. The software comes as an ISO-file which you will have to burn to a CD-ROM.

 Tip: You can also get the software when you have a subscription to VMware Technology Network.

Next, you will need hardware. You can not just rip a PC from your company's PC graveyard or from your basement which is filled with old hardware. You will need real server class hardware to run VMware ESX Server. First of all, this is because there are some special requirements that you need to meet. One of them is that you must use an SCSI disk to store the special VMFS file system. You can not do that on an IDE disk. In addition, you will also need the correct disk or host bus adapters and network adapters to work with VMware ESX Server. They are typically available in the server class hardware which you will find on the requirements list on VMware's website at the following URL:

`www.vmware.com/support/resources/esx_resources.html`

 Note: It is still possible to use an older server that has an SCSI controller or RAID adapter for a testing environment or to use it when you want to learn how to get started with the VMware ESX Server. But it is definitely not what you want to do for your production environment. Last but not least, you will experience a lack of support from VMware if you do not stick to their list of supported hardware.

Hardware requirements
A fully detailed hardware configuration guide is beyond the scope of this introductory section. To set up the hardware for your environment, for example when choosing the amount of memory you need or disk space requirements, there are many parameters that you need to take into consideration. You will need to look at how much memory your virtual machines will use, how much data they need to store, etc. However, I will give you a short list of what hardware you need to set up an ESX Server in general.

Processor
VMware requires a minimum of two CPUs, as you can see on their website. The software does, however, run with one single CPU. Not that I recommend that option for your production environment, but for testing and educational purposes, you can install with only one processor.

Other requirements

For the rest, you need this hardware for a minimal installation:

- 512 MB RAM
- Two Ethernet controllers. Supported types are:
  - Broadcom NetXtreme 570x Gigabit controllers
  - Intel PRO/100 and PRO/1000 adapters
  - 3Com 9xx based adapters
- Disk controller:
  SCSI:
  - Adaptec
  - LSI Logic
  - most NCR/Symbios adapters
  RAID:
  - HP Smart Array
  - Dell PercRAID
  - ServeRAID
  - Mylex RAID
  Fibre Channel:
  - Emulex
  - QLogic
- SCSI disk or assigned LUN from your SAN

With the above hardware, you can set up a basic ESX Server. But you probably realize that with 512 MB RAM there is not much memory left for running the virtual machines. So, you will at least need to add more RAM. One Ethernet adapter will be used for the Service Console and the other one for the virtual machines.

It is always best not to share resources with the virtual machines environment if it is not necessary. This would leave one Ethernet adapter that all your machines are using. It is better to have more network adapters to divide the load, especially for virtual machines that generate a lot of traffic.

It is also preferable to have multiple disks, and it is even better to have multiple disk controllers. It is not hard to understand that four virtual machines reading and writing to their virtual disk files on one single disk will not be as efficient as the same virtual machines that write to virtual disk files which are on separate disks.

You might notice that only SCSI disks are listed in the hardware requirements list. So, does that mean that you can not install VMware ESX Server on a machine with only IDE devices? The answer is yes, but! The operating system part of VMware ESX server for running the Service Console could run on an IDE hard disk. However, the VMFS file system to which you need to store your virtual machine virtual disk files can only be created on SCSI devices.

39.1 Installing VMware ESX Server

At this point, I am assuming that you have your hardware set up and configured and that you have the VMware ESX Server installation CD-ROM available. The most recent version at the time of writing this book is ESX Server 2.5.1, build number 13057.

You start the installation by booting your server from the CD-ROM. After booting the Welcome screen, displayed in Figure 39.1, it will prompt you to select your preferred installation method.

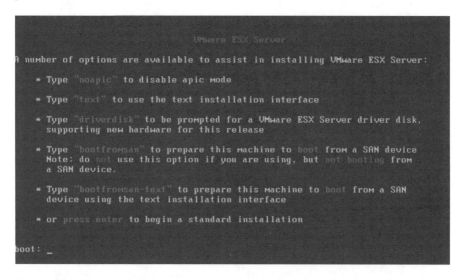

Figure 39.1: The welcome screen lets you choose from several installation options.

If you do not select any of these options, then the installation will automatically continue with the graphical installation interface.

If you have any problems with graphics during the installation, select the text installation option for a non-graphical installation. Other installation options, such as configuring booting from a SAN are beyond the scope of this introductory section.

 Tip: You might ask yourself: how did he create those screenshots of a bare metal installation process? The answer is simple: you can run through the installation of VMware ESX Server in a VMware Workstation virtual machine.

Follow the these steps to go through the ESX Server installation. These steps assume that you are running a normal graphical mode installation.

1. After selecting the installation type, the graphical welcome screen will be displayed. Click **Next** to continue.

2. Next, select a default or custom installation.

3. If you have selected a custom installation, you will be prompted with a keyboard and mouse configuration screen. Select the correct keyboard layout and click **Next**.

4. In the next screen, select the correct mouse type and click **Next**.

5. The End User License Agreement is displayed. Read and click the checkbox if you accept the agreement. Click **Next** to continue.

6. The next screen is the Serial Number screen. Enter your ESX Server serial number and the Virtual SMP serial number if you have bought this additional product. You can skip this step and enter the serial number later. But, you will not be able to start any virtual machines.

7. In the next screen, you must set up your hardware devices. Figure 39.2 shows an example of the hardware configuration screen.

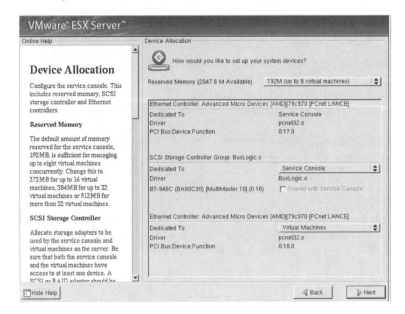

Figure 39.2:   During installation, you must assign hardware to the service console or to the virtual machine environment.

With VMware ESX Server, you must always use at least two network adapters. You can see that one of them is assigned to the Service Console. This is where you connect to for management with the Management Interface and VirtualCenter. Disks can also be used for the Service Console only or the virtual machine environment; but, you can also share the disk space between them.

Also displayed in Figure 39.2 is the memory reservation for the Service Console. The default assignment is 192 MB, which is based on running eight virtual machines. Table 39.1 shows your options, when assigning memory to the Service Console:

Table 39.1: Memory selection for the Service Console.

Amount of RAM	Number of Virtual Machines
192 MB	Up to 8 virtual machines
272 MB	Up to 16 virtual machines
384 MB	Up to 32 virtual machines
512 MB	More than 32 virtual machines
800 MB	Maximum amount of virtual machines

8. In the next screen, you must choose between manual or automatic partition. With the automatic selection, the installation process will propose a partition scheme for your disks. With the manual selection, you will have to create all partitions from scratch. The default partition table for the automatic installation is displayed in Figure 39.3.

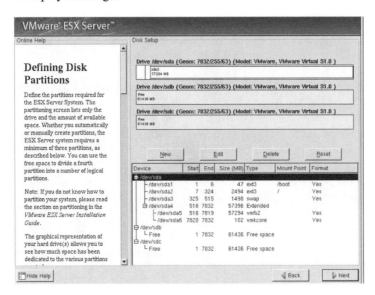

Figure 39.3: The default partitioning scheme for automatic partitioning.

You will need at least these partitions, listed in Table 39.2.

Table 39.2: Required partitions for an ESX Server installation

Function	Mount point	Type	Size
Boot partition	/boot	ext3	50 MB
Root partition	/	et3	2500 MB
Swap partition	swap	swap	2 x amount of RAM assigned to the Service Console

9. The next screen allows you to specify the network specifications for the first network adapter. Other adapters will be configured after the installation. You can choose between a DHCP configuration, and a static configuration. It is common practice to use a fixed address for your servers in general.

    You could configure your DHCP server to assign the IP address based on the host's MAC address to always use the same address. Or, you can use a host name in your DNS server that is dynamically updated by your DHCP server. However, I really think that a fixed IP address is just as simple and practical.

10. In the next screen, select the time zone where your server is located.

11. You will now be prompted for a root password. In this screen you can also create additional user accounts. It is always a good idea to create at least one account that you will be using to work with your server. It is not good practice to work with the root account on a daily basis.

12. After setting up the user accounts, a new screen will let you start the actual installation. It also shows you where the installation log file will be located. By default, this location is /tmp/install.log. The installation program will also write the choices that you have made during installation to a Kickstart file called /root/anaconda-ks.cfg.

13. After all the packages have been installed, the system can be rebooted to start the ESX server.

When the ESX Server is rebooted after installation, the welcome screen (shown in Figure 39.4) is displayed. It will tell you what the host name of the ESX server is and how you can access it with Management Utility. You will also see a message which tells you that you can login to the service console locally, by pressing Alt-F2. This will open a new TTY terminal, where you can login. When you are logged into another terminal, you return to the initial welcome screen by pressing Alt-F1.

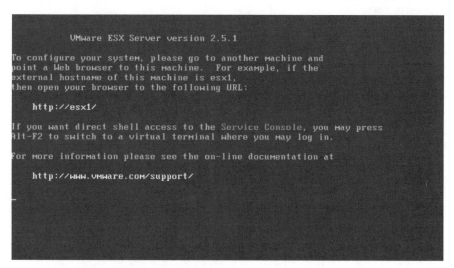

Figure 39.4: The welcome screen explains how to access the ESX Server.

To manage your ESX Server, login to Management Interface by pointing your browser to http://ipaddress or http://hostname. You should login as the root user.

39.2 Post Installation Tasks

When you login to the Management Interface for the first time, you will see two warning messages that will tell you what you need to configure after the installation is complete:

- Swap space

- Virtual Ethernet Switches

- Configure ESX Server storage

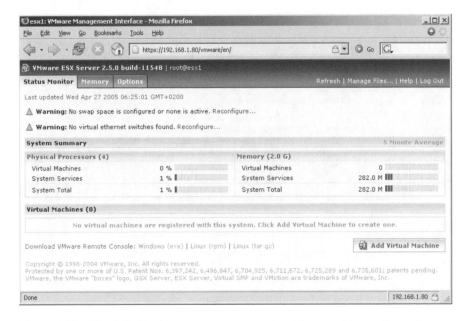

Figure 39.5: After initial login swap space and networking must be configured.

Configuring swap space

Click the link next to the error message to assign swap space for your ESX Server environment. If you remember, you also created a swap partition during the initial installation. That one, however, was for use by the Service Console. The swap space that you are going to define here is for the virtual machine environment itself.

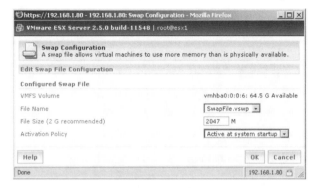

Figure 39.6: After installation, create swap space for your virtual machine environment.

The configuration screen will suggest a minimum amount of swap space. I recommend that you create a swap file that is at least twice the size of the amount of memory that you have available in your server. But you probably need more. If you ever add memory to the server, you do not want to spend a lot of time creating a new larger swap file. For example, if you have installed 4 GB of RAM, you should create an 8 GB file. But I would just create a 16 GB swap file. That way, you will not run into too many problems when expanding the server's memory.

Configuring Virtual Ethernet Switches
Your VMware ESX Server should at least have one virtual Ethernet switch. When you select the reconfigure link next to the warning message, you will be guided through the switch configuration. The configuration screen will suggest a network name and will list the available physical adapters. You must assign at least one adapter to your new virtual switch.

Configure ESX server storage
Your virtual machines must be stored on volumes that are of the VMFS type. You can configure these after the installation from the Options tab in the Management Interface. Click the link Storage Management to configure VMFS volumes to store your virtual disks.

39.3 Upgrading your ESX Server
From time to time there will be upgrades or patches for the ESX Server. It depends on your own environment if you need to install them, but a general rule is to always keep your systems up to date. Patches in general can help you prevent possible problems or performance bottle necks. ESX Server patches come as a compressed tarball. For example, `esx-2.5.1-13057-upgrade.tar.gz` upgrades it to the latest patch level for ESX Server 2.5.1.

After downloading the patch, copy it to your ESX Server or when it is on a Windows Server or Linux host use a Samba or NFS mount to access the package.

Note: To install the package, you must start the ESX Server with the regular Linux kernel. The VMkernel must not be running.

Unpack the file with the following commands:

1. Make a temporary directory, such as /tmp, your present working directory:

    ```
    cd /tmp
    ```

2. Extract the file with the following command:

    ```
    tar zxf esx-2.5.1-13057-upgrade.tar.gz
    ```

3. Make the subdirectory, where the package is extracted to, the present working directory and execute the upgrade script. There will also be a README which you must read. It will tell you how to do the installation and it will warn you about any possible issues.

    ```
    cd esx-2.5.1-13057-upgrade
    ```

    ```
    more README
    ```

    Tip: You do not have to enter the entire path. Just type the first letter and use tab to use the auto complete feature in Linux.

    ```
    ./upgrade.pl
    ```

4. The script will start to run and when it is finished it prompts you to reboot the server.

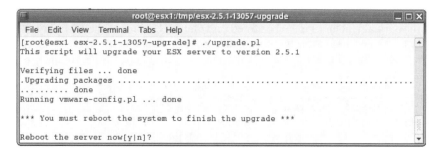

Figure 39.7: ESX Server upgrade.

40 Managing Virtual Machines

This chapter contains information on the management part of VMware ESX Server. Almost no management is performed locally; everything is done via the Management interface or with Remote Console. In chapter 42 I will also introduce VMware VirtualCenter to manage the ESX Server.

40.1 Using the Management Interface

The Management Interface is always installed on your ESX server. It is important to get to know this utility because it is where you can configure everything for your ESX Server environment. If you have one or more servers, which may be combined with VMware GSX Servers in your environment, then you will probably want to look into VirtualCenter to manage your VMware servers. How to use this management application is explained in chapter 42.

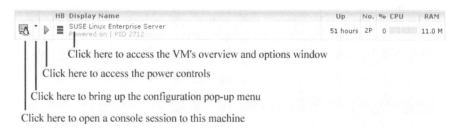

Figure 40.1: Overview of the controls and information in the Management Interface.

When you are logged in to the Management Interface for the first time, there will be no virtual machines configured. Once you have configured your first machine, you can use the controls that are shown in Figure 40.1. In addition to using these controls, you can also see how long the virtual machine has been up, how many processors the machine uses (if you have the Virtual SMP product), and what the CPU and RAM usage is.

Heartbeat
One of the things I would like to explain about the Management Interface is the meaning of heartbeat, which is displayed next to the power control button of the virtual machines (in the HB column). When you have the VMware tools loaded inside your virtual machine, it will continuously send heartbeats to the ESX Server.

When all the heartbeats have been received, within the minute before the screen was refreshed, the percentage of received heartbeats is 100% and the indicator will be green. When all the heartbeats are not received, the percentage drops and the indicator will be orange. When the tools are not loaded, the indicator will be greyed out because in that case the heartbeat is not available at all.

Tip: If you notice strange heartbeat behavior, such as when the percentage is low but the virtual machine is actually performing very well by itself, check whether you have the correct version of VMware tools loaded inside the guest operating system.

Adding a virtual machine

When you are at this point in the configuration, I expect that you have already created you first virtual machine. In the Management Interface, click the link for Add Virtual Machine and follow the instructions. I will not go into a lot of detail about creating virtual machines here. The information about virtual machines in the first part of this book regarding installation of Windows, Linux, and NetWare and the installation of the guest OS tools is identical for virtual machines that you create for your ESX Server. There are a few specific configurations that I would like to discuss, because they are ESX Server specific.

Using multiple processors

This is one of the first additional configuration options which you will see when creating virtual machines. If you own a license for VMware's additional product Virtual SMP, then you can assign a maximum of two CPUs to the machine for the guest to use.

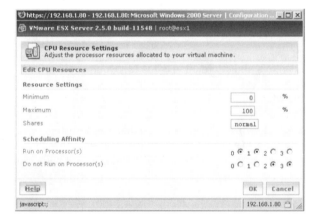

Figure 40.2: A virtual machine can be configured to run on specific processors.

When the virtual machine is created, regardless of whether you have the Virtual SMP product, if you have multiple processors, then you can configure which CPUs can be used by the virtual machine and which ones can not. This can be done from the CPU tab in the virtual machine configuration screen.

Adding virtual disk files

The next step in creating a virtual machine is to assign a virtual disk. You can choose to use an existing one or to create a new one. If you have a SAN, you can also assign physical LUNs to a virtual machine to be used.

A difference that you will notice if you have worked with other VMware products is that you can not store the virtual machine files in a directory hierarchy. You can only select available storage from the ESX server and assign a name to it. The files are just stored in the root of the partition. Another thing is that hard disk space is always pre-allocated to the virtual disk file. The dynamically growing scheme does not apply for ESX Server.

Figure 40.2: Adding disk to the new virtual machine.

40.2 Using ESX Server Remote Console

Access to the console of the virtual machines on your ESX Server is provided with the Remote Console utility. The easiest way to get this software is to click the download link at the bottom of the Management Interface web page.

Windows installation
To install the client application on a Windows computer, you should simply run the executable that you download. At the time of writing this book, this is the file VMware-console-2.5.1-13057.exe. After installation, you can simply start the application by selecting the **VMware virtual machine Console** shortcut from **Start → Programs → VMware**.

Linux installation
The easiest way to install the client application on a Linux computer is to download the RPM package (VMware-console-2.5.1-13057.i386.rpm) and let it install automatically with a package manager.

Many recent Linux distributions come with the RedCarpet client. When you choose to download the RPM from a browser, one of the choices you will have is to open the file with RedCarpet. If you do that, the only extra step left is to click **Continue** in the summary window as displayed in Figure 40.4.

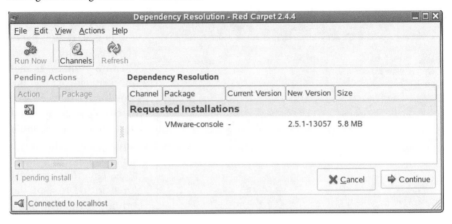

Figure 40.4: Using RedCarpet is the easiest way to install the Linux version.

You can also manually install the RPM version by using the following command:

```
rpm -Uhv VMware-console-2.5.1-13057.i386.rpm
```

The version number in this example can of course be different if you are using a newer version of the software.

If you do not have RedCarpet or for any other reason, you do not want to install the application from RPM, you can download the tar version (VMware-console-2.5.1-13057.tar.gz).

If you have the tar archive on your system, you have to decompress and extract it. You can do that simultaneously, by using the z and x parameters:

```
tar -zxf VMware-console-2.5.1-13057.tar.gz
```

The archive will be extracted into a subdirectory called vmware-console-distrib. Use the cd command to enter that directory and start the installation from there:

```
vmware-console-distrib
```

```
./vmware-install.pl
```

This will start the VMware virtual machine console installation script. I have listed the questions and the default answers here, for your reference. In most cases, you can leave the defaults in place. First, you need to read and accept the end user license agreement.

1. In which directory do you want to install the binary files?
   `/usr/bin`

2. In which directory do you want to install the library files?
   `/usr/lib/vmware-console`

3. In which directory do you want to install the manual files?
   `/usr/share/man`

4. In which directory do you want to install the documentation files?
   `/usr/share/doc/vmware-console`

After the installation has been completed, you will be prompted to run the configuration script. You can answer yes. Or, you can run the script later with this command:

`/usr/bin/vmware-config-console.pl`

The only configuration script question that you will be asked is: What port do you want the remote console to use to connect to the server? The default answer is: 902.

41 Some Extra Tips on Using VMware ESX Server

Once you get started with VMware ESX Server, most of the features you need are self explanatory. Or, you can also check the VMware online documentation. There are a few practical tips that I would like to give you to make your task of administering ESX server easier.

41.1 Accessing the ESX Server's File System Remotely

When you get started with VMware ESX Server, you definitely need to become familiar with Linux. This product is based on Linux and uses all of the commands, utilities, and configurations that are common in the Linux environment. One of the specific items that you need to get used to is to access the ESX server's file system from your Windows host, in many cases.

A very easy and secure protocol to do this is SSH. It is available by default on all Linux hosts and there are many tools available for the Windows environment as well. A good starting point for any SSH related software is www.openssh.com. To use a secure shell session to your host, you can use PuTTY, which is available from www.openssh.com/windows.html.

For transferring files, the utility WinSCP, based on Secure CoPy command (SCP) is very useful. You can download this tool from winscp.net.

41.2 Creating an ISO Vault

When you start installing operating systems, you probably want to do it by using ISO images. If you have only one ESX Server or GSX Server, then it is simple: just copy the files to that server and you are done. But most administrators have more than one server and you may already have a Windows or Linux server that stores your collection of ISO files.

In either case, it is a good idea to point your ESX Server to that central location. If it is a Windows server, you can do this with the Samba protocol, and if it is a Linux host you can use NFS.

 Note: Since it will be a single point of failure, there are a few things to keep in mind when you use a central ISO storage location. Make sure to only connect ISOs to virtual machines during installation. Disconnect them when the machine is completely installed. If you leave them connected and the ISO is not available, it will result in an error message and the virtual machine might not start.

Samba

To create the Samba share, use the mount command following this syntax:

```
mount -t smbfs -o username=<user>,password=<pw>
              //<ip | host>/sharename <mount point>
```

To mount the share to /mnt/iso as a special user with read-only rights:

```
mount -t smbfs -o username=iso,password=secret
                  //isosrv/isoshare /mnt/iso
```

Alternatively, when you want to set this up to be loaded automatically when your ESX Server boots, you want to add the following to your /etc/fstab file. As an example for the previous command line:

```
//isosrv/isoshare   /mnt/iso    smbfs
        ip=isosrv,username=iso,password=secret,noauto 0 0
```

NFS

When your files are on another Linux host, or an ESX Server, you can set up an NFS export, to which your ESX Server can point to. On the host where the files reside, create the export manually with the following command:

```
exportfs <host>:/path
```

To share the /iso directory with the host called esx2:

```
exportfs esx2:/iso
```

To permanently add this NFS export to your host, add it to the /etc/exports file in the following, commonly used format:

```
/iso/ esx1(ro,root_squash,sync)
```

On the server, where you want to configure access to the files, you first have to make sure that the two necessary daemons are loaded. You can do this manually with the following commands:

```
/etc/init.d/netfs start
/etc/init.d/portmap start
```

When the daemons are loaded, use the following command to manually mount the NFS location to a directory:

```
mount -t nfs <ip | host>:/path <mount point>
```

To access the previously exported share on host esx1:

```
mount -t nfs esx1:/iso /mnt/iso
```

To permanently add this NFS mount to your server to be activated every time it starts, add the following line, based on the example, to the /etc/fstab file:

```
esx1:/iso /mnt/iso  nfs    ro,rsize=1024,wsize=1024,noauto 0 0
```

41.3 Maintenance and Troubleshooting Mode

When the ESX Server boots, it uses the LILO boot loader to start the operating system. In the boot loader screen, you can choose to start ESX (default), or Linux.

Use the Linux part to perform configuration and troubleshooting on the ESX server when needed. In this mode, virtual machines will not be started. So, if there are any problems during the boot process, use this mode to investigate and troubleshoot.

Figure 41.1: The LILO Boot loader allows you to start the Linux part only.

 Tip: You can check which mode the server is started in, if you check the message on top of the second terminal (Alt-F2). When booted in ESX vmkernel mode, it will say: VMware ESX Server 2.5.1 (or any other version number). When booted in Linux, it will just say: Linux on the first line.

42 Introduction to VirtualCenter

In a multi VMware server environment, with GSX Servers, ESX Servers, or in a mixed environment, the management can very easily become very complex. To manage virtual machines, you must access several Management Interfaces on individual hosts. Also, accessing virtual machine console requires access to several hosts with the Virtual Machine Console utility. And when multiple administrators need to have rights to servers, which of course will be different levels of rights, it requires a lot of work to configure all them on individual hosts.

To solve these manageability issues, VMware has created the VirtualCenter. With this application you can manage a mix of VMware GSX and ESX Servers. And it is also the platform that you must use when you want to use the vMotion application to perform transfers of virtual machines to other hosts.

Another important feature of VirtualCenter is that it helps you evaluate the load of your virtual machine environment. Within one central location, you can monitor what all the servers are doing, and when the problems occur, and you can take the right action. VirtualCenter even enables you to assign actions to typical events and warn you, for example when CPU load reaches a threshold. Last but not least, VirtualCenter supports easy deployment of new virtual machines based on templates.

 Note: As was the case in chapter 1, which covered the ESX Server, this chapter is not a complete VirtualCenter manual. My intention is to get you started with the application in a clear and simple manner.

Before we get into the installation of the product itself, there is some terminology that you need to be familiar with.

VirtualCenter Server
This is a Windows-based application that runs on a Windows Server platform. It is the central node in the entire VirtualCenter infrastructure. It communicates with the VirtualCenter agents on the hosts and the administrators attach to this server with their client application.

VirtualCenter Client
This is the Windows based application that an administrator runs to manage the virtual machine environment. The client application communicates with the VirtualCenter server.

VirtualCenter Agent
This is the software that runs on every VMware GSX Server and ESX Server. It collects the information that is sent to the VirtualCenter Server and it performs the actions that are sent by the server.

VirtualCenter Web Service

This is an optional component that can be installed to provide access to the VirtualCenter environment for third party developers, by using the Software Developer Kit.

42.1 Installing VMware VirtualCenter

This software must be installed on a Windows server. This server can be a physical one, but the VirtualCenter software itself can also run inside a virtual machine. Of course you will loose management capability when the host where that machine resides is off-line (unless you use vMotion first). But since you already have the VMware platform to consolidate all these servers that are typically not doing very much, it makes sense to look into a virtual VirtualCenter server.

The latest version of the software is VMware-vpx-1.2.0-12684.exe and can be downloaded from VMware's website if you own a license. Or, it can be obtained when you have a subscription to the VMware Technology Network.

The installation is very straightforward so I will not cover it here. When the VirtualCenter server is installed and you start it for the first time, you are prompted to enter the serial numbers. VirtualCenter is licensed on a per host basis. So you enter a license for every GSX Server or ESX Server host that you want to manage.

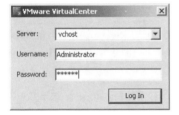

When the server is up and running, you can use the same installer to install the client on your workstation. When you start the application you are prompted to login. The user account you can use to log in is from the VirtualCenter Windows Server.

Figure 42.1: VirtualCenter login.

After your first login, you must create a "farm" of servers and add your hosts to your VirtualCenter environment. Perform the following steps to configure your environment:

1. Right click **Server Farms** and select **New Farm**.

2. Enter the name of your farm and press **Enter**.

3. Right click the newly created farm and select **Add Host**.

4. Specify the hostname or IP address for the GSX Server or ESX Server and the port number. This will be the same port (902 by default) which is used for VMware virtual machine console connections.

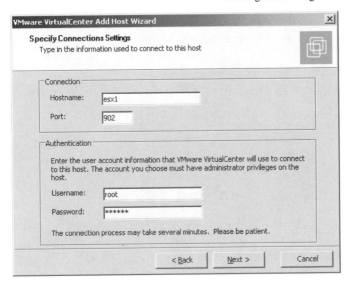

Figure 42.2: To add a host, specify the IP address or hostname, and the port and provide a username and password.

5. You can now organize your virtual machines in VirtualCenter. You can combine machines from different hosts into groups of virtual machines.

42.2 Creating Virtual Machines with VirtualCenter

VirtualCenter offers you full control over your GSX Server and ESX Server environment, including the creation of new virtual machines. You need to have permissions to create new machines. This will be discussed later.

Before you start creating virtual machines on a GSX Server host, you must specify where the virtual machines will be stored. On an ESX Server, this is on your VMFS volumes. However, for the GSX Server you must specify the path in VirtualCenter if you want to create machines from this application. Right click the host that you want to configure and select **Properties**.

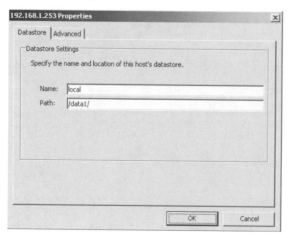

Figure 42.3: For GSX Server, you must configure where the virtual machines will be stored.

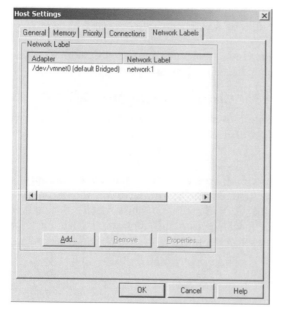

On a GSX Server you must also specify a network label for the networks you that have in the machine.

This can be done from the local server console or the VMware Virtual Machine Console. It is the method used in Figure 42.4. The network configuration can also be set up from the Management Interface.

Define a name for the network which you can easily identify when working with the VirtualCenter application.

Figure 42.4: For GSX Server, you must configure a network label for the configured virtual networks.

To create a virtual machine, perform the following steps:

1. In your Farms view, select the GSX Server or ESX Server where you want to create the new virtual machine. Right click the host and select **New virtual machine** or select **New virtual machine** from the **File** menu.

2. In the virtual machine wizard, select a typical or custom method. For this example, I have decided to use the custom method.

3. Next, select where to place the virtual machine in VirtualCenter. Virtual machines can be grouped together; for example based on operating system, location, department, etc.

Figure 42.5:   VMs can be grouped to keep your
VirtualCenter environment organized.

4. Select which operating system you will be installing inside this virtual machine.

5. Enter a name for your virtual machine and select the VMFS datastore that you want to store the virtual disk files (ESX) to, or the datastore that you have defined for your GSX Server that you want to store the machine's files to.

6. Select the number of processors to be used in this virtual machine. This is only available if you are configuring the machine for an ESX Server that has Virtual SMP installed.

7. Assign memory to the virtual machine.

8. Select the type of network for the virtual machine.

9. Select the SCSI bus type for this virtual machine: Buslogic or LSI Logic.

10. Select a disk type to add to the virtual machine.

11. Select the size for the virtual machine.

12. Select a disk mode for the virtual machine.

13. A window will be displayed, explaining that VirtualCenter is ready to submit the task to the ESX Server.

42.3 Managing Virtual Machines with VirtualCenter

After creating the virtual machine, you can manage it with the VirtualCenter client. Figure 42.6 shows an example of the VirtualCenter management interface.

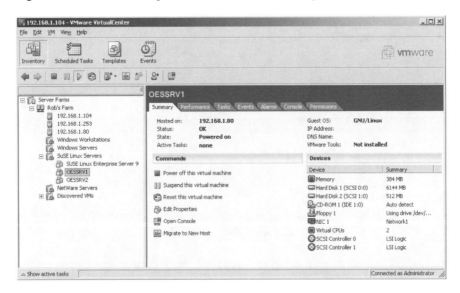

Figure 42.6: An example of the VirtualCenter Client application.

To access the console of a virtual machine, you can select the Console tab in the client application. But you can also open a separate window with the console, if you right click the virtual machine and select Open Console from the popup menu. Or, you can select **Open Console** from the **VM** menu. Using the extra console instead of the one that is integrated in the Console tab allows you to access multiple virtual machines at the same time.

42.4 Cloning a Virtual Machine

A virtual machine which is configured on an ESX Server or GSX Server can be cloned within the same host or to another host. This process will create an exact copy of the machine on the destination host. However, there are a few limitations to what is possible and a few things to keep in mind:

- A virtual machine must be powered off before it can be cloned.
- You can not clone a machine with an IDE hard disk from a GSX Server virtual machine to an ESX Server.
- You can only clone machines within a farm, not to other farms.

To clone a machine, perform the following steps:

1. Right click the virtual machine in VirtualCenter and select **Clone** or select the **Clone this Virtual Machine** option in the machine's summary screen.

2. The Virtual Machine Clone Wizard will be started. The first thing you need to do is to specify the destination host for the virtual machine.

3. Next, specify a group where the machine will be placed in the destination farm.

4. Provide a name for the virtual machine to be used on the destination.

5. Select a location for the virtual machine. For a GSX Server, this is one of the data stores that you configured initially. For an ESX Server, it is one of the available VMFS file systems. The checkbox to automatically start the virtual machine after creation is enabled by default.

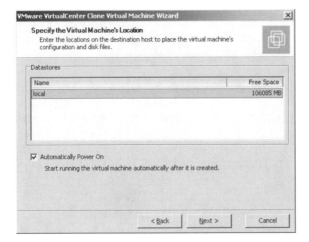

Figure 42.7: Select a destination for the virtual machine.

6. Specify the network to which the host will be attached.

7. Specify the memory size for the clone.

8. The last choice that you have to make is about customizing the guest operating system. You have three options:

    - Starting the guest customization wizard
    - Importing customizations from an XML file
    - Not customizing the guest operating system

    The guest customization helps you change the identification information for your guest. For Windows, this is workgroup and domain information, including the computer name, networking configuration, and the SID. For Linux, it is the host name, the dns domain suffix, and the networking configuration.

    To prepare for Windows guest optimization, download the sysprep package from www.microsoft.com/windows2000/downloads/tools/sysprep/default.asp and store the extracted files in the following files for the specific operating system versions:

    `C:\Program Files\VMware VirtualCenter\resources\windows\sysprep` followed by these subdirectories:

    ```
    \resources\windows\sysprep\1.1\
    \resources\windows\sysprep\2k\
    \resources\windows\sysprep\xp\
    \resources\windows\sysprep\svr2003\
    ```

    For Linux, the files must be stored in `C:\Program Files\VMware VirtualCenter\resources\linux\tools`. The tools can be downloaded from the following URL: `www.vmware.com/download`.

9. When you choose not to configure the guest, the wizard ends here. When you do want to configure the guest operating system, the wizard for Windows or Linux starts to help you specify the information needed for the new virtual machine's identity.

10. When the clone process is submitted, you track it in the Tasks tab of the VirtualCenter application.

42.5 VirtualCenter Permissions

For individual GSX Server and ESX Server hosts, you can configure user accounts and grant permissions to administrators for managing the virtual machine environment. With VirtualCenter, you can configure this on a central location and there is no longer a need to create local accounts on your server. You can create user accounts on the local server where VirtualCenter is installed, or you can use your existing Active Directory domain.

Permissions can be assigned to the following objects:
* Farm
* Farm Group
* Host
* Virtual Machine Group
* Virtual Machine

To assign permissions, right click the object where you want to assign rights to, and select **Add Permission**. From the dialog box (see Figure 42.8), select the users or groups that you want to assign rights to and click **Add**. Or, click **Remove** to delete previously assigned rights.

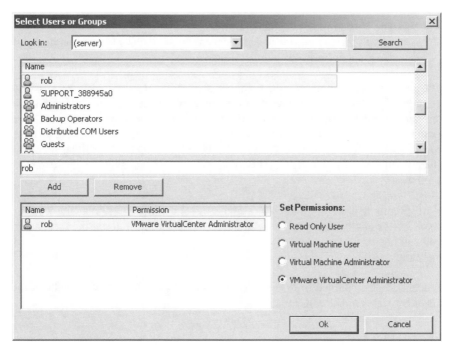

Figure 42.8: Users and groups can be granted permissions for VirtualCenter.

There are four permission levels you can configure:

- Read Only User
  Users with this permission can view the state of virtual machines, hosts, farms and groups.

- Virtual Machine User
  With this permission a user can perform power operations and interact with the virtual machine console. The user can not modify any properties of the virtual machine.

- Virtual Machine Administrator
  Users that are assigned this permission can:
  o Connect and disconnect virtual machine devices, migrate with VMotion, clone, remove, and configure virtual machines.
  o Create, import, and deploy templates.
  o Add and remove hosts from farms.
  o Create, remove, or modify farms, farm groups, and virtual machine groups and their content.
  o Cancel running operations.

- VMware VirtualCenter Administrator
  A user with this permission has all rights to the VirtualCenter environment and can also grant permissions to other users.

The permission assignments use a hierarchical model with inheritance. Permissions assigned to a farm will also apply to all objects within that farm. This feature provides you the capability to assign rights to administrators in various ways. For example, when you have a group of database administrators that need to have console access to their database servers, you can give them the Virtual Machine User permission for the virtual machine group that contains all the database servers.

 Note: Rights that are configured at a higher level can not be restricted at a lower level. For example, once you are a virtual machine administrator at the farm level, you can not be assigned as a Read Only User at an individual virtual machine in that farm.

When a user is removed from the Windows accounts database, that user also loses his or her rights in VirtualCenter.

42.6 Working with Events and Alarms in VirtualCenter

VirtualCenter provides a central location for accessing all the events on your GSX Server and ESX Server hosts. In the events window, you can see informational messages, warnings, and critical errors. You can view events for all systems by clicking the Events button in the main toolbar. Or, you can look at events on a farm, group, host, or virtual machine level.

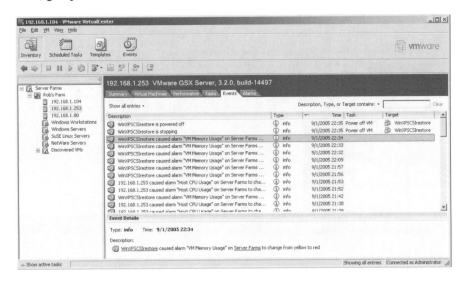

Figure 42.9: VirtualCenter collects events from all hosts in your environment.

When browsing through the events list, you can select individual events to get more information about the event in the **Event Details** window.

Alarms

The events are based on the built-in alarms, among other things. You can also define custom alarms in VirtualCenter. You can define triggers that you want to monitor. When the specified event occurs, or when a configured threshold is reached, the alarm will be triggered and the defined action will be executed.

You can define alarms at the farm, group, host and virtual machine level. Only when you select the farm option, you will have to choose between a virtual machine alarm, and a host alarm. In all other cases when you select a host, it will be a host alarm and when you select a virtual machine or group it will be a virtual machine alarm.

Alarms are applied by using a hierarchical system where alarms will not be overwritten by alarms that are configured at a lower level. The alarm settings are cumulative when looking at the effective alarms for an object.

There are four triggers that you can use to monitor your virtual machines. They are listed in Figure 42.10:

- VM CPU Usage
- VM Memory Usage
- VM Heartbeat
- VM State

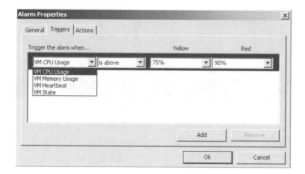

Figure 42.10: Triggers for virtual machine alarms.

There are three triggers that you can use to monitor your ESX Server or GSX Server host. They are listed in Figure 42.11:

- Host CPU Usage
- Host Memory Usage
- Host State

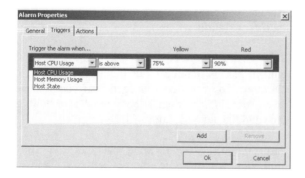

Figure 42.11: Triggers for host alarms.

When defining a trigger, you need to specify the percentage below or above the threshold when the indicator will turn yellow or red.

Next, in the Actions tab, you should specify what action will occur when the indicator turns from one state to another; i.e., yellow to red. The default setting is that the action is executed when the indicator goes from yellow to red. Multiple actions can be configured for an alarm. You can, for example, run a script and also have an e-mail sent to you.

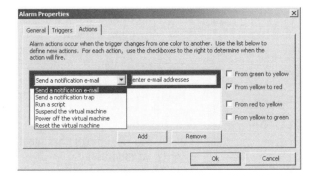

Figure 42.12: Actions for virtual machine alarms.

There are six different actions that you can configure for a virtual machine alarm. They are listed below as well as in Figure 42.12:

- Send a notification e-mail (SMTP)
- Send a notification trap (SNMP)
- Run a script
- Suspend the virtual machine
- Power off the virtual machine
- Reset the virtual machine

The first three actions listed for virtual machines are also available for the host alarms. These are also listed in Figure 42.13.

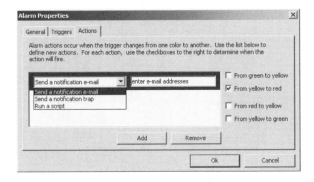

Figure 42.13: Actions for host alarms.

Sending an e-mail or a notification trap requires configuring the VirtualCenter Settings for SMTP and SNMP.

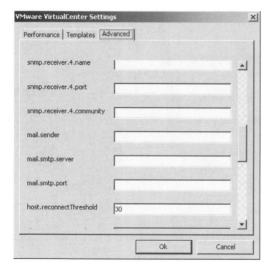

Open the **Virtual Machine Settings** window from the **File** menu. For SNMP, you can specify up to four hosts that can receive traps from your VirtualCenter environment. You must specify the IP address or hostname, the port, and the community string for each receiver.

For the SMTP settings, you must specify an identifier that will be used as the sender of the e-mail. For the delivery of the message, configure an SMTP host and port.

Figure 42.14: SNMP and SMTP settings for VirtualCenter alarms.

Index